SOLIDARITY

Wildcat: Workers' Movements and Global Capitalism

Series Editors:
Immanuel Ness (City University of New York)
Peter Cole (Western Illinois University)
Raquel Varela (Instituto de História Contemporânea (IHC) of Universidade Nova de Lisboa, Lisbon New University)
Tim Pringle (SOAS, University of London)
Peter Alexander (University of Johannesburg)
Malehoko Tshoaedi (University of Pretoria)

Workers' movements are a common and recurring feature in contemporary capitalism. The same militancy that inspired the mass labour movements of the twentieth century continues to define worker struggles that proliferate throughout the world today.

For more than a century, labour unions have mobilized to represent the political-economic interests of workers by uncovering the abuses of capitalism, establishing wage standards, improving oppressive working conditions, and bargaining with employers and the state. Since the 1970s, organised labour has declined in size and influence as the global power and influence of capital has expanded dramatically. The world over, existing unions are in a condition of fracture and turbulence in response to neoliberalism, financialization, and the reappearance of rapacious forms of imperialism. New and modernized unions are adapting to conditions and creating a class-conscious workers' movement rooted in militancy and solidarity. Ironically, while the power of organized labour contracts, working-class militancy and resistance persists and is growing in the Global South.

Wildcat publishes ambitious and innovative works on the history and political economy of workers' movements, and is a forum for debate on pivotal movements and labour struggles. The series applies a broad definition of the labor movement to include workers in and out of unions, and seeks works that examine proletarianization and class formation; mass production; gender, affective and reproductive labour; imperialism and workers; syndicalism and independent unions, and labour and leftist social and political movements.

Also available:

Choke Points: Logistics Workers Disrupting the Global Supply Chain
Edited by Jake Alimahomed-Wilson and Immanuel Ness

Just Work? Migrant Workers' Struggles Today
Edited by Aziz Choudry and Mondli Hlatshwayo

The Spirit of Marikana: The Rise of Insurgent Trade Unionism in South Africa
Luke Sinwell with Siphiwe Mbatha

Wobblies of the World: A Global History of the IWW
Edited by Peter Cole, David Struthers and Kenyon Zimmer

Southern Insurgency: The Coming of the Global Working Class
Immanuel Ness

Working the Phones: Control and Resistance in Call Centres
Jamie Woodcock

Solidarity

Latin America and the US Left
in the Era of Human Rights

Steve Striffler

First published 2019 by Pluto Press
345 Archway Road, London N6 5AA

www.plutobooks.com

British Library Cataloguing in Publication Data
A catalogue record for this book is available from the British Library

ISBN 978 0 7453 9920 1 Hardback
ISBN 978 0 7453 9919 5 Paperback
ISBN 978 1 7868 0191 3 PDF eBook
ISBN 978 1 7868 0261 3 Kindle eBook
ISBN 978 1 7868 0260 6 EPUB eBook

This book is printed on paper suitable for recycling and made from fully managed and sustained forest sources. Logging, pulping and manufacturing processes are expected to conform to the environmental standards of the country of origin.

Typeset by Curran Publishing Services, Norwich

Simultaneously printed in the United Kingdom and United States of America

Contents

Acknowledgements

This project is the product of a political engagement and scholarly curiosity that began well over a decade ago with Aviva Chomsky. Avi's experience, knowledge, insight, and friendship have shaped this project from conceptualization to completion. Although she cannot possibly be blamed for errors of fact or interpretation, most of what is of value in the following pages is due to her direct influence and political commitment. I cannot thank her enough.

Our ongoing engagement has included more than ten years of solidarity work around Colombia, which has put me into contact with union leaders, community activists, and others whose thoughts and actions have taught me much about how power and solidarity work in an unequal world. Likewise, Avi and I organized the "Empire and Solidarity in the Americas" conference at the University of New Orleans between 2008 and 2016. The conference profoundly influenced my understanding and knowledge of the history of Latin American solidarity. I thank all of those who participated over the years.

Adolph Reed Jr. has deeply shaped my own thinking about politics and history, and his comments on the manuscript were invaluable. Likewise, Lesley Gill's work and example continue to inspire, and her reading of an earlier version was immensely helpful. Jana Lipman commented thoroughly on the entire manuscript, and I cannot thank her enough for her incredibly careful reading. Dan La Botz provided extremely useful feedback, and generously shared his own work. Thomas Adams, John French, and Gavin Smith have also positively shaped the book through direct feedback as well as their own work. Thanks to everyone.

I also thank participants from the Boston-Area Working Group for Historians of Latin America and the Caribbean, who provided thoughtful commentary on a key portion of the manuscript. Special thanks to Kirsten Weld for organizing us and Harvard University for hosting.

The team at Pluto Press has done a wonderful job shaping, editing, and moving the manuscript along. Immanuel Ness was my initial connection to Pluto, and his advice and suggestions proved indispensable throughout the process. David Shulman has been a fantastic editor both as a careful reader and consistent motivator. Peter Cole also provided insightful commentary.

Finally, many thanks to my family, including my wife Karon, whose passion, energy, and love make life so much better; to my father Chuck and (late) mother Nancy, whose lifetime of support I appreciate more and more; and to Allie, Brad, and Tara whose young lives remind me there is hope for the future.

Steve Striffler

Introduction

My scholarly interest in the history of Latin American solidarity comes from a political engagement around Colombia during the past 15 years. Like much of Latin American solidarity, the campaign I have been involved with began when Latin Americans—in this case, indigenous and Afro-Colombian communities from the northern province of La Guajira—reached out to international actors. They sought allies in the global North to support their struggle against the rapid expansion of an exceptionally large coal mine owned by Exxon, which in the early 2000s violently evicted the community of Tabaco from its ancestral lands.

Had the Cerrejon mine been owned by a less prominent company, or chosen a less conspicuously violent path for destroying a village, it is quite possible that community efforts to acquire foreign allies would have been unsuccessful. Even with the egregious violation of human rights by a prominent multinational corporation, the communities still struggled to find overseas allies and capture international attention. In an age of information overload, characterized in part by a seemingly endless supply of human crises, it is not easy to get on the global radar.

They eventually did, however, and ever since then a small group of activists from Europe, the United States, and Canada have supported the affected communities during an evolving conflict with the mine's owners and the Colombian state.[1] The campaign has utilized a range of tactics to put pressure on the mine's owner by bringing global attention to its horrid behavior. As we will see, this strategy of "naming and shaming," whereby activists shine a global spotlight on companies or governments in order to alter their practices, has a long history within international solidarity. In our case, we pursued this strategy through a number of tactics. We took international delegations to Colombia in order to witness and publicize the devastation caused by the mine.[2] We have brought Colombians on speaking tours to educate

I

and alert US audiences to the true cost of coal. We held conferences to publicize abuses and deepen alliances between communities and other actors. We pressed the mine's owners at shareholders' meetings and mining conferences. And we produced films, articles, and books in order to raise the profile of the cause both in Colombia and abroad.

These efforts generated concrete gains. When we began, the mine barely recognized the existence of the communities, and insisted that the eviction of Tabaco had been handled legally and properly. The matter was closed. The campaign not only forced the mine to reopen the case of Tabaco and address issues of compensation and relocation, but also shaped how the mine dealt with other communities as the enterprise expanded. The campaign served to connect communities with each other as well as with allies within and outside of Colombia—and provided a political education for everyone involved.

At the same time, given the incredible imbalance of power, there have been real limits not only to how much the mine's actions can be influenced, but on the capacity of the campaign to improve the situation of the communities. The mine continues to expand and largely calls the shots in the region. The communities remain politically and economically marginalized, living under exceptionally difficult circumstances in a region where mining has made an already precarious existence nearly untenable.

In a larger sense, then, this campaign confronts many of the same challenges faced by much of Latin American solidarity work. To begin, the broader model of solidarity relies heavily on the ability of Latin Americans to capture the attention of international allies, who must then find ways to pressure corporations by garnering media attention, influencing shareholders, or accessing state power. Their capacity to do so, in turn, is a function of many factors, some of which are quite arbitrary. Most communities, for example, do not have the "benefit" of being exploited by a prominent global corporation such as Exxon.

Likewise, because international attention tends to be drawn to crisis and spectacle, and can require communities to display extreme suffering before a global audience, it can be fickle and fleeting as crises subside or simply fail to attract or sustain attention. A model of solidarity that relies on crisis or public outcry for its fuel can be prone to move from one fire to the next, addressing the most egregious aspects of particular cases before moving on to the next disaster. Typically, this leaves the underlying issues that produced the crisis in the first place unaddressed, and can have the effect of excluding most people from the political equation altogether, since relatively few people are exploited in ways that will ever place them on the public's radar.

Even more, as much as these campaigns embody and are sustained by remarkable human commitment and energy, they tend to work from very limited political and economic power on both ends of the solidarity equation. The needs of those we work with in Colombia are overwhelming, and far outstrip any capacity that we—as international allies—possess or could realistically develop in the future. Indeed, the communities sought international support in the first place because they could not depend on the Colombian state to defend their interests against foreign mining companies.[3] Nor could the communities mobilize sufficient allies or tap into social movements in Colombia to alter the mine's practices, influence the government, or otherwise advance their cause. The pursuit of international support, although courageous and creative, signaled the weakness of their overall position. The balance of power was and is stacked against them.

At the international end, although a committed group of activists from a number of different countries have been working on this campaign for well over a decade, we have few financial or human resources. In comparison with the communities, we no doubt seem, and in some ways are, "powerful." But we are a small group with no permanent staff, little budget, and limited political power. We have contacts and allies in numerous countries, and have (along with the communities) become skilled at identifying and accessing the mine's pressure points. But there is no political base or larger movement that we can tap into for support or resources.

Nor are we alone. Although this "campaign" model of political engagement, whereby a relatively small group from the global North attempts to support the struggle of a poor and isolated group in Latin America, is not the only form that contemporary solidarity takes, it has become sufficiently widespread to warrant historical and strategic reflection. How, in a sense, did we get here—to the point where this important, but relatively limited, form of intervention has become such a common form of solidarity? And, more importantly, how can we build effective international solidarity, particularly in a context where progressive forces are so politically marginalized? How do we practice and build revolutionary solidarity in the absence of revolutionary movements? What kinds of immediate, urgent, and (often) short-term struggles might help establish the building blocks for political movements that not only address moments of crisis or egregious cases of human rights abuse, but advance working-class power with the capacity to address broader issues of political and economic inequality—the very inequalities that make crisis and abuse such chronic features of everyday life in the first place?

Latin American Solidarity and Left Internationalism

These political questions led me to explore the broader history of Latin American solidarity in order to better understand how current forms of solidarity came to be, and how past efforts have or have not shaped or diverged from more recent struggles. Why and how did people in the United States embrace and transform a range of internationalisms, including anti-imperialism, anti-colonialism, socialism, labor, peace, religious, and human rights, when framing and engaging in solidarity with Latin America? What practices and strategies, forms of organization, and strands of internationalism have us-based activists adopted when participating in "solidarity" with Latin America? How have understandings and practices of solidarity changed over time, why has it mattered, and how has this international engagement shaped the us left?

The following is by no means a comprehensive history of Latin American solidarity. Such a book may one day be written, but the nature of Latin American solidarity will make this a particularly difficult enterprise. A broad range of us actors, often for quite distinct political and personal motivations, have practiced international solidarity throughout us history in a wide array of changing sites, organizations, institutions, and movements. Most of these efforts have not been centralized or coordinated by large or prominent organizations, and although this book attempts to trace the connections between various people, organizations, and campaigns, a defining feature of Latin American solidarity has been its ideological differentiation, lack of institutional continuity, and inconsistent presence.

The ongoing struggle for Latin American solidarity to cohere and gain consistent political traction is partly explained by the fact that much of its core has always been opposed to American empire, an opposition that has never been particularly easy or popular in the United States. Opponents to empire have not only had to confront the material forces of US political and economic power, but have also faced the uphill ideological battle of convincing Americans that the United States is, in fact, an imperial force. As a result, those from the United States who opposed US empire often found themselves isolated from American society, attacked by the US government, and even divided and disconnected from each other. They have, at times, been quite effective in capturing public attention, and have even secured important victories, but their struggles have been by their very nature pitted against dominant political currents. They have participated in campaigns that were tough to get off the ground, difficult to sustain, harder to grow, and whose impacts are hard to gauge. Writing a "complete" or comprehensive account of this history will be no easy task.[4]

And yet, for a number of reasons, the time is right for a history of Latin American solidarity. For one, the scholarship now exists to support such an endeavor. During the past two decades, academics have produced numerous studies focusing on particular solidarity campaigns and struggles.[5] Collectively, these fine-grained analyses allow for a broader history to be told. We also have more sweeping, global, histories of internationalism, particularly with respect to the human rights movement[6] and black internationalism.[7] This book draws heavily upon this superb scholarship.

More importantly, this is a particularly apt moment for a critical examination of the US left, especially its internationalist expressions. Since the end of the Second World War, the United States arguably has been the most powerful country in the world, both in its military reach and as the leading architect of a global capitalism that has delivered massive inequality and environmental destruction across the planet. If this imperial power is going to be constrained, reversed, or even overcome, we need to rebuild the US left. The construction of an effective left, with a strong internationalist current, is not only important for working people in the United States. It is imperative for the entire world.

This is hardly news to Latin Americans. They have been on the receiving end of US imperialism for well over a century, and have struggled against US military and economic aggression in their own countries. As a result, they know quite well how important a US left is—or rather could be—for restraining American empire. An oft-told story in solidarity circles reflects this very sentiment. When asked how US activists could help the Latin American cause, many Latin Americans have responded with some version of the following: "The best thing Americans can do is change things in the United States, fix your own country and government." As we will see, this mandate can be interpreted in a number of ways, emanates from a wide range of political orientations, and does not mean that on-the-ground solidarity in Latin America is not appreciated, welcome, or meaningful. But it does speak to the powerful influence of the US government and corporate interests in the region, as well as to the most important role that Latin American solidarity occupies: namely, to shape how US power operates in the Americas.

Much of the following, then, explores how, when, and why solidarity actors have attempted to advance this project. In the process, it is suggested not only that a left internationalism rooted in the United States is important for the future of the world, but that progressive forays into internationalism provide particularly revealing points of entry for understanding the US left as a whole, including its general decline and uneven disappearance from public life since the 1970s. Internationalism is not just a good measure of US empire. It is a good barometer of the left.

Indeed, the decline of the US left and revolutionary movements in Central America after the 1980s has limited the very forms that internationalism could take in recent decades. Solidarity that depended on mass mobilization, traditional left institutions, or even a critical mass on the left was largely off the table. US-based activists have long struggled over what it means to "be in solidarity" with Latin

Americans, but this ongoing challenge became even more difficult to navigate once revolutionary movements, institutions, and hopes were decimated in El Salvador, Guatemala, and Nicaragua. This was further complicated by the continuing decline of the US left and labor movement during the same period. There was simply less to connect to on both ends as activists struggled to get their bearings across the hemisphere.

Without a left, or at least without one possessing the capacity to influence state power or public debates, international allies have tended to engage in what can be best understood as defensive struggles to help Latin Americans "negotiate the best possible terms of their defeat"[8]—that is, to navigate a political landscape defined by weakened social movements and a particularly savage form of capitalism. In our work in Colombia, we pursued this path not so much because we, or our Colombian counterparts, could not imagine grander forms of internationalism, but because the range of options has been quite limited in a climate devoid of a left with meaningful political power. This is not to say these struggles have been insignificant. In many cases, helping allies make the best of a bad situation can represent an important, if partial, victory.

But it is to say that the ongoing decline of the left—of a force with the capacity to open up the political space necessary for addressing inequality—has made it much more difficult to imagine, let alone actively pursue, efforts to "scale up" political projects in a way that significantly, or even modestly, alters the balance of power for Latin Americans. What, in a political sense, are relatively localized, often isolated, typically under-resourced, and frequently short-term struggles trying to build in the long term? The decline of the left has made it difficult to pursue long-term projects, and challenging to even ask these types of strategic questions, in part because a vibrant left creates the spaces where those questions can be addressed. The relative absence of the left—and the corresponding rise of the right—has also allowed for the emergence of a political economy characterized by constant crisis, in which marginalized groups are often forced to act now (in order to survive) and think later. Under such circumstances, it is often difficult to connect immediate struggles to longer-term political projects.

Organization, Argument, and History

This book attempts to understand recent solidarity efforts histor-
ically by tracing the ongoing evolution, relationship, and struggle
between moderate and left-wing strands of internationalism within
the broader current of Latin American solidarity, and what this has
meant for the US left as a whole. The first part, Chapters 1 through
3, explores the long period from the 1800s until the onset of the Cold
War, an era during which solidarity was channeled primarily through
an anti-imperialism that was at times inflected by pacifism, black internationalism, and radical labor solidarity. Although we now tend
to associate anti-imperialism almost exclusively with the radical left,
it found a mainstream home during this period in part because imperialism was largely associated with Europe and the establishment of
overseas colonies, and thus taken up quite comfortably by US politicians, leading literary figures, and even the core of an emerging labor
movement. By the end of the nineteenth century and the first decades
of the twentieth, imperialism was seen as inherently un-American by
liberal sectors of the political establishment.

As European colonies receded from the Caribbean, however, and
the United States itself became an (overseas)⁹ imperial power during
the late 1800s and early 1900s, this common sense anti-imperialism
became harder to maintain, especially as many "anti-imperialists"
sought to justify a strong US presence in the Caribbean in order to
further national economic interests. Even so, lining up behind imperialism, which included rethinking how to understand it, proved
to be an uneven transition. Anti-imperialism retained a mainstream
foothold in the United States through the first half of the twentieth
century, and arguably played a role in limiting the nature and length
of US military occupations in the Dominican Republic (1916–24),
Haiti (1915–34), and Nicaragua (1912–33).

It was also during this period, however, that a revolutionary or
emancipatory internationalism—rooted in more radical understandings of anti-imperialism—emerged first around the Haitian
revolution, persisted unevenly through the 1800s around the global
struggle against slavery and the Cuban fight for independence,
and then intensified during the early twentieth century around the

8

Mexican Revolution and US military occupations in the Caribbean. As we will see, this revolutionary internationalism itself flowed through two semi-distinct, semi-intertwined, streams, defined on the one hand by a black internationalism that linked ongoing oppression at home with US imperialism abroad, and on the other hand by a (whiter) radical-socialist tradition that sought to make similar connections between the domestic and the international. The protagonists of revolutionary internationalism, regardless of from which tradition they came, were more likely than their mainstream counterparts to work or identify with Latin Americans, and saw their project not solely in terms of stopping US military intervention overseas, but in terms of a shared struggle to transform the world. What that new world would ultimately look like was not always clear or agreed upon, but revolutionary internationalism assumed a collective notion of liberation that would produce a fundamentally different order.

The ongoing development of revolutionary internationalism during the first decades of the twentieth century was fueled by the expansion of a broader US left that (for example) made connections between labor exploitation on both sides of the US–Mexico border; or between forms of oppression in the Jim Crow South and the racist nature of US imperialism in the Caribbean. It included a deeply internationalist element that was informed by (and at times in solidarity with) causes such as the Spanish civil war (1936–39), the Italian invasion of Ethiopia (1935–39),[10] and strikes in the Caribbean and West Africa in the late 1930s. There was also an important communist and anarchist presence within what was becoming a powerful labor movement, particularly in the Industrial Workers of the World (IWW, or Wobblies) and the mass-production unions of the Congress of Industrial Organizations (CIO). Put simply, the lines between labor and the left were much blurrier than they became during the Cold War. Indeed, it was precisely the interwoven nature of "domestic" and "internationalist" currents within the left, as well as the vibrant exchange and blurred boundaries between labor and the left, that made the prospects for the emergence of a powerful left rooted in labor and the working class so great during the 1930s.[11]

It was also the uneasy alliance, or at least willingness to work together and find common ground, between liberal and left anti-imperialists that made anti-imperialism a considerable force in American politics during the first half of the twentieth century. Part of this was tied to a period in which left ideas, actors, and organizations were (uneasily) accepted as part of the broader political milieu, but it was also because the language of anti-imperialism often meant different things to different people, and hence could house a variety of political projects. Not unlike human rights in the 1970s, the malleability of anti-imperialism served as a political umbrella that could welcome and mobilize a range of groups with differing political ideas and visions.

This would not last. The Second World War and the Cold War deeply disrupted the uneven development of international solidarity. During the war, much of the United States, and especially liberals, mainstream unions, and the left, set aside concerns about US empire and participated in the anti-fascist struggle.[12] This was reasonable enough given the importance of the fight and the fact that the US government itself was preoccupied with Europe, and hence not intervening as aggressively in Latin America. However, once the war was over, and anti-fascism quickly gave way to anti-communism, left internationalism in the United States was not simply slow to rebound. It was largely destroyed by a full-scale assault. This Cold War dismantling was true of the left in general, but the space for radical internationalism was particularly limited during the Cold War, especially from the end of the Second World War through the early 1960s.

The United States emerged from the war a superpower, its imperialism turbo-charged by anti-communism, and there was very little in the way of domestic opposition to empire. Opponents either acquiesced to, or were silenced by, imperial power. Many liberals—both African Americans and their white counterparts—joined the fight against communism, either because they saw it as part of a broader struggle against "totalitarianism," or because they simply realized that the political space for anti-imperialism was quickly disappearing as the Cold War heated up—and narrowed their political horizons accordingly. Liberals and leftists who stayed course found themselves under attack, and in many cases paid a dear price.

The labor movement, a central target of McCarthyite attacks, responded to the threat by purging most of the left from its ranks and embracing Cold War anti-communism both at home and abroad.[13]

This ensured that the core of labor, led by the AFL-CIO, did not participate in (and at times actively opposed) progressive internationalism
in the Americas for the next 50 years. It also meant that what remained
of the left was substantially disconnected from an increasingly conservative labor movement. As labor purged its left, what remained of
the US left lost and became disconnected from labor.

But labor was hardly the only space where liberals severed connections with the left at the onset of the Cold War. It was this separation,
which included a liberal shift to the right and the concurrent dismantling of the left, that undermined progressive politics in the United
States in general, and essentially destroyed the broad current of anti-
imperialism that had emerged during the first half of the twentieth
century. What this meant in concrete terms is that when US-backed
Cold War violence swept over Latin America beginning in the 1950s
and 1960s, the very forms of internationalism that might have been
expected to offer a challenge were either absent or severely debilitated. This decimation of left internationalism, in turn, created space
for the emergence of alternative internationalisms that could survive
in the politically hostile world of Cold War anti-communism, while
also being sufficiently meaningful and effective for solidarity activists
looking to extend a hand to Latin Americans. With violence sweeping
Latin America, and US-based left internationalism in retreat, there
was something of a solidarity vacuum.

The second part of the book, Chapters 4 and 5, explores the path
by which human rights filled this vacuum during the Cold War, in
effect tracing how modern Latin American solidarity blossomed
through human rights at roughly the same time as left internationalism struggled to survive. What was it about human rights that
allowed it to thrive when other forms of internationalism were being
"disappeared" by the Cold War? What made it so attractive to US
activists as a way of framing, imagining, and mobilizing solidarity
during the 1970s and 1980s? And why were human rights, as opposed
to other currents of internationalism, the dominant vehicle through
which modern Latin American solidarity emerged as an identifiable
political project?

In retrospect, the close association between Latin American solidarity and human rights may seem almost inevitable to those of us

who can hardly imagine a solidarity landscape without human rights at its core. By the 1980s and 1990s, the two were deeply intertwined, as many activists simply saw human rights as the way to engage in progressive internationalism. Yet, as late as 1970, the capture of internationalism by human rights was far from assured. Human rights were barely on the map and not part of mainstream discourse.[14]

What this part of the book argues,[15] in essence, is that the ascent of human rights within Latin American solidarity was possible not only because it offered a compelling way of confronting forms of violence that could be tied to US actors and policies, but because it was not a form of left internationalism—an internationalism premised on the notion that collective struggle is undertaken with the goal of generating deep transformation and addressing material inequality. As mainstream human rights became rooted in the professional collection and distribution of information about torture and false imprisonment, it actively distanced itself from political projects, including those of so-called human rights victims. In a sense, it had to. In order to be seen as a neutral, objective observer, one that could be trusted to reliably identify and denounce human rights abuses, human rights organizations actively divorced themselves from any politics, but particularly from an identifiably left politics aimed at reducing inequalities. It was the very limited nature of this political project—one that did not so much challenge the Cold War consensus as reaffirm it—that allowed human rights to not only survive during the Cold War, but blossom through it.[16] In this sense, while the anti-communism of the Cold War made it very difficult for internationalisms rooted in economic justice to thrive, the violence of the Cold War helped create a set of conditions that enabled more narrowly focused interventions around what came to be understood as international human rights.

This was important for the long-term trajectory of international solidarity. Although human rights cannot possibly be held responsible for the inability of left internationalism to re-emerge in the decades immediately following the Second World War,[17] its emergence as the standard-bearer of internationalism made it more difficult to re-establish (more ambitious) left internationalisms. This was not simply because human rights gobbled up all the oxygen in the proverbial internationalist room. It was that human rights displaced or crowded out a range of internationalisms that assumed collective struggle would fundamentally change the world with a form of solidarity that was actively divorced from transformative political projects altogether. In so doing, it altered the political calculus while limiting the horizon of international solidarity. This transformation was never complete, and more radical understandings and uses of human rights certainly persisted, but it nonetheless represented a significant shift.

Human rights also contributed to a solidarity landscape defined in part by relatively small campaigns with limited political goals. It encouraged, if not institutionalized, a model of solidarity managed by professional organizations (NGOs) which engaged in short-term campaigns that were intended not so much to build political power as to capture international (media) attention in order to respond to urgent crises, abuses, and needs. In this sense, it was not simply that political visions and projects narrowed with the disappearance of the left, but that narrowed modes of solidarity such as human rights filled political spaces that both were a product of the left's decline and contributed to its further marginalization. A contracted political horizon, generated in part by the decline of the left, helped produce the human rights movement, but the human rights movement also made it more difficult to imagine and pursue more revolutionary forms of internationalism.

The rise of human rights did not, however, mean that left internationalism disappeared completely. In fact, although the re-emergence of a left anti-imperialism within Latin American solidarity was overshadowed in relative terms by the ascendance of human rights, it too experienced a resurgence during the 1980s through engagement around Central America. This was substantially because of the presence of revolutionary movements in El Salvador, Guatemala, and Nicaragua, which animated and inspired US leftists who sought to advance socialist revolution abroad at a time when it was not possible at home.

Central American revolutions also captured the attention of Ronald Reagan, however, who backed repressive military regimes and essentially guaranteed the continuing relevance of the human rights movement. The proliferation of human rights violations and associated activism both raised the profile of international solidarity and had a radicalizing effect on many activists. Targets of human rights violations in Latin America were generally on the left, and many were engaged in a politics that challenged the social order in fundamental ways. As a result, Americans who were drawn to activism by the human tragedy often became engaged in (or at least sympathetic towards) transformative political projects. In this sense, there was a productive tension between human rights and left internationalism that helped fuel the dramatic growth of the Central American peace movement during the 1980s.

At the same time, part of why the peace movement, including its left wing, figured so prominently in the US political landscape of the 1980s was that the broader left was itself disappearing from public life. With so little hope on the domestic front, many activists turned their energies to international issues in the 1980s. The bleakness of the moment, characterized by the ongoing decline of the labor movement, the rightward slide of American society, and the "end" of socialism, served to exaggerate the size of the peace movement while hiding the extent to which it was politically isolated. Just as the peace movement could not reverse the ongoing decline of the left, the left was not in a position to bolster the peace movement by altering the broader political landscape that produced Reagan and a resurgent Cold War foreign policy in the first place. Despite all its energy and innovation, as well as its considerable impact on the US Congress, Latin American solidarity struggled to alter the fundamentals of US–Latin American relations even during its height in the 1980s, and had difficulty sustaining a presence after Reagan left office, the civil wars came to an end, and military regimes relinquished power in Central America. This speaks partly to the difficulty of sustaining left internationalism when the broader left is in steep decline.

The third part of the book, Chapters 6 through 8, explores the trajectory of Latin American solidarity from the 1990s through the early 2000s. Latin American solidarity went through a period of retrenchment and reorientation after the peace movement dissipated, but the urgency associated with the neoliberal crisis provided the fuel for continued solidarity. The focus was now less around human rights abuses than a series of economic and labor-related issues that were tied to the neoliberal assault on working people. This included the growing focus on trade in progressive circles in the late 1980s and 1990s, beginning with opposition to the North American Free Trade Agreement (NAFTA) and the ongoing development of "fair trade" (Chapter 6); as well as solidarity efforts around the Zapatistas, the global justice movement, anti-corporate campaigns, and the anti-sweatshop movement (Chapters 7 and 8). In the process, the chapters collectively suggest that as diverse as these efforts have been, they all were products of the neoliberal moment in at least three senses.

First, although these political initiatives have long historical roots, they all responded to the policies and consequences of neoliberalism by the 1990s. In the case of NAFTA and the Zapatistas, where opposition coalesced around a free trade agreement, this seems fairly obvious. But fair trade, corporate campaigns, and anti-sweatshop activism also were refashioned and energized by the devastating impacts of neoliberalism on working people in Latin America. North Americans witnessed the disastrous consequences of the Washington Consensus, felt responsible, and wanted to support Latin American struggles.

Second, all emerged in a landscape, partly produced by neoliberalism, in which traditional large-scale oppositional movements were in decline, debilitated, or absent from the scene altogether. This political vacuum created opportunities, but also generated a solidarity that inherited much from the human rights movement, including a focus on the most extreme and high-profile of abuses, and a highly fragmented organizational infrastructure rooted heavily in NGOs that was ill equipped to deal with neoliberal capitalism. Neoliberalism created a seemingly endless number of crises, but in the absence of a broader left it proved difficult not only to connect these issues, but to name the problem or mobilize a relatively coherent opposition around them. Latin Americans would do this throughout much of the region starting in the mid to late 1990s with the rise of the "pink tide," but an anti-neoliberal bloc did not emerge in the United States during this period.

Third, and most importantly, although all of these political initiatives opposed neoliberalism, they also shared in its logic by embracing a politics that moved away from the state as a key site of activity and struggle. This anti-statism, which in some ways was built into attempts by the human rights movement to restrain state power (often through independent monitoring from stateless entities), really took off in the 1970s as the state came to be seen as part of the problem. The broader neoliberal attack on government during the 1980s furthered this tendency, and made it politically and ideologically difficult to develop a positive vision of the state, particularly one in which government was understood as possessing the capacity to mold an economy for the benefit of its citizenry. This assault, when coupled by the absence of left movements with the capacity to capture or significantly shape state power, encouraged a range of progressive political initiatives that attempted to side-step the state as a political site. In different ways, the Zapatista struggle, along with fair trade, anti-corporate, global justice, and anti-sweatshop movements, all adopted this logic as standard operating procedure during the 1990s and early 2000s. The result was an internationalism that was channeled through organizations and strategies that were not equipped to deal with the very problems and forces it opposed.

A Note on the Meaning of Solidarity

Solidarity is very difficult to define at any particular moment, to say nothing of the fact that its meaning changes over time. It is a contested and somewhat vague concept which continues to mean different things to different people who are often advancing quite distinct goals and visions. Depending on context, it can be a claim, aspiration, argument, political vision, way of including/excluding particular groups, or all of the above and more.

The term itself is surprisingly recent in origin. "Solidarity" only took on a political meaning in the late 1700s during the French revolution, when revolutionaries began to use the term instead of "fraternity" to indicate and create a sense of political community. From there, it went in a variety of directions within Europe, but was most notably adopted by workers and religious communities to deal with the social dislocation and fragmentation associated with industrial capitalism.

The notion of working-class solidarity developed in this context, and served to popularize the broader concept while taking it in a radical direction. The interests of the individual worker became fused with those of the collective, which in this case was understood in terms of class. Here, solidarity was rooted in sameness, an abstract universalism. Workers, by virtue of their mutual experiences and similar socio-economic location in society, were said to share common interests that were opposed to the capitalist class. This was an aspirational claim about how a particular group, in this case an entire class, should see themselves and the world. It did not mean that working-class solidarity actually existed. Divisions around nationality, religion, geography, race/ethnicity, gender, and a whole series of other lines have always made it difficult to achieve working-class solidarity. Indeed, despite early claims of transcending nation, and a compelling slogan (Workers of the World Unite!), generating international working-class solidarity has always been particularly difficult, existing more as an aspiration and political vision than as a concrete reality. Solidarity has to be forged.

Likewise, the claim that workers' interests were opposed to capitalists did not necessarily lead to a shared goal or agreed set of methods for advancing their interests. Some, particularly within the socialist tradition, sought to defeat the capitalist class for the benefit of society as a whole. Others wanted to build cooperatives or alternative economic forms to compete with or replace factories, while still others sought to resolve class conflict through peaceful reforms. What was ultimately radical about working-class solidarity was that it offered a quite different basis for cohesion or solidarity, one that required active organizing and was rooted not in family, village, nation, or religion, but in class—an openly political category that challenged other claims of solidarity, particularly nation and religion, while pointing to an inherent conflict between working people and their oppressors.

Religious communities, and particularly the Catholic Church, were also worried about the alienation, competition, and upheaval brought by industrial capitalism. Rejecting both liberalism and (especially) socialism, Christian solidarity sought to integrate workers, employers, and others into a peaceful and harmonious world. As a method for integrating society, Christian solidarity initially looked more like charity and had little to say about inequality, but as society's ills outstripped the capacity of families and voluntary organizations, religious institutions increasingly recognized the importance of the state for ensuring a just society, including fair wages and working conditions. Workers were not to make claims against their employers.

Such advocacy was to be carried out by more privileged sectors, and insure social integration while removing the need for workers and the poor to take political action. As the concept of Christian solidarity developed during the twentieth century, it saw government playing an even more forceful role in alleviating inequality, and at times (as we will see with liberation theology in Latin America) came to share more with a solidarity rooted in notions of class conflict.[18]

By the early 1900s, solidarity was also being applied and asserted within the international context of supporting anti-colonial or anti-imperialist struggles. Here, international solidarity could mean supporting the right to self-determination for colonized (or previously colonized) people by working to keep colonial-imperial powers out of what came to be known as the Third World. But it could also include more racially rooted claims of being in solidarity with African and Asian people against a global system of exploitation. Solidarity with "Third World" peoples at times worked from a global understanding that saw race and class oppression as intertwined, and produced through racialized processes of capitalism and imperialism. Even in the hands of committed socialists such as Che Guevara, who in some ways personified the 1960s notion of a revolutionary forged through solidarity, internationalism blended revolutionary working-class solidarity with the anti-imperialist solidarity of Third World peoples.

Indeed, one of the questions that international solidarity brought to the fore was, how do we enter into solidarity with people who on the surface are so different? Solidarity rooted in race or class asserts sameness, whereby "we," regardless of geographic location, engage in solidarity with people who are "like us" because of a shared experience of oppression and/or a common socio-economic location. This claim continued to inform international solidarity throughout the twentieth century, particularly among socialists and radical people of color in the United States who found common cause with people of African, Asian, and Latin American descent. But it was increasingly accompanied by solidarity that was rooted less in a common experience or economic position than in a series of other concerns and goals that ultimately reflected how actors see the world and envision the future.

For revolutionaries such as Che, who did not come from working-class backgrounds, solidarity was rooted not so much in sameness as in a shared political commitment to radical transformation, a tendency with a long history that many within the us left shared and (often) developed during the post-war period through international engagement around the Cuban revolution, South America during the 1970s, and Central America in the 1980s. This radical project was, however, difficult to rebuild and sustain in the United States during the post-Second-World-War period for reasons discussed below, including the onslaught of the Cold War, a broader political shift to the right, the rise of neoliberalism, and the demise of socialism and the Soviet Union. Indeed, although the end of the USSR ultimately allowed for a more open and vibrant discussion of socialism, in the short term the Soviet Union's demise weakened the egalitarian ideal—the notion that governments, even those of capitalist countries, should facilitate a modicum of economic equality. In this sense, the increasingly small space occupied by revolutionary internationalism and the us left as a whole was part of a broader shift away from forms of solidarity that sought to shape or capture state power with the purpose of redistributing wealth—something that previous solidarity efforts had largely assumed.

International solidarity nonetheless persisted, and took many forms during the post-war period, but did so within a restricted political space that led to, and in some ways forced, narrowed visions and less ambitious political projects. For many religious and secular actors solidarity meant aligning themselves with those who suffered from us intervention. Solidarity in this case was motivated not out of the sameness of experience, or necessarily a shared political project, but by a sense of responsibility that the us government or economy was causing suffering in other places, and that such suffering could not be disconnected from the privileges enjoyed in the United States. The goal here was to alter the us presence in the region, reduce the suffering, and perhaps allow Latin Americans to chart their own political and economic course. In a world defined by massive global inequality, this type of solidarity, regardless of the radicalness of its politics, often contained a degree of humanitarianism and assumed hierarchy, whereby one group "gives" and another group "receives" solidarity. The goals and motivations driving solidarity shape, in turn, the methods and forms that solidarity takes, ranging from active support of revolutionary groups and opposition to US policies to creating alternative economies, delivering development aid, or providing sanctuary for exiles and refugees.

All of this and more is included and discussed in this history. As a piece of scholarship, the book makes no claims of being comprehensive, but does work from a fairly expansive understanding of what has constituted "Latin American solidarity" over time, including for example those who might have opposed US foreign policy but could in no way be said to have been (or saw themselves as) "in solidarity" with Latin Americans in the sense of advancing a shared political project. The book points to the strengths and limitations of various initiatives that had something to say or do about the presence of the United States in the western hemisphere. But it spends little time judging whether certain efforts did or did not constitute solidarity at a particular moment in time.

As a political intervention, however, this account points to the importance of developing a revolutionary international solidarity that helps build deep and continuous movements with the capacity to radically restructure local, national, and international political-economies by shaping or capturing state power. Markets need to be restructured, political power reordered, and wealth radically redistributed. This requires the state, and also has to occur on multiple levels, including globally—which is why a left internationalism that is less aspiration and more substance is so important. This is a tall order, and one that requires an expanded US left that can not only engage more effectively in struggles that put out fires or alleviate crises, but lead short-term fights that help us sustain long-term struggles and movements. By supporting political efforts in other countries, and engaging in shared struggles across borders, US left internationalism can not only be part of the global fight against capitalism, but also part of the process through which the left, including its domestic and internationalist expressions, is reconstituted. What the following explores is how left internationalism developed in the distant and recent past with an eye towards building a better future.

I

US Empire, Anti-Imperialism, and Revolution

From the beginning of the 1800s through the early 1900s anti-imperialism was the driving force within (progressive) US-based internationalism in relation to Latin America. The prominent, mainstream, version of this current was rooted primarily in a liberal political class that associated imperialism with Europe and foreign colonies. Understood this way, US politicians, sectors of the intelligentsia, and the core of an emerging labor movement opposed those who pushed for US empire. They were "anti-imperialist" in that they wanted Europe out of what was increasingly seen as an "American" hemisphere, and that they were opposed to the United States establishing its own overseas colonies.

This current was itself quite differentiated. Some felt US military intervention was a betrayal of US history and democratic values, while others grounded their opposition in a broad commitment to peace. For still others, opposition to overseas colonies was rooted in more re-actionary motives, like not wanting to incorporate "tropical peoples" into the nation-state because either they would dilute the genetic pool or they could never be assimilated. Despite internal differentiation, this opposition nevertheless mobilized against proponents of empire who pushed for a stronger US military presence overseas.

This was an oddly imperial form of anti-imperialism which was by and large not internationalist, was often racist and paternalistic, rarely engaged in active solidarity with Latin Americans, and typically worked from an understanding of imperialism that was defined primarily in terms of US military intervention. Assuming that the United States had fundamentally good intentions, and that the overall presence of the United States in the region was benevolent, main-stream anti-imperialism generally took it for granted that the United States should intervene in all sorts of ways that extended American power in the region. If the United States simply refrained from estab-lishing foreign colonies and kept rogue corporate actors in check, a greater American presence in the hemisphere would be good for the United States and Latin America.

A more radical anti-imperialism also emerged during this period, however, and in some ways predated its mainstream counterpart. Revolutionary or emancipatory internationalism shared in the oppo-sition to US intervention, but pushed anti-imperialism to the left in two important respects. First, it tended to define imperialism not only in terms of US military intervention, but as a larger system of oppression that negatively impacted people in both Latin America and the United States. How that oppression was understood—in racial, class, or an-ti-democratic terms (or some combination)—could vary, but it was seen as central to how the United States operated at home and abroad. Second, the revolutionary current also tended to be more interna-tionalist in the sense of understanding the fight against imperialism as a collective project to be carried out with allies in Latin America. Overall, then, what this meant is that revolutionary anti-imperialists began to see themselves as advancing a collective project to transform the world.

Chapter 1 begins and ends with revolution and revolutionary in-ternationalism. As a world event that ushered in the 1800s, the Haitian revolution generated an international solidarity which recognized that global processes of colonialism and slavery had profoundly shaped the world, and that people living in very different places had all seen their lives negatively disrupted by forces and people of European origin. In the United States, this internationalist impulse was often led by African Americans who suggested that people of African de-scent throughout the world, and colonized peoples more broadly, could engage in a collective struggle to radically transform the world. Such visions sought to deepen and extend notions of freedom and liberation associated with the French and American revolutions.[1]

After the US civil war, this US-based internationalism—rooted in anti-colonial, anti-slavery solidarity—channeled its energy towards

Cuba's decades-long struggle for independence during the second half of the 1800s. Seeing the end of slavery in the United States as but one step in a broader struggle, sectors of African Americans helped coordinate international support for Cuban rebels. They advocated against direct US intervention, which they suspected would lead the United States to occupy the island and impose a Jim Crow style of rule on the Cuban people. They argued instead that Cubans were more than capable of repelling the Spanish by themselves if given material aid.[2] Likewise, although sectors of the broader left were initially skeptical of the Cuban struggle because of the support it received from more mainstream actors in the United States, they too eventually became some of Cuba's strongest supporters.

The attraction of the Cuban struggle went well beyond African Americans and the left, however, and produced a more moderate anti-imperialism which was pushed by a broad range of politicians, intellectuals, pacifists, religious leaders, labor organizations, and the like. This differentiated current supported Cuban independence from Spain for a multiplicity of reasons, including to advance US business interests on the island. The use of US troops to push the Spanish out and control Cuba was debated, and solidarity with Cuban rebels was understood in fairly instrumental terms. All of this was shaped by widespread support throughout US society for Cuban freedom from Spanish rule.

By the start of the 1900s, Marx's growing presence was felt as revolution swept over Mexico, and along with it a radical, cross-border, labor solidarity rooted in socialist and anarchist traditions. Here, like Haiti, international solidarity with Mexico was an avenue for developing a revolutionary praxis that saw collective struggle as a path not simply for replacing governments, but for restructuring society. That revolutionary solidarity emerged in a border region defined by the conspicuous presence of US capital and a particularly aggressive and exploitative form of economic development is not entirely surprising.

The point here is not that solidarity during this period was deep or wide, evolving neatly in any particular direction, or somehow more ideologically pure or radical than what came later. It was that not only did mainstream anti-imperialism keep more aggressive calls for a colonial empire in check, but forms of revolutionary internationalism began to emerge and promote transformational political projects, visions, and agendas. Such projects were, to be sure, incomplete, inconsistent, and muddled on a number of levels, but they nonetheless assumed that the world should be ordered in fundamentally different ways. They were political not simply in the sense of being partisan, or in the recognition that power and wealth were unequally distributed, but in that they were implicitly or explicitly grounded in collective notions of liberation that would usher in a new world.

Global Inequality, Global Solidarity

The massive global inequalities produced by colonialism, slavery, and the industrial revolution generated ideas and movements about human equality and justice, about the place of collective action in transforming society, and about what solidarity across borders might look like in a modern world. Part of what made these issues so urgent, and part of what made the modern world so revolutionary in terms of creating inequality and challenging it, was that colonialism, slavery, and industrialization all worked to draw or force millions of people out of traditional societies. Modern forces ruptured these worlds in profound ways, disrupting rural societies that had their own inequalities and hierarchies, but that nonetheless often possessed quite distinct worldviews and forms of social organization which led people to openly challenge the new reality of global empires, capitalist expansion, and violent displacement on ever-increasing scales.

The formation of the United States was itself very much part of this broader process of imperial reach, colonial expansion, and violent dislocation. The US government shifted from treating Native American tribes as foreign entities and signing treaties with them, to incorporating them as domestic subordinates. African Americans went from being excluded from citizenship to being granted it, but in compromised ways. Latin America shifted from colonial status to independence, with northern Mexico subsequently being incorporated into the United States, creating a new population of second-class citizens and semi-incorporated Native American groups. All of these processes and policies, in turn, created opportunities for solidarity between allies within the United States and colonized, incorporated, and/or enslaved peoples within and around the emerging nation-state.

In this sense, although international solidarity—as solidarity among people of different countries or nation-states—could not be based in the United States prior to 1776, the formation of the United States itself generated opposition that created opportunities for transnational solidarity between colonized peoples and sympathetic colonizers (or between slaves and white allies). Put another way, the earliest examples of us-rooted "solidarity" that proposed a different form of social organization, and linked those inside and outside of the United States against empire, were those connected to Africans and Native Americans before and after 1776. Those who opposed the policies and practices of imperial expansion and slavery were (at times) challenging the very basis of the emerging nation-state, and/or listening to voices within Native-American and slave communities that offered alternative visions of organizing society.

The extent and nature of such solidarity can, of course, be easily overstated. The widespread belief in white superiority, and a deeply entrenched paternalism, made forging real solidarity between white allies and Native Americans or enslaved people extremely challenging during this period. In the case of Native Americans, it was not really until after western expansion had been essentially completed, and most Native Americans massacred through genocidal campaigns, that much in the way of "solidarity" emerged. And even then, reformers held a wide range of perspectives, with some advocating that (the remaining) Native Americans should be sovereign and independent, and others pushing for assimilation, education, and enhanced rights within the system. Either way, it was generally assumed that "Indians" needed to be civilized and their societies rehabilitated through the introduction of Christianity or other modernizing projects. Likewise, white abolitionists also framed their work with slaves in quite varied, but often paternalistic, ways which generally assumed white superiority.

Free blacks and enslaved Africans, by contrast, consistently challenged these views, arguing that the American revolution itself should deliver freedom to all.[3] Indeed, it was in many ways among free blacks in the United States during this revolutionary period that the seeds of a black internationalism rooted in the idea of universal emancipation were planted.[4] What emancipation would look like was not always agreed upon and would evolve over time, in part because its religious and secular foundations could be quite varied, but it often went well beyond abolition to include liberation for colonial and oppressed peoples the world over.

Haiti

The first instance of us-based solidarity across international borders within the Americas occurred not long after 1776, and was sparked by the Haitian revolution. The Haitian revolution (1791–1804) was a struggle by blacks to overthrow colonialism/slavery and claim full citizenship before a world audience. As such, it inspired and actively fomented rebellion and revolution across the hemisphere. It was also an early precursor to post-Second World War anti-colonial movements which took revolutionary nationalism in internationalist directions.[5]

us-based attempts at solidarity with Haiti were constrained, in part by the difficulty of travel during this period, and in part because white reaction to the Haitian revolution was defined largely by fear and horror. The threat posed by the revolution to slavery and colonialism, the bulwarks of European and us power and wealth, made it intolerable. Indeed, one response to Haiti was what Ashli White called "transatlantic racial solidarity," a counter-revolutionary solidarity, as whites in the United States raised funds and tried to help refugees fleeing the revolution.[6] Most "white observers saw Haiti as a place of equality perverted and run amok."[7] Mainstream opinion, fueled by stories of black violence from white refugees fleeing Haiti, confirmed the idea that blacks "were a separate and degraded people" who could not possibly manage an economy, much less run a country or develop a functioning civil society.[8] For its part, the us government would not recognize Haiti's independence until 1862.[9]

For many blacks, however, Haiti served as a revolutionary inspiration, and it is here—in the early expressions of what we came to think of as black liberation—that the modern origins of a revolutionary

26

solidarity within the Americas can be found. As Michael West and William Martin argue:

> For the black international, the events in Saint Domingue were iconic. The Haitian Revolution represented a culmination of decades of armed struggle by enslaved Africans in the Atlantic world, even as it heralded exciting new developments in the black quest for universal emancipation. Like no other event before or since, the Haitian Revolution electrified African-descended people all over the Americas, the enslaved majority along with the nominally free minority. Haiti became the bellwether of black freedom in the Atlantic world, albeit one that would not be replicated, although not for want of trying. Haiti's symbolic value to black internationalism was a primary reason for the hostility and isolation it faced from slaveholders and white powers everywhere.[10]

Haiti inspired by example, contributing to rebellious impulses in the United States in the form of the Pointe Coupee Conspiracy in Louisiana (1795), Gabriel Prosser's revolt in Virginia (1800) and Denmark Vesey's rebellion in Charleston (1822).[11] The Haitian revolution's anniversary and heroes were celebrated by African Americans throughout the 1800s, allowing them to connect "the fate of their own freedom with emancipation of people in Latin America and the Caribbean."[12] As Frederick Douglass told an audience at the World Columbian Exposition in Chicago in 1893, Haiti was "the original pioneer emancipator of the nineteenth century."[13] For sectors of African Americans, anti-slavery and anti-imperialism were deeply intertwined, and animated a collective struggle for an expansive vision of liberation.[14]

Although broader solidarity was severely constrained by the fact that Haiti terrified most whites, there were a few white abolitionists who recognized and applauded the revolutionary potential of Haiti, seeing it as part of a longer democratic push.[15] In a series of three essays entitled "The rights of black men," Abraham Bishop of Connecticut offered support for the Haitian rebels which prefigured many of the arguments of later-day solidarity movements, including an interesting blend of secular and religious ideas. "Like a handful of other antislavery advocates," historian Tim Matthewson writes,

Bishop "sympathized with the antislavery thrust of the Haitian revolution because he saw it as part of the great global revolution which
began in 1776 and would soon sweep away the last vestiges of barba-
rism and slavery."[16] Bishop began by justifying the need for armed
struggle on the part of the slaves. "They are asserting those rights
by the sword which it was impossible to secure by mild measures."[17]
Abolitionists, Bishop claimed, were hypocrites if they failed to extend
support to revolutionary Haiti.[18] Important as such dissident voices
were in articulating a more radical form of liberation, Bishop and
fellow abolitionist Theodore Dwight were rather lone voices among
US whites.

Latin American Wars for Independence and the US Invasion of Mexico

The Latin American wars for independence from Spain were understood in a more positive light by most people in the United States than
was the Haitian revolution. Although Haiti continued to trouble, the
universal ideals of freedom and democracy that the United States was
theoretically founded upon continued to inspire, and were the lens
through which Latin American independence was understood during
the period from 1810 to 1825. As Caitlin Fitz has so ably documented,
people in the United States not only paid considerable attention to
Latin American independence, but "took republicanism's southward
spread as a complement to themselves, seeing it as proof that their
own ideals really were universal."[19] In celebrating Latin American
independence, then, Americans were celebrating themselves.[20]

During this relatively brief moment, white observers were fairly
open to not only the anti-colonialism embodied in Latin American
struggles, but abstract notions of abolition and racial equality. This
commitment to the egalitarian principles of the American revolution
allowed them to "embrace a group of multiracial Catholic revolutionaries whose battles were at once anticolonial and antislavery."[21] US
observers "rarely dwelled on the insurgents' Catholicism," and "re-
acted to news of the Spanish-American antislavery efforts and black
leadership with casual acceptance rather than outraged alarm."[22]

This solidarity was often passive, and did not seem to produce
a critical engagement around slavery and white supremacy in the

United States. It was also at times a little shallow, as Americans named their livestock, towns, and sons after Spanish-speaking statesmen, or toasted hemispheric independence on July 4. But Americans also sent disaster relief, sold arms and ammunition to rebels, and even "risked their lives under rebel flags as mercenaries and privateers."[23] More than this, there was a generally positive view of Latin America, even if it had more to do with how Americans were coming to understand their own nation than with what was going on in the rest of the hemisphere.

By the mid-1820s, however, this brief love affair with Latin American independence, and the uneven commitment to universal principles of equality embodied in it, gave way to the rhetoric of white US exceptionalism.[24] Latin American freedom came to be seen as dangerous once it was understood through a racial lens, in which darker-skinned people broke free from Spanish rule. Given that US leaders ruled over a slave society, it is not surprising that they came to see Latin American independence this way, or that it made them uncomfortable. This led to the tendency, especially among Southern Democrats, to draw an increasingly sharp distinction between the noble cause of the American revolution and the "savage" wars in Latin America.[25] In a sense, the conceptual gap between Latin American wars and the Haitian revolution was narrowing. For future President John Adams, the American revolution was a "war of freemen" whereas those in Latin America were "savage" "[w]ar[s] of Slaves against their masters."[26] African Americans, not surprisingly, saw Latin American emancipation in much more positive terms.[27]

This shift towards a more negative, paternalistic, and ultimately racist understanding of Latin America was also tied to the fact that as European colonialism faded, US influence in the region grew and became increasingly imperial. This, in turn, yielded attempts—almost always rooted in US exceptionalism and assumed superiority—to justify why a strong US presence would benefit the rest of the hemisphere. That is, it became harder to place Latin American events, ideas, and peoples on a par with those in the United States as the region became a primary target of US empire.

This backdrop colored the intense opposition that emerged around the prospect of US involvement in the war with Mexico (1845–48), in which the United States ultimately occupied and annexed over half of its southern neighbor. Before the war started, opposition to US adventurism was fairly widespread and—on the eve of the US Civil War—quickly linked to efforts to expand slavery into new US states or territories. Members of Congress quickly labeled the conflict "Mr. Polk's War," charging that President James K. Polk provoked the war in order to generate public hysteria, stampede a war resolution through Congress, acquire land from a weak neighbor, and expand to the south and west in order to extend slavery and augment the power of the slaveholding South. Journalists and other critics pointed out that Polk's request for Congress to recognize the war had the facts completely reversed: It was not Mexico that was the aggressor, but the United States.[28]

Ralph Waldo Emerson, Henry David Thoreau, and other well-known literary figures voiced strong opposition to the war. Thoreau's 1849 essay "Civil disobedience," which was subsequently taken up by both Gandhi and Martin Luther King, emerged out of his opposition to what he understood as an imperialistic war which sought to expand slavery.[29] And organizations like the American Peace Society and the American Anti-Slavery Society wrote, petitioned, and protested. Most reformers had little, if any, contact with Mexicans, and some were openly anxious about the racial implications of Latin American independence movements more broadly. But they successfully exposed the hypocrisy behind the US government's justification for starting an unprovoked war.[30]

African Americans went further, quickly connecting the war to the expansion of slavery, but also linking their own struggles to long-standing efforts by Latin Americans to break free from both slavery and colonialism. They were much more likely to see Latin Americans as fellow travelers in the struggle against imperialism and slavery. As Paul Ortiz writes, "Inundated with propaganda about the superiority of Anglo-Saxon institutions, [African American] freedom fighters against slavery looked to Haiti, Mexico, and other nations in the Global South for political wisdom on how to grapple with racial capitalism."[31] Frederick Douglass denounced the invasion of Mexico as a "'disgraceful, cruel, and iniquitous war' that doomed Mexico to be 'victim of Anglo-Saxon cupidity and love of domination.'"[32] He saw this as "a war against freedom, against the Negro, against the interests of workingmen in this country."[33]

For working people, many of whom were recent immigrants, the war was experienced through the competing prisms of class and race. Aspirations to whiteness led many to rally to the imperialist cry. However, as Paul Foos notes, "common soldiers realized that their part in conquest would be as wage-earning guardians of the propertied classes, Mexican and Anglo, with their 'glory' collected in the form of atrocities against the poor and dispossessed."[34] Indeed, the desertion rate was higher than for any war in US history, punctuated by the desertion of Saint Patrick's battalion, a division of soldiers that actually abandoned the US army to join the Mexican side.[35]

Once the fighting began, however, support for the war became fairly widespread, and dissident voices became more difficult to hear. For a nation of farmers, including many aspiring landowners, the acquisition of millions of acres in the West no doubt proved seductive. Vocal opposition was largely confined to the north-eastern united States, and was a mixed bag. Many opponents feared expansion or empowerment of the slave South, while others did not want more non-whites admitted as citizens, or simply did not believe Mexicans had the capacity to be governed as a colony or protectorate. A small minority did see the war as a US conquest of foreign territory, and denounced such actions as immoral and belonging to feudal Europe, but even this minority saw Mexicans as inherently inferior to Anglo-Saxons. In the end, US aggression produced a politically muddled and differentiated opposition, and actual solidarity with Latin Americans was not yet part of the equation.

Cuba's Struggle for Independence

Long before the US war with Spain formally commenced in 1898, "possession of Cuba became a fixture of U.S. policy."[36] States in the North wanted access to Cuba's tropical products, while those to the South saw the island's potential as a valuable addition to the slaveholding states. Cuba came to be understood as US destiny, as fundamental to national interests. As Thomas Jefferson wrote to James Monroe in 1823, Cuba's "addition to our confederacy is exactly what is wanting to round out our power as a nation to the point of its utmost interest."[37] After numerous failed attempts to purchase the island, however, the United States reluctantly accepted Spanish sovereignty, and in fact guaranteed it by declaring that the United States would not allow control over the island to transfer to another European power.

Cubans, however, continually pushed for independence from Spain through a series of insurrections during the second half of the 1800s. Although none toppled Spanish rule, they did serve to elevate the cause of Cuban independence on the island and within the United States. They also revealed a fundamental feature of the Cuban resistance which appealed to a portion of international allies while ensuring that US powerholders never fully embraced the notion of a free Cuba. As Ada Ferrer documents, Cuba's rebel leaders put together a multiracial army that denied the existence of race while waging a war against colonialism and racism. Cuban rebels spoke of a raceless nation during a period when racial hierarchy defined American society.[38] This political project in which Cubans, regardless of color, unite behind a free Cuba, had been the vision of José Martí, the intellectual architect of Cuban nationalism. The idea that blacks might rule Cuba, a territory that US leaders assumed belonged to the United States, terrified the US political establishment and made it very difficult for them to get behind Cuban independence.

During the 1860s and 1870s when Cubans were just beginning the push for independence, some of the first allies in the United States were radical abolitionists. For them, Cuba became a key site in the global struggle against slavery immediately following the Civil War, a struggle whose goals overlapped with anticolonial efforts by Cubans to end Spanish rule. The victory against slavery in the United States, particularly from the perspective of African Americans, was part of a longer struggle to defeat slavery and subjugation on a global level. The Civil War had served to elevate the notion that the fate of African Americans was linked to oppressed people in Latin America and the Caribbean.[39] And, in part because of its proximity, Cuba was the primary site through which this understanding took shape through "the connections between Black abolitionists and Cuban revolutionary emigres in the United States."[40]

It was black organizers who built a Cuban solidarity movement throughout the United States during the 1860s and 1870s, which was rooted in both anti-colonialism and anti-slavery. The Cuban Anti-Slavery Committee circulated a petition supporting Cuban independence at meetings and gatherings throughout the United States. The anti-slavery campaign mobilized enough black voters to "convince legislatures in key Southern states, such as South Carolina, Louisiana, and Florida, to pass strongly worded resolutions in support of Cuban liberation that would then be sent to the White House."[41] Organizing centers emerged across the country, and by the early 1870s the Cuban Anti-Slavery Committee had achieved sufficient prominence that it was able to secure a meeting with President Grant. When it was clear that Grant would not support Cuban freedom with sufficient commitment, black Americans organized protests and other actions. For his part, Frederick Douglass was an early and enthusiastic supporter of the Cuban cause, even encouraging young African Americans to renounce their citizenship and join the fight in Cuba.[42]

These early efforts by African Americans to support Cuban independence facilitated and were eventually engulfed by a broader wave of support for the Cuban cause once the final conflict began in 1895. By 1897 there was little support in the United States for Spanish rule, in part because it was clear to everyone that Spain's days as a colonial power were numbered. More than this, there was growing sympathy, and active solidarity, around the Cuban cause. With Spain on its way out, the question largely came to revolve around how (and why) the United States should respond in a way that undermined Spanish colonialism and/or supported the Cuban cause.

The US government, and particularly the McKinley (1897–1901) and Cleveland (1893–97) administrations, did not want Spain to transfer sovereignty to Cubans any more than they wanted control to pass to another European country. Control over Cuba should shift to the United States. Aside from this serving US economic interests, Cubans were seen as not capable of governing themselves. A free Cuba would bring with it political chaos, upheaval, and racial conflict.[43] As McKinley's minister to Spain noted, "I do not believe the population is to-day fit for self-government." Independence would result in a "continuous war of the races" and a "second Santo Domingo,"[44] invoking the specter of Haiti. It was the duty of the United States to preserve order, a rationale that was repeated, fine-tuned, and applied in the coming decades as the United States extended its imperial reach into the Caribbean—and sought to distinguish its own noble involvement from European colonialism.[45]

The problem for US administrations, however, was that by 1898 the cause of Cuba Libre "had obtained widespread popular support, manifested most dramatically in periodic congressional resolutions calling for the recognition of Cuban independence and threatening war in its behalf."[46] And there was good reason to believe that congressional advocates had the support of most Americans. At the very least, a range of groups sought to provide the rebels with material aid, even if they were against direct US intervention because they feared the United States would never leave, felt it was too costly, or simply thought Cubans should be allowed to claim a victory they had earned.

Support for independence was strong in part because Cubans worked tirelessly to attract material and moral aid from potential allies in the United States. Through mass meetings, carnivals, speeches, fundraisers, Cuban-American fairs, the publication and distribution of newspapers and pamphlets, the influencing of reporters, and the establishment of contacts with important political figures, Cubans helped create a favorable opinion of their struggle against Spain.[47] Cuban revolutionaries had great appeal as underdogs, and were trying to defeat an enemy that was seen by most as a cruel and despotic European power. As Philip Foner notes, "a majority of the American people supported the Revolution, wished to assist it themselves, and desired to see their government give it the recognition they believed it was entitled to. Sympathy for Cuba was expressed in editorial columns, plays, and pamphlets, preached from the pulpit and platform, and voice in poetry." "Support for the Cuban cause was expressed by men and women in all classes of society, and in all sections of the country."[48]

The cause at times produced strange bedfellows with diverging motives. Many anti-imperialists, including leaders of the Anti-Imperialist League, opposed US intervention and supported Cuban independence on racialist grounds. The United States should not possess colonies that might add racially inferior peoples to its population. William Jennings Bryan opposed "expansion which secures us alien races for future subjugation," while insisting that the United States "reserve a harbor and coaling station ... in return for services rendered."[49] Andrew Carnegie's opposition to annexation and involvement in the Anti-Imperialist League was based on financial, strategic, and racialist grounds.[50]

For its part, the AFL called upon the US government to recognize the Cuban belligerents, and to follow the example of France in the American revolution by providing "recognition and aid" to the rebels.[51] The AFL was against actual military intervention, however, on the principle that "Labor is never for war .... Who would be compelled to bear the burden of war? The working people. They would pay the taxes, and their blood would flow like water."[52] The AFL also opposed any further expansion or annexation, in principle, on both racial and labor grounds.

At the same time, the AFL—led by Samuel Gompers—also argued quite strongly for US global economic domination. "The nation which dominates the markets of the world will surely control its destinies," Gompers asserted. "We do not oppose the development of our industry, the expansion of our commerce, nor the development of our power and influence which the United States may exert upon the destinies of the nations of the earth." This could be accomplished, though, without actual annexation of lands like the Philippines with their "semi-savage population." "Neither its gates nor those of any other country of the globe can long be closed against our constantly growing industrial supremacy .... We are and will continue to be the greatest conquerors of the markets of the world."[53]

Thus, although the AFL advocated material aid for the Cuban rebels, it was rooted in a rationale which was by no means an anti-imperialism that most on the left would identify with today. It did, however, reflect a key component of what became labor's internationalism during the twentieth century. US labor would support Latin American labor unions that worked well with business. This was a labor unionism that was not anti-imperialist, particularly militant, nor antagonistic to capitalism—and could be a staunch enemy of workers and organizations who promoted such radicalism.

The US government eventually navigated the complicated political terrain of Cuban freedom by pursuing what the McKinley administration dubbed a "neutral intervention"—one that would end a war between two hostile parties while simultaneously acknowledging and postponing the question of independence until a future moment when Cubans were ready to govern. With this, and the attack on the USS *Maine*, the United States was able to rally public support for its splendid little war. And, predictably given the US orientation towards Cuba since the early 1800s, once the war was over promises of independence gave way to the higher "duty" of a superior nation to set an inferior one on the right track. In short, the United States was there to stay, a fact that was institutionalized through the 1901 Platt Amendment's formal appropriation of Cuban sovereignty.

The Cuban struggle represents an important turning point for both solidarity and empire. In terms of solidarity, although a strong current of anti-imperialism ran through the United States, it still associated imperialism with European colonialism, whereby European powers physically occupied colonies. It was not yet associated with economic imperialism. The position articulated by Gompers—that US business should endlessly expand abroad—was uncontroversial, except perhaps within fringes on the far left. Not only was the United States still emerging as an economic force, and hence not seen as an imperial power in the European sense, it was widely accepted within the United States that the spread of American business benefitted the rest of the hemisphere (and their inferior peoples) in a way that European colonialism had not.[54]

However, if debate around Cuba did not expand conceptions of imperialism to include economic imperialism, it did serve to move understandings beyond colonial occupation in the narrow sense. Where the real debate around Cuba emerged, and intensified as the United States tried to expand its influence in the Caribbean, was over the question of US military intervention outside of permanent territorial occupation. If formal colonies were not the norm, or at least did not represent the path forward, what was the role for the US government in promoting business interests abroad? If US economic expansion was accepted as an unqualified good, how might the US government—without establishing colonies—facilitate this process while supporting US economic interests?

This question—should the United States intervene, and how—was central to debates around Cuba, and was fundamentally about how different groups within the United States saw themselves and their nation in the larger world. The answer achieved institutional form through Cuba in the form of the Roosevelt Corollary to the Monroe Doctrine in 1904. Here, rather than territorial expansion or imperialism, the United States was effectively positing an intervention that was to be understood as an international police/humanitarian action to provide peace and stability for people in need of US aid. Once intervention was defined in these terms, one's position came to grow out of one's stance towards the United States and its foreign policies and practices. If you believed the United States to be an inherently benevolent actor, and an exceptional one when judged in relation to European colonizers, interventions could be seen and explained as altruistic (even more so if you assumed, as many people did during this period, that as an Anglo-Saxon nation the United States was inherently superior to its darker-skinned neighbors). In this sense, despite the fact that after 1898 the United States was a colonial power with territories in the Pacific and Caribbean, a humanitarian spin allowed people to understand intervention apart from colonialism or imperialism.

At the same time, if you did not see the United States as a benevolent actor, then you were generally opposed to intervention. Consequently, as this tension evolved through the Mexican Revolution and US interventions in the Caribbean, opposition to intervention became more and more the domain of the left, and often intertwined with a larger critique of US institutions and capitalism itself. Still, as we will see, through the first half of the twentieth century a moderate anti-imperialism persisted in relation to its radical counterpart and put a check on US adventurism.

Mexican Revolution and Radical Labor Solidarity

Between 1898, when the United States firmly inserted itself into the Cuban struggle for independence, and 1934, when it finally withdrew from Haiti, the United States militarily intervened or occupied Panama (1903), the Dominican Republic (1916–24), Mexico

(1914), Nicaragua (1912–33), Haiti (1915–34), and Cuba (numerous times). US willingness to wield the "Big Stick" throughout the hemisphere grew, and was in fact institutionalized through the Roosevelt Corollary to the Monroe Doctrine in 1904, which declared that the United States had the right to play the role of international police when the "impotence" of governments in the Americas paved the way for European intervention and threatened US interests. From here on, or at least until the Cold War shifted the calculus, the United States justified its continual intervention in the region by melding the "defense of US interests" with a paternalistic (and not so subtly racist) benevolence that claimed the duty of the United States was to provide order and stability to a region that was incapable of governing itself.

After Cuban independence, the US government no longer flirted with supporting Latin American revolutionaries. Going forward, and beginning with the Mexican revolution in 1910, the United States intervened directly against Latin American rebels. This generated opposition not only in Latin America, but at home as well. By the early 1900s, not only did significant numbers of Americans tend to oppose overseas intervention in general, but Latin American revolutionaries, and the ideals of freedom and equality they were fighting for, held a certain appeal for sectors of the US population. This created the potential for an anti-imperialism that was not only opposed to US adventurism, but that actively supported (and engaged in solidarity with) Latin Americans who were opposed to US intervention.

In the first decades of the twentieth century there was significant opposition to US incursions into Mexico, the Dominican Republic, Haiti, and Nicaragua, including from groups that actively sought and developed solidarity with Latin Americans. This differentiated strand of solidarity responded to the US expansion of the moment, but it also drew on a political context which included growing labor agitation and organization, the spread of explicitly internationalist thought and movements like communism and anarchism, guerrilla resistance in occupied territories, an increasingly self-conscious pan-African identity,[55] and the early association of anti-colonial movements with socially revolutionary uprisings.

The Mexican revolution nonetheless proved a challenge for solidarity. While the Cuban struggle for independence developed fairly widespread support throughout US society, Mexico's revolution was very different. Cuban independence fighters were seen by broad sectors of the US public as victims of Spanish oppression. Their victory would not only be virtuous, but open up the Cuban economy to US capital. A win-win. By contrast, Mexican revolutionaries were more often portrayed as threatening bandits, particularly by business sectors that had considerable investment in mining, agro-business, and railroads, and had long benefitted from the 35-year rule of Porfirio Díaz (1876–1911). In other words, unlike Cuba, support for US economic interests meant intervention against, rather than for, revolutionaries. This was a sign of things to come.

As a result, unlike in Cuba, where rebels enjoyed widespread support, meaningful solidarity with Mexican revolutionaries became largely the domain of the far left in the United States.[56] Such solidarity directly challenged the overall direction of US policy and economic investment in the region, and hence meant that supporters of Mexican revolutionaries were by and large opposed to the US government in quite fundamental ways. Anti-imperialism, as a left current opposed to not only US intervention in the narrow sense, but the very nature of US economic involvement in the region, was slowly beginning to emerge, taking on anti-capitalist tendencies, and would eventually become an important component of Latin American solidarity as it developed during the twentieth century.

That some of the earliest examples of radical solidarity took place in the border region should come as no surprise given that the US economic presence in Mexico was so much greater than anywhere else in Latin America during early 1900s. The border economy that grew after 1848 was based on an influx of US capital to develop railroads and mines. Attracted by mineral resources, generous concessions, and a cheap labor force, US capital flowed into Mexico during the Porfiriato, a rule that was characterized by the dispossession of the peasantry, the spread of agrarian capitalism, and rapid industrialization. Díaz's free market policies gave US investors control over Mexican railroads as well as large mining, timber, ranching, and agriculture enterprises.

For Mexican workers, many of whom had only recently been forced off the land, Díaz's regime meant increasingly long work days, poor working conditions, inadequate housing, low pay, and brutal repression, especially if they tried to organize. The rapid entrance of foreign capital brought with it the added insult of extreme wage differentials between us and Mexican workers. The harsh conditions, combined with the sheer growth in the number of industrial workers and the increased circulation of radical political ideas, created a powder keg that was an opportunity for radicalism and cross-border solidarity.[57]

On the us side of the border, the Industrial Workers of the World (iww or Wobblies) became an important catalyst to labor organizing among Mexican workers. On the Mexican side, the Partido Liberal Mexicano (PLM) played a similar role—less a political party than a vehicle for organizing a revolutionary movement. They did so within in a context where Mexican and American workers were rapidly organizing into unions—Railway Brotherhoods, Western Federation of Miners, the iww, etc.—on both sides of the border, particularly within the rapidly expanding mining sector. In 1894, there were all of 40 American mines in Mexico; only a decade later there were over 13,000. Mexican workers responded by organizing and striking.[58]

In one exemplary case, workers at a mine in Cananea, Sonora, which had been set up by Colonel William C. Greene with the aid of Porfirio Díaz, went on strike in 1906. Americans at the mine received up to three times what Mexicans doing the exact same work were paid. Greene asked for the help of the Arizona Rangers to break the strike, which they immediately did after the governor of Sonora swore the entire ranger contingent into the Mexican army as "volunteers." Díaz contributed Mexican rural guards to the cause, the workers were mowed down, and the strike crushed.[59]

Linked to the great mining strikes in Mexico during this period, and attempting to foment a broader revolution, the leaders of the PLM fled to the United States where they were pursued by agents of the infamous Pinkerton Detective Agency.[60] Their arrests and continued persecution in the United States served to stimulate international solidarity, and pushed the PLM and their us allies towards an understanding of internationalism rooted in working-class revolution—whereby they started to see themselves as part of a worldwide struggle against capital.[62] "This PLM–IWW connection would prove to be the most important link between Mexican and American labor radicals in the first two decades of the twentieth century."[62] By 1914, the PLM had some 6,000 members on the US side of the border, and in Los Angeles its Spanish-language newspaper, *Regeneración*, had over 10,000 readers.[63] For its part, and in communication with the PLM, the IWW was organizing workers, including those of Mexican descent, throughout the US Southwest.[64]

As a result of continued persecution, the PLM leaders were constantly on the run, often fleeing to the United States where they were harassed by both American and Mexican authorities. When Juan Sarabia, the vice president of the PLM, was kidnapped in the United States and taken to Mexico by Mexican officials working with US authorities, the legendary organizer Mother Jones started a public campaign to free him. He was returned to Arizona in eight days. When other PLM leaders, including Ricardo Flores Magón, were subsequently arrested in Los Angeles, she began a campaign to have them released. "They were patriots," Mother Jones insisted, "like Garibaldi and George Washington—these Mexican men in jail fighting against a bloodier tyrant than King George against whom we revolted."[65] The PLM leaders remained in jail for over a year before their trial began, during which time Mother Jones raised funds to support their legal battle, expanding the campaign to include other Mexican revolutionaries/exiles as they were imprisoned and persecuted. The Western Federation of Miners and the IWW also supported their cause, with the Los Angeles branch of the IWW insisting that the imprisoned Mexicans were a "working class movement and nothing else, and it is for us who are revolutionists to help them in the fight."[66]

"Big Bill" Haywood appealed to socialists, Wobblies, and AFL unionists, reminding them that the persecuted Mexican leaders were their "comrades, men who dared to speak for liberty, men who were fighting for political freedom and struggling to overthrow the system of peonage."[67] The Socialist Party of America also passed a resolution, sponsored by Eugene V. Debs, supporting the prisoners and insisting they were "comrades in the social revolution."[68] The *Appeal to Reason*, an influential socialist newspaper, devoted an entire issue to the PLM and published Flores Magón's scathing attack on US prison conditions.[69] And Emma Goldman, the well-known anarchist, gave speeches in support of the PLM rebels.[70]

Mother Jones and John Murray, a Los Angeles socialist and labor leader, established the Mexican Revolutionists Defense League and worked to convince Gompers, president of the AFL, to support the cause. Murray, who subsequently devoted his life to the Mexican cause, convinced Gompers that the PLM was essentially liberal (i.e. not too radical), and argued that it would not be wise for the AFL to "allow the IWW and the Socialist Party to get all the credit among workers in Mexico, and Mexican-Americans in the U.S. Southwest." Gompers subsequently got the 1908 AFL Convention to adopt a supportive resolution.[71]

John Kenneth Turner, a socialist, reporter, and author of the well-known *Barbarous Mexico*, also joined the cause. Turner raised an issue which was of special concern to US trade unions. "American capitalists," Turner wrote, "support Diaz because they are looking to Mexican cheap labor to help them break the back of organized labor in the United States, both by transporting a part of their capital to Mexico and by importing a part of Mexican laborers in this country."[72] This issue, which would obviously become central for labor solidarity through the present day, was not understood in intensely nationalist terms, but framed with the (implicit) recognition that the broader threat posed by capital should be challenged through a radical internationalism.

Despite sustained support from the left both within and outside of US labor circles, the PLM leaders were found guilty and sentenced to jail, after which Mother Jones obtained a meeting with President Taft and demanded a pardon. Unfortunately, Taft—like all US Presidents of the period—was a strong supporter of Porfirio Díaz. Nevertheless, by the spring of 1910, a coalition of progressives and unionists convinced William B. Wilson, a Congressman from Pennsylvania and former leader of the United Mine Workers, to ask Congress to investigate the harassment of Mexican exiles, which contributed to the prisoners' ultimate release.[73]

Regardless of the outcome, this was a very early instance of sustained, significant solidarity in which US actors—led by radical sectors within the labor movement—actively engaged with counter parts in Latin America. This was not simply Americans opposing US foreign policy without regard to Latin Americans. This was an internationalism that substantially involved working people, was fundamentally rooted in labor and the left, and was based in a shared and radical political project between people in two different countries. If that project was never fully articulated or realized, it was nonetheless a product of the intense economic exploitation associated with a border region where US capital operated with near impunity. It was also a solidarity that understood imperialism not in terms of direct colonial rule, but in terms of the broader impact of foreign capital. As such, it tended to not only oppose the policies and practices of the US government and businesses, but was quite often anti-capitalist in a larger sense of a shared struggle against capitalism.

Conclusion

It is important to stress that the revolutionary internationalism that was emerging during this period was not isolated to the IWW or Mexico. Although US-based solidarity around the Mexican Revolution was largely driven by the radicalism of the IWW, these efforts were part of a broader emergence of revolutionary nationalism and internationalism in the 1910s, 1920s, and 1930s around the Caribbean basin. Some of the more conspicuous expressions of this will be explored in the next chapter with respect to the US occupations of Haiti, the Dominican Republic, and Nicaragua. Yet, as Margaret Stevens and others have documented, a left internationalism shaped deeply by communists and fellow travelers was developing throughout the "black Caribbean," a geopolitical space that included not only the United States (particularly New York City) and Mexico, but parts of the British West Indies, Haiti, Cuba, Puerto Rico, the Dominican Republic, Panama, and other countries in the region. Many of the organizations that emerged during this period, such as the Anti-Imperialist League, the American Negro Labor Congress, and the International Trade Union Committee of Negro Workers, were created in order to carry out the strategy of the Communist International. Comintern strategy vacillated considerably between the mid-1920s and late 1930s, but anti-racism remained central to the shifting efforts, and black radicals with ties to the Caribbean were at the heart of revo-lutionary struggle throughout the period. This included an explosion of strikes and continuous efforts to establish communist organiza-tions in the Caribbean as well as ongoing international solidarity that flowed both north and south throughout the period.[74]

Much of this internationalism would have mixed results as initia-tives stalled, could not be sustained, or failed to get off the ground. But a significant sector of the US left was nonetheless coming to see itself as part of a broader anti-capitalist struggle—involving people throughout the world but particularly in the Caribbean basin—that was inextricably linked to a system of racist imperialism. And, although they remained a minority, this radical left maintained a working relationship with a much larger liberal establishment that could not only be critical of empire, but increasingly accepted the notion that government should at least constrain capital while pro-tecting working people from the worst excesses of the market. This uneasy liberal-left alliance was both hopeful and politically meaningful.

2

The Caribbean under US Occupation

The three-plus decades between 1898, when the United States hijacked Cuban independence, and 1933, when President Roosevelt (FDR) announced the Good Neighbor policy and initiated the withdrawal of US troops from Nicaragua and Haiti, was a high period of direct US military intervention in Latin America. Whereas the United States could try to pass off its involvement in Cuba as a benevolent, even anti-imperialist, effort to remove Spain from the island, it became much more of a challenge to put a positive spin on its presence in the Caribbean during the first decades of the twentieth century. The United States was no longer expelling a European colonial power from the hemisphere. It was invading sovereign countries with the purpose of achieving hegemony over the region.

After the defeat of Spain in 1898, the United States took control of Cuba and Puerto Rico (as well as the Philippines), and began to aggressively extend its presence in the Caribbean basin. As early as 1905, the United States had established financial control through customs receiverships over the Dominican Republic, Nicaragua, and Haiti, and would have done so in Honduras had the US Senate not blocked it. In this sense, although the US occupations examined in this chapter, including the Dominican Republic (1916–24), Haiti (1915–34), and Nicaragua (1912–33), were particularly lengthy and complicated, they were not so much anomalies as part of a broader pattern of direct intervention and imperialism in the Caribbean basin. The United States would not only send significant numbers of troops for long periods of time, including some 2,000 to Haiti, 3,000 to the Dominican Republic, and 5,000 in Nicaragua, but took over many of the most basic functions of the state in what ultimately were failed attempts at nation building.[1]

Not surprisingly, the occupations produced intense opposition within Haiti, Nicaragua, and the Dominican Republic. The brutality of the marines insured that whatever resistance there was to the initial interventions intensified during the course of the occupations themselves. As historian Alan McPherson aptly states, the "overall style of US occupation in Latin America—brutal, acquisitive, disrespectful, and racist—transformed much of the initial relief and hope of some occupied peoples into disappointment, fear, and eventually rage."[2] Opposition to occupation would come in many forms, from armed uprisings by peasants in the countryside to nonviolent resistance by members of the political class and other sectors of society. Yet, with the possible exception of Nicaragua, where Sandino's anti-imperialist crusade generated a large-scale armed rebellion, opposition remained fragmented and uneven. Indeed, part of the reason the United States intervened in the first place, and could justify its presence, was that all three countries were ruled by small groups of elites who were internally divided, unable to build effective central governments, and did not possess the capacity to forge nations. When combined with US concerns about instability exposing the Caribbean to European control, the fact that Caribbean elites struggled to govern effectively and were assumed to be racially inferior paved the way for US intervention.

What this internal political division within Caribbean countries also meant, aside from constant turmoil and fiscal crisis, was that domestic resistance alone did not possess (nor could it develop) the military or political capacity to end the US occupations. The brutality of the US presence generated an opposition that would come in many forms and from multiple sources, but it could not produce coherent nationalist movements in countries that were deeply divided along racial, geographic, and class lines. Armed struggle against a better trained and equipped military force could not by itself expel the United States from the Caribbean. Nor could non-violent forms of political resistance.[3]

In short, Caribbean opposition to US intervention would require international support to amplify the cause and repel the United States—to mobilize world opinion in Latin America, Europe, and the United States in order to isolate the United States and force a change in policy. Not surprisingly, Latin Americans throughout the region, including political leaders in most countries, opposed the occupation, which concerned policymakers in Washington who evaluated the cost of intervention at least in part against the animosity it created in its own backyard. Likewise, Europeans also proved more than willing to challenge US justifications for military intervention. The cost of occupation increased as world opinion turned against the United States, which served to fuel opposition within the United States itself.

The emergence of opposition within the United States was not a given, and depended heavily on the ability of people in the Caribbean to both wage armed resistance against the US military and make their case internationally. Delegations from the countries, as well as exiles living in the United States, would prove key in all three cases. The well-worn justification that US interests had to be protected and order restored in places that could not govern themselves continued to be a persuasive one within the United States during the first decades of the twentieth century. US foreign policy did not garner much attention, few Americans saw the United States as an imperial power, and most people assumed Latin Americans to be inferior. More than this, there were powerful forces in the US government that sought to establish political systems within the Caribbean basin that were beholden to US (and not European) interests.

And yet, as we will see, widespread opposition emerged from a range of groups across much of the political spectrum. A current of moderate anti-imperialism, led by mainstream politicians, church leaders, pacifists, the AFL, and others would question US justifications for intervention and eventually oppose the occupations themselves. Some within this camp would actively support the efforts of moderate actors within the Caribbean, particularly Dominican nationalists who mounted an international campaign to expose the true nature of the US occupation. In general, however, moderate anti-imperialists were more focused on the fact and nature of occupation than building alliances with Dominicans, Haitians, and Nicaraguans.

African Americans would be among the earliest, most consistent, and most vocal opponents. Like Americans in general, US blacks held a variety of opinions about people in the Caribbean basin, with some even arguing that US tutelage would benefit the region. Yet African

Americans' first-hand experience with racism not only led many to question US motives more quickly, and generally assume that US occupation brought racist repression, but made them more ready to see those who resisted occupation as rebels and patriots to be honored and supported. It also led them increasingly to understand the struggles of black Americans and those of colonial peoples as being inextricably linked—that is, towards a critical black internationalism. That they were able to voice opposition to US imperialism and openly support rebels during a period in which oppression against black people was intensifying throughout the United States and the Caribbean basin is a remarkable testament to their courage and commitment—but also to the transnational world they had built through migration within and between the United States and Caribbean basin.[4]

There was also a radical left made up of communists, intellectuals, and others who built alliances to both oppose occupation and (at times) act in solidarity with people from the region. Their political importance outweighed their numbers, in part because the entire period falls under the shadow of the Bolshevik revolution and the Third International. Founded right after the revolution, the Communist International (Comintern) insisted that anticolonial movements were central to the broader struggle against imperialism, and hence pushed for an alliance between working people in advanced capitalist countries and oppressed peoples in the colonies.[5] But more than any other political movement, communists pushed for black liberation through a socialism that confronted racial oppression.

By putting the "Negro question" at the heart of its politics, and offering an analysis and plan for realizing black liberation, the Comintern attracted large numbers of black radicals during this period. That this project coincided and existed in healthy tension with a black political revival, defined in part by Garvey's Universal Negro Improvement Association and the Pan-African Congresses organized by W. E. B. Du Bois, gave it even more energy. Garvey's project in particular, regardless (or perhaps because) of its pro-capitalist politics, helped move international solidarity beyond a class of middle-class activist-intellectuals and into the mainstream of black America. The broader point is that the internationalism of the

48

left during this period was deeply engaged with black politics, and opened up space for black leftists.[6] As such, communists served as an important link between black and white radicals within the United States and across the hemisphere in the fight against US imperialism in the Caribbean.[7]

In this sense, the broad contours of Latin American solidarity in many ways took shape during the first decades of the twentieth century in the Caribbean basin. This included the development of an opposition to US intervention in both Latin America and the United States that, although diverse and ever-changing, came to include what would become a familiar cast of liberals, leftists, journalists, intellectuals, exiles, workers, and peasants. At times, in Latin America, this opposition would be armed, challenging both the US military and its proxies on the battlefield. More often than not, however, these were political-ideological battles over how the US presence was to be implemented and understood, with the US government and its Latin American allies promoting a familiar set of justifications while opponents mounted what we now think of as "campaigns" to re-frame US involvement as an imperialist intrusion, and force the United States to change course or withdraw.

Although such efforts did not force the United States to end military occupations quickly, international solidarity would experience considerable success by the end of the period. It was an important factor in forcing the withdrawal of the United States from the Caribbean basin. The United States that departed Haiti and Nicaragua in the mid-1930s left with a sullied reputation as an imperial power. Fewer Latin Americans saw the United States as a positive, or even benign, force in the region, and more Americans joined in that assessment. The breadth and depth of this opposition can, of course, be overstated. Likewise, it was an opposition that ultimately lacked staying power, largely dissipating as US foreign policy in Latin America pivoted under FDR, the depression consumed the country, the Second World War heated up, and the Cold War forever changed international solidarity and the left. Nevertheless, criticism of, and opposition to, US involvement in the region both widened and deepened as a result of solidarity around the Dominican Republic, Haiti, and Nicaragua.

Dominican Republic

The immediate justification for the US occupation of the Dominican Republic in 1916 centered around a cycle of insurrections that produced ongoing political turmoil. US claims that intervention was required in order to stabilize the Dominican Republic no doubt served to hide its own motive of insuring that the Caribbean was open for business and under US control. But there was nonetheless a bit of truth to the claim. Some sectors within Dominican society even initially accepted the US intervention in the hope of removing corrupt leaders.[8]

This initial acquiescence was, however, never widely shared nor long-lasting, and undermined by the heavy-handed nature of the US presence. When President Wilson's demand for control over basic government functions was refused, the United States cut off funds for the Dominican government and denied recognition of the provisional president chosen by the country's Congress. The United States then simply took control, outlawed gun ownership, censored speech, cancelled elections, suspended the Dominican Congress, and slowly turned over a good chunk of the country to US sugar companies.[9] It was not a subtle rule.

Nor was it surprising that widespread resistance emerged almost immediately, in two broad forms. On the one hand, Dominicans rejected the US call to turn in their weapons, and instead carried out armed resistance in the countryside throughout the occupation. At times, particularly in the eastern part of the country, this opposition would achieve a degree of cohesion. But for the most part it consisted of roaming bands of armed actors who were attempting to hang onto local power. Their presence not only caused continual problems for the United States, but tended to bring out the worst in the marines, whose abuses did little to win over the population while causing a public relations problem abroad.[10] Nevertheless, because armed resistance was sporadic, small scale, and portrayed by United States as simple banditry, it remained largely isolated from international attention or attempts to forge broader oppositional movements in and outside of the Dominican Republic.[11]

On the other hand, non-violent opposition also emerged from the country's divided political class, originating first among a small group of moderate nationalists tied to the Dominican president whom the United States had deposed in 1916, then expanding to include more radical groups, and finally incorporating a significant portion of Dominican society. This was never an armed struggle, and relied heavily on developing allies outside of the Dominican Republic in order to pressure the United States to withdraw. It proved somewhat effective. A relatively small group of Dominicans, whose primary goal was to rid the country of US troops and control, built coalitions and gained international allies in the United States, Latin America, and Europe. This global campaign, which eventually turned the occupation into a *cause célèbre* and embarrassed the US government, was helped by the nagging persistence of armed resistance and the fact that the military government itself was quite repressive.[12] It was also facilitated by the fact that remarkably similar events—including US military misdeeds—were playing out in Haiti and Nicaragua.

Carried out over an eight-year period, the moderate, nationalist campaign made it increasingly difficult for the military government to rule, raised questions about the competence of the United States in managing Dominican affairs, brought the issue onto the front pages of US newspapers and into the 1920 Presidential campaign, and was amazingly successful at fomenting international opposition from governments, political leaders, and other groups throughout all of Latin America, much of Europe, and elsewhere. Dominican leaders toured Latin America and succeeded in getting Latin American countries to voice opposition to the US occupation. The campaign exposed abuses by the US military government, sullied the reputation of the United States, and turned the occupation into an international embarrassment.[13]

The success of Dominicans in altering the perception of the occupation, and organizing considerable international opposition, is all the more remarkable given that before and during the First World War few in the United States seemed to care—and those who did supported the occupation. With the almost lone exception of *The Nation* and the African-American press, both of which were becoming aware of what US aggression looked like in neighboring Haiti, those in the United States who voiced an opinion generally backed military intervention.[14] Prior to and during the First World War the respectable press largely accepted the US government's version of events, seeing intervention as a benevolent gesture and a duty of the United States.[15] As historian Alan McPherson notes, even as late as 1919, US publications "were largely in favor of the Haitian and Dominican occupations, expressing belief that self-government was impossible among people of color, disgust at the history of violent insurrection, fear of European intervention, and concern for protecting US investments."[16]

By the start of the 1920s, however, Dominicans (as well as Haitians and Nicaraguans) found a more receptive audience not only in Latin America and Europe, but in the United States as well.[17] The horrors of the First World War, brought about in large part by European nationalism and colonialism, created space for a progressive internationalism (rooted in an emerging Third World nationalism) to develop around opposition to overseas intervention by the United States. US policymakers may not have soured on intervention, but there was a significant current of anti-imperialism running through the US public that was "not swayed by arguments about race or geopolitical self-interest" and saw the evils of occupation as "incompatible with the identity of the United States."[18]

More than this, in the aftermath of war, President Woodrow Wilson's global declaration in support of self-determination, and his promise of a peaceful new world order defined by sovereign, independent countries, stirred the hopes of people throughout the world. Wilson would not deliver on this liberal internationalism, and in fact shared the belief that most of the world's non-European peoples were simply incapable of self-rule and would require years of tutelage before being allowed to self-govern. But the language of self-determination captured the global imagination after the First World War, was difficult to put back in the bottle, and was sufficiently vague that it not only appealed to a wide range of people but could be taken in far more radical directions than Wilson intended. Most immediately, it helped stimulate an anti-colonialist wave in which non-European, non-white peoples appropriated Wilson's language and claimed the right to self-determination. This was a radical idea at the time, and one that resonated with African Americans as well. Longer term, as this anti-colonial nationalism developed it would be shaped as much by Lenin and the left's understanding of imperialism as it would by

Wilson's more moderate offering.[19] But for now it opened up space for anti-colonialism and independence in the non-European world.

It was in this context, then, that a small group of Dominicans vigorously advocated the sovereignty of their nation to members of the US Congress, the State Department, the diplomatic community, labor unions, and Latin Americans living in the United States. As a result, increasingly sympathetic articles started to appear not only in *The Nation* and African American newspapers, but in a range of publications including the *New York Times*, the *Washington Post*, the *Yale Review*, and the *Journal of International Relations*. A majority of US newspapers were now against the occupation.[20]

This shift was made possible at least in part by on-the-ground solidarity. *The Nation* and the National Association for the Advancement of Colored People (NAACP), aligned with Dominican nationalists, formed the Haiti–Santo Domingo Independence Society to force the United States to withdrawal from the entire island. This society "waged an active campaign for the immediate re-establishment of constitutional government, the immediate withdrawal of the marines, and the negotiation of an equitable treaty."[21] Academics began to hold conferences criticizing the occupation. The Popular Government League argued the intervention had been motivated by the interests of US banks. The Foreign Policy Association of New York and the Anti-Imperialistic League of Boston condemned the occupation. US senators and representatives now demanded investigations, and Republican presidential candidate Warren Harding used the issue to great effect in the 1920 election.[22] Referring to FDR, who was running as the Democratic vice-presidential candidate and was the former assistant secretary to the Navy, Harding quipped: "If I should be elected President … I will not empower an assistant secretary of the Navy to draft a constitution for helpless neighbors in the West Indies and jam it down their throats at the point of bayonets borne by the United States marines."[23]

Samuel Gompers, President of the AFL, also took up the Dominican cause and became one of its strongest allies. This occurred in large part because a representative from Dominican labor, José Eugenio Kunhardt, attended the Second Congress of the Pan-American Federation of Labor (PAFL), an international organization started by the AFL and run by Gompers.[24] After Kunhardt outlined a series of complaints about the US military occupation, the PAFL sent two US labor leaders to the Dominican Republic to investigate, which in turn led to a report asking the United States for major changes in its military occupation. In its third congress (1921), PAFL then passed a resolution demanding that the United States withdraw from the Dominican Republic—which Gompers dutifully delivered to the President, who was predictably annoyed.

The Dominicans' efforts to influence US labor were further supported by labor leaders from other Latin American countries, who pushed Gompers to take a stronger stand. What is interesting about the involvement of Gompers and the AFL is that it gave the Dominican cause an immediate audience with the President. Unlike today, where we assume US labor leaders have very limited access to political power, in the 1920s inquiries from the most powerful labor leader in the country required responses from the US government and provided an avenue for Dominicans to push their cause. The mainstream core of labor had a seat at the table. More than this, the willingness of Gompers to take up the fight signaled how mainstream the Dominican cause itself had become. This was due in part to the Dominicans' success in pushing their case, but it was also tied to the fact that there was a strong current in US society that opposed, or at least seriously questioned, US military intervention abroad.[25]

As a result of this broad-based campaign, in which Dominican nationalists successfully shaped world opinion and developed important allies in the United States, the Wilson administration committed to the general principle of withdrawal, stating that the United States had succeeded in its mission and the Dominican Republic was ready for self-rule. This attempt to save face belied the fact that the United States would leave the Dominican Republic a mess, had been embarrassed, and was now concerned that continued intervention could hurt US political and economic interests in Latin America and elsewhere.[26] The United States had intervened in order to establish a stable representative democracy and instead paved the way for three decades of military rule under Rafael Trujillo.

It is worth noting that the opposition to occupation that emerged within the Dominican Republic was never particularly revolutionary.

Moderate calls to rally around the nation produced modest results in terms of forging domestic opposition. Anti-imperialist appeals were similarly subdued, framed less in terms of empire than in principles of sovereignty and self-determination. Armed resistance was widespread, but sporadic, localized, and rarely reflecting political convictions or ideologies. On the whole, the dominant core of Dominican opposition did not advocate revolutionary transformation. It focused instead on getting US troops out of the country and returning control over the government to nationals.[27]

Yet Dominicans were remarkably effective in taking their cause beyond the country's borders, where its message resonated with audiences that were already predisposed to understand the struggle in terms of nationalist liberation, self-determination, anti-colonialism, and anti-imperialism, and to therefore be critical of US justifications for intervention. And because the Dominican struggle could not help but be understood in relation to occupations in Haiti and Nicaragua, its message was amplified. More than this, it worked— if slowly and unevenly. The internationalism of the struggle was a key factor in not only repelling the United States from the island, but bringing an end to a period characterized by direct US military occupation in Latin America. Its presence also nurtured currents of anti-imperialism throughout the Americas, and supported struggles in Haiti and Nicaragua.

Haiti

The US military occupied Haiti from 1915 to 1934 through a brutal, racist, military dictatorship. From the outset, the US government worked hard to portray the military occupation as a humanitarian mission that was necessary to stop violence in Haiti, put an end to anarchy, and protect US lives and property. This was by now a familiar refrain. The United States was selflessly helping the Haitian people and building democracy in the Caribbean through military occupation.[40]

As with the Dominican Republic, this benevolent image was uncritically embraced early on by the mainstream US press. As one editorial put it:

The United States at present is collecting the customs, preserving order, and acting as confidential and respected adviser to the Haitian government. It has taken the United States a very long time to intervene in Haiti. To find in recent history an example of greater forbearance, greater patience would be difficult. Having exhausted every possible resource in giving the Haitians time and repeated occasions to put their own house in order, now that we have gone in to do that work for them we are going to do it properly and thoroughly.[29]

Framing the occupation as a duty of the US government was not uncommon: "the great experiment of a great government trying to help a small government help itself, the great experiment of minding your neighbor's business better than he can mind it himself, of holding and directing the dark brother's hand...."[30] This paternalism, and the notion that it was the obligation of the United States to help smaller nations develop into liberal democracies, was an underlying assumption held by the Wilson administration and US policymakers during this period—one that was frequently articulated in openly racist terms. As Secretary of State Robert Lansing explained in 1915, the experience of Haiti shows "that the African race are devoid of any capacity for political organization and lack of genius for government. Unquestionably there is in them an inherent tendency to revert to savagery and to cast aside the shackles of civilization which are irksome to their physical nature."[31]

Such views necessarily obscured the fact Latin American countries had their own histories of democratic intuitions and ideas, as well as the fact that the United States was not helping countries establish democracy. It was looking to ensure that the Caribbean basin remained under US control and served American economic interests. In the case of Haiti, the United States did not deliver democracy but "forced through its own authoritarian, antidemocratic system," effectively eliminated an elected legislature, undermined the judicial system, used forced labor, and legally protected any and all acts of the occupation.[32]

Although the United States would justify intervention in terms of restoring order to a country defined by continuous turmoil, the actual presence of the United States created unrest by stimulating armed resistance throughout the countryside while alienating an elite that had been running the country. In rural areas, resistance came in the form of localized insurrections which, although not highly centralized or coordinated, continually flared up and proved difficult for the US marines to manage or eliminate.[33] Because these insurgencies generated and exposed marine brutality and racism, they also served to increase opposition. Haiti's political class was not only frustrated by their loss of power, but quickly came to oppose the occupation, as US racial contempt became transparent and Jim Crow segregation was imposed. This, in turn, would eventually generate more national responses from groups like the Patriotic Union (UP), a major political force in the Dominican Republic that came to oppose the occupation.[34]

African Americans—led by the NAACP, black press, and black churches—were among the earliest to pay attention, and would help lead the challenge against occupation, in part by continually pointing to the giant gap between official portrayals of the US presence and on-the-ground reality. Prior to the end of the First World War, however, some black Americans shared the opinion that Haitians were an uncivilized people in need of discipline, enlightenment, education, and uplift, even if they were generally less open to occupation. Booker T. Washington "published an article in which he celebrated the occupation of Haiti as the only way to civilize the blacks of that country."[35] According to Brenda Gayle Plummer:

> Aside from the handful of intellectuals who gloried in Haiti's revolutionary past and in the unique culture of the people, most blacks looked upon the occupation as a logical consequence of that country's chronic political turbulence. Others shuddered at the lurid accounts of voodoo that frequently appeared in the popular press. Texas educators E. L. Blackshear condemned both the civil disorder and the religious heresy and in 1912 urged the formation of an international peace-keeping force to occupy Haiti.[36]

Even W. E. B. Du Bois, who would ultimately be quite critical of the US presence, suggested the initial occupation was good for Haiti, and simply urged the United States to send black troops instead of white ones.[37]

After the First World War, however, which itself had demonstrated how poorly the colonial powers treated their subjects, civil rights organizations began to blossom, black nationalism went through a resurgence, and African Americans became less accommodating and more openly critical of racist ideas and practices in general. Haiti moved onto the political agendas of many blacks, who increasingly made connections between the racism they experienced at home and the action of the US military in Haiti. As Plummer notes, "Increasing numbers of blacks abandoned the notion of participation in the regime as they came to see it as undemocratic, racist, and unproductive. They foreswore the belief that Haitians could profit from accommodationism, as they likewise rejected this formula for themselves."[38]

At times this support came from black radicals who had emigrated from the Caribbean, such as Claude McCay and Cyril Briggs. A communist, Briggs founded the Comintern-inspired African Blood Brotherhood in New York in 1919, which eventually grew to several thousand members and sought the liberation of blacks everywhere.[39] Yet, as Alan McPherson notes, solidarity and sentiment flowed from a wide range of African Americans, from "capitalists such as Robert Moton of the Tuskegee Institute, to feminists such as Addie Hunton, who in 1919 founded the International Council of Women of the Darker Races (ICWDR), which investigated the lot of Haitian women and children." The breadth of support among black Americans was remarkable:

> In 1919 Madam C. J. Walker allied with A. Philip Randolph to found the short-lived but important International League of Darker Peoples to oppose the occupation. Margaret Murray Washington, wife of Booker T., presided over the ICWDR. Visitors to the black republic included some of the brightest lights of the Harlem Renaissance and 1920s civil rights—Langston Hughes, Zora Neale Hurston, William Scott, and Arthur Spingarn. They linked the cause of Haitian independence to larger struggles for racial justice.[40]

Perhaps the most significant questioning of the US mission in Haiti was generated by the 1920 investigation conducted by the NAACP. Up until this time, the NAACP had concentrated largely on national issues, fighting for racial equity at home and developing a strong campaign against lynching. However, as James Weldon Johnson rose through the ranks of the organization, he began to widen the NAACP's scope. Weldon was "convinced that the issue of racism was not confined to the borders of the continental United States, but was rooted as well in American policy toward black nations. For him, Haiti was a prime example of American racism exported overseas."[41]

The NAACP sent Johnson, who spoke French, was of partly Haitian descent, and had diplomatic experience in Venezuela and Nicaragua, to investigate the US occupation of Haiti in 1920. He went with Herbert Seligman, a journalist, author, and member of the NAACP board. Johnson was there for three months, during which time he not only traveled and interviewed political leaders, peasants, and a few marines, but encouraged everyone he met to organize against the US invasion.

On returning, Johnson published a series of articles in *The Nation*, as well as *The Crisis*, the official organ of the NAACP, and a number of other periodicals. It was Johnson's investigation that ultimately helped bring the hypocrisy of the US occupation onto the front pages of major newspapers. Seligman also published a powerful exposé for *The Nation* that demonstrated the racist nature of the occupation, revealing that US marines talked about killing "Gooks."[42] *The Nation* was particularly important in the propaganda war because it not only "bridged the worlds of progressive blacks and whites,"[43] it became an important organizing center—through its key role in the Haiti-Santo Domingo Independence Society—for the anti-imperialist opposition.[44]

These investigations and actions exposed three important aspects of the US endeavor to the broader public. First, the occupation was not, as the United States maintained, a "peaceable intervention" that had come at the invitation of the Haitian government. In fact, Haitians had twice rejected US overtures. As a US soldier observed upon arrival, "We were not welcome. We could feel it is as distinctly as we could smell the rot along the gutters. There was not a smile in sight."[45] It was only after the Marines landed in 1915 that Haiti was forced to sign an agreement that "invited" the United States to intervene and take control of just about everything (Haitian finances, the military, public works, education, health services, etc.). Second, Johnson exposed the fact that National City Bank of New York, whose vice president effectively controlled the State Department's Haitian policy, held monopoly control over the Haitian economy by controlling the only bank in the country. This revelation undermined US claims that the occupation was a humanitarian mission in both intent and practice.

Third, and perhaps most crucial in terms of garnering the interest of the respectable press and developing popular opposition to the occupation, Johnson exposed the brutality of the marines. He recounted a particularly one-sided slaughter in which marines had killed some 3,000 "bandits" who had risen in opposition to the occupation. He also revealed press censorship, horrible conditions in the countryside, and the US reliance on force to maintain control.[46] Although not widely reported during the early stages of the occupation, such brutality was not surprising given the racism of the US military. One high ranking US officer described soldiers as "bad niggers" and referred to their leaders as "shaved apes, absolutely no intelligence whatsoever, just plain low nigger."[47] The US military routinely harassed, tortured, and murdered Haitians, and established forced labor for public works projects. As one Haitian pointed out when asked why he used the term slavery to describe the system of forced labor: "One, the work isn't paid. Two: you worked with your back to the sun, wearing nothing but pants. Three: they only sent you home when you were sick. Four: You didn't eat enough, just corn and beans. Five: You slept in a prison or at the construction site. Six: When you tried to run away, they killed you. Isn't that slavery?"[48]

The brutality of the occupation would not be fully revealed until years later, but Johnson's investigation helped shift the terms of the debate and opened the flood gates—well beyond African Americans. Reports of racism and brutality on the part of the marines, as well as mismanagement by the United States, widespread corruption, and the repression of political dissidents, began to surface and were at times confirmed by US soldiers. For the first time since the marines had landed, the Wilson administration was not only forced to discuss the occupation, but was on the defensive. Warren Harding, the Republican candidate during the 1920 election, seized Haiti as a campaign issue when Democratic vice presidential hopeful FDR boasted that he (as assistant secretary of the Navy) had written the Haitian constitution. Harding, who quickly promised to withdraw the marines from Haiti if elected (and then failed to do so once in office), took Roosevelt's admission to be the "most shocking assertion that was ever emanated from a responsible member of the government of the United States" and as an "official admission of the rape of Haiti and Santo Domingo by the present administration."[49] The *New York Times* demanded an inquiry into military inefficiency and mismanagement, and reported on how the marines fired machine guns from airplanes at defenseless Haitian villages.[50]

As a result of these efforts, disapproval of the occupation moved well beyond black leaders to include much of black America and large numbers of whites during the 1920s. Black churches were particularly vocal, demanding the release of political prisoners, the restoration of civil liberties, and the end of the occupation. Black political groups, ranging from the pro-Communist to the National Colored Republican conference, came out against the occupation.

> The intense fighting between U.S. Marines and the Haitian revolutionaries, called "cacos," was highlighted weekly in both pictures and words by the *Afro-American Leader*, the *Cleveland Gazette*, the *New York Age*, the *Washington Bee*, and other African American newspapers. The press championed the Haitian revolutionaries as freedom fighters in the tradition of African American abolitionists such as Gabriel Prosser, Denmark Vesey, and Nat Turner.[51]

Eventually, as Mary Renda documents, opposition went well beyond African-American groups, spreading to the liberal press, the international women's movement, the radical left, and the small Haitian immigrant community in the United States.[52] Like Cubans before them, and Chileans, Argentineans, and Central Americans after them, exiles from Haiti came to occupy an important place in the emerging solidarity campaign. "As nationalists promoting a nationalist cause, they fired the imagination of those who saw Haiti as part of a larger African world which must be redeemed from white control."[53] The Haitian community organized with American blacks, staged protests, and rarely missed an opportunity to make the connections between Haiti and the plight of blacks in general. As Bishop John R. Hurst, an American-educated Haitian who headed the Episcopal Church in

Haiti, noted, the Haitian problem "is but the Negro question in a new form."[54]

A wide range of anti-imperialists now approached Haiti from a variety of directions, arguing that US imperialism benefited only a small group of US businesses, that it went against basic US principles of democracy, and that instead of bringing enlightenment to the Caribbean it delivered atrocity. Nor was this solidarity without impact in Haiti itself. Perhaps the most powerful effect of Johnson's investigation was the role his visit to Haiti played in revitalizing the Haitian opposition. Johnson's trip contributed greatly to the reorganization and revitalization of the Patriotic Union, which had been effectively eliminated under a treaty in 1916. The UP was reconstituted, became a powerful force for national liberation, and set up 14 chapters throughout Haiti. It was after Johnson's visit that the UP began sending delegations abroad, with the NAACP's New York offices serving as the US headquarters for the UP. In Haiti, the UP kept up its campaign against the occupation and challenged the censorship imposed by the US military dictatorship. When US senators came to investigate the situation in Haiti, it organized a huge protest against the occupation and pushed the investigation in a more critical direction.[55]

Such efforts made the occupation increasingly unpopular in the United States by the mid-1920s, and created space for expanded opposition in Haiti. In the end, a series of uprisings in Haiti in the late 1920s, combined with protests in the United States, made US rule simply untenable and forced the slow withdrawal of the United States.[56]

Nicaragua

In 1912 the United States sent a force of almost 3,000 marines in order to ensure that Nicaragua was ruled by a government sympathetic to its interests. The military victory was quick. The occupation was not. A marine contingent would remain in Nicaragua for most of the period between 1912 and 1925, and then returned in 1927 to confront an armed rebellion led by Augusto Sandino. It would take six years, but by 1933 the popular rebellion—sustained and strengthened by international allies—would force the United States to withdraw its troops from Nicaragua.[57]

The military occupation was bumpy from the start, in part because of all Latin Americans, Nicaraguans "perhaps most resented the long-term economic and strategic control that Washington and Wall Street arrogated" over the region."[58] This embryonic anti-imperialism was the product of both a long history of US involvement in Nicaragua and the nature of the occupation itself. The conspicuous presence and violent behavior of the marines served as a visible reminder of US control. Worse yet, any initial hope that the US occupation would deliver some sort of "development" was quickly dashed. The overly generous concessions bestowed upon US companies only fueled the growing resentment.

In this sense, although a similar set of concerns drove resistance to US occupations throughout the Caribbean, including inequality, concentrated political power, and the nature of US rule, Nicaragua was a particularly receptive site for the kind of anti-imperialist nationalism that Sandino would espouse in forging rebellion. Armed resistance appealed to not only workers and peasants, who "grasped Sandino's message of class warfare,"[59] but resonated with people from all over the world. As one commentator noted, Sandino's uprising generated "a never before seen explosion of global publicity."[60]

Latin American media outlets were among the quickest to point to the shortcomings of the US occupation and to the virtues of the Nicaraguan resistance—suggesting that Sandino and his followers should be placed alongside the likes of Bolívar and Martí. But Europeans, Japanese, Chinese, and others across the globe were also critical of US involvement and/or applauded Sandino's struggle. The US government felt this pressure acutely, especially as it was taken up by the news media and political actors in the United States.[61]

In the United States, sectors of African Americans were again central to the emerging opposition, in part because many were already primed by similar events in Haiti and the Dominican Republic. "The black press, from Marcus Garvey's *Negro World* to the NAACP's *Crisis*, edited by W. E. B. Du Bois, gave extensive and favorable coverage to the rebels, and Garvey's Universal Negro Improvement Association had a significant pro-Sandino membership on Nicaragua's Caribbean coast."[62] "African Americans cheered the Nicaraguan resistance against the United States invasion. Black media exposed the ugly reality that the US Marines were in Nicaragua to defend the profits of the United Fruit Company...."[63] Indeed, according to the *Pittsburgh Courier*, a US triumph would mean slavery for Nicaraguans through increased exploitation from US banks and corporations. African Americans organized workshops to learn about resistance movements in Nicaragua and Haiti, while the black press provided favorable coverage of Sandino, equating his followers to those of George Washington.[64]

Even before Sandino was on the radar in the late 1920s, however, mainstream US newspapers, including the *New York Times*, began to question the wisdom of the occupation itself, and suggested the presence of "imperialistic motives."[65] Consequently, once Sandino emerged it did not take long for the press to question the government's claim that Sandino was a common bandit. Carlton Beal's reporting in *The Nation* was particularly important for altering public/media understandings of the Nicaraguan rebel.[66] Once Sandino was understood in political (and not criminal) terms it was not a giant leap to conclude that US marines were slaughtering Nicaraguans in order to squash a patriotic rebellion (as opposed to simply restoring order). Sandino became something of an icon, one who wore anti-imperialism on his sleeve and always seemed ready with a good quote: "The sovereignty of a free people is not to be discussed; it is to be defended with gun in hand."[67]

US-based opposition groups, both those who supported Sandino's cause and those who simply wanted to end the occupation, informed and fed off the press coverage. In addition to Honduras and Mexico, both of which became important international sites of Sandino solidarity, New York City emerged as a hub of transnational support. Home to significant numbers of radicals and Latin Americans (and some Latin American radicals), New York became not only a key place for protests, but a "conduit of much of Sandino's transnational money."[68] Faith-based organizations, as well as secular pacifists, began to stress the ethical costs of occupation. Scholars and eventually policymakers entered the fray, and growing sectors of civil society argued for non-intervention, while sympathizing with those living under occupation. Congressional leaders put pressure on the President to withdraw. In short, solidarity and opposition to the occupation had gone mainstream. As Van Gosse recounts, "Sandino excited a worldwide admiration that infested surprisingly large numbers of North Americans. Sympathy with the Nicaraguan guerillas, and disgust at the brazen North American occupation, was hardly confined to the radical fringe, but came from groups all over the political map."[69]

In many ways, it was the figure and vision of Sandino that ignited global interest and served to highlight the distinction between two semi-distinct currents of anti-imperialism that were emerging during this period. The first, as Richard Grossman outlines, is best understood as anti-interventionist, and was comprised of groups that opposed US intervention in Latin America without being (actively, necessarily, or at all) in solidarity with Latin American rebel movements led by the likes of Sandino, Castro, Allende, the FMLN, or the FSLN. This current dates back to the US occupation of Mexico in the mid-1800s, but as we saw it really came together in a coherent form around the Spanish–American–Cuban War at the very end of the nineteenth century. Led by organizations like the Anti-Imperialist League, which could count among its diverse members such notables as Grover Cleveland, Andrew Carnegie, Samuel Gompers, and Mark Twain, this group saw intervention as a betrayal of US history, its professed commitment to democracy and anti-colonialism, and the US constitution.[70]

Progressives and pacifists also played central roles in this anti-interventionist current. Some, such as the Fellowship for Reconciliation and the American Quakers, were religious in origin and could trace their pacifist roots back to the First World War. The Women's International League for Peace and Freedom also opposed US intervention and even "economic imperialism." Collectively, these groups wrote letters to the White House, worked to inform the public, and sent people to Nicaragua to investigate. Their demand was clear. They wanted US Marines out of Nicaragua. Such efforts helped energize opponents of intervention in the US Congress, who in turn forced vigorous debates about the role of the US military in Central America and the Caribbean. Much like today, opposition within Congress was at times intense, often centering on the question of whether the President was required to seek Congressional support before committing combat troops, but never reached the level of cutting off funds for the war. Such pressure did, however, contribute to President Hoover's decision to withdrawal troops in 1933.[71] This anti-interventionist tendency has typically been the more dominant and mainstream of the two, and would continue to be at the heart of opposition to US foreign policy during the Cold War.

There was, however, a second tendency that shared the first group's opposition to US intervention, but took one step further by opposing US imperialism, and supporting Sandino and efforts to expel the United States from Nicaragua. Given limitations with communication and transportation during this period, much of this support was often symbolic, coming in the form of newspaper articles and declarations of solidarity—important contributions which shaped how Sandino and the rebellion were understood. At times, however, solidarity with Nicaraguan rebels was quite concrete and material. Communists, specifically the Workers Party of America and its front organization the All-American Anti-Imperialist League, built support for Sandino by developing alliances with a wide range of actors on the liberal-left (following the strategy of building a United Front). Events in Nicaragua animated the All-American Anti-Imperialist League, and in 1928 it held a convention in New York with some 400 people, including John Brophy from the United Mine Workers as well as representatives from the ACLU, *The Nation*, and Chinese and Filipino associations opposed to US imperialism. Attendees developed a plan for actively helping Sandino which included not only protests and efforts to educate people in the United States, but direct forms of aid to Sandino's cause. The FBI reported that the league sent Sandino nearly $50,000, and Sandino himself remained in contact with them.[72]

In the end, what this all meant is that in 1927 when the marines tried to subdue Sandino's rebellion, they not only confronted an opponent who was able to bring together large numbers of armed combatants (in part by articulating a compelling vision of anti-imperialist nationalism), but fairly quickly faced a transnational opposition that supported the uprising and isolated the US government. Although Sandino's cause would lose some of its international luster by the early 1930s,[73] the armed rebellion itself could not be subdued, and served to focus enough negative attention on the United States that the costs of occupation became too great.

Before leaving Nicaragua, however, the United States placed the Guardia Nacional in the hands of a loyal ally, Anastasio Somoza, who would insure that US military intervention was no longer necessary. Somoza would assassinate Sandino in 1934, and the Somoza family—with the full support of the US government—would bring the people of Nicaragua almost five decades of brutal dictatorship. Indeed, because of the fierce and intensely nationalist resistance that Sandino offered, as well as the remarkable solidarity that he garnered both within and outside of Nicaragua, the United States became increasingly reluctant to deploy troops, the conspicuous presence of which galvanized the opposition both in Latin America and at home. Sandino, in this sense, reinforced an important lesson that led to a strategic shift in the way US power operated in the region. Rather than sending US troops, why not create and back repressive right-wing dictators and Latin American armed forces that supported and were beholden to US interests? US troops were no longer needed as long as the United States could operate through loyal proxies. This shift would have a dramatic impact on Latin America and the landscape of solidarity during the post Second World War period.

Conclusion

With varying degrees of size, intensity, and coherence, widespread opposition to US military occupation emerged in the Dominican Republic, Haiti, and Nicaragua, including armed resistance and international campaigns. With the slight exception of Sandino, whose fiery anti-imperialism drew upon class antagonisms within Nicaragua, this opposition was largely focused on repelling the United States and restoring self-rule. With the exception of small numbers of radical leftists, most opponents were not advocating the revolutionary transformation of their societies, even if the US presence often stoked nationalist anti-imperialism while exposing the class interests of domestic elites. The brutal nature of the occupations not only allowed opponents to expose US narratives about benevolent motives and a soft touch, but revealed the imperial and racist nature of the US presence in Latin America. This, in turn, fueled both anti-imperialism and nationalism throughout the region.

In the United States, anti-imperialism was fairly broad based during this period, and was by no means restricted to what we think of as the radical left. Relatively mainstream actors, including US Congressmen, the AFL, the NAACP, churches, civil rights organizations, prominent newspapers, the Anti-Imperialist League, and the like were all part of a political current which opposed imperialism not simply in the increasingly dated sense of colonial possession. They had also come to understand and oppose imperialism at least in terms of the US military presence, and in some cases could be quite critical of US capital, especially when it took the form of monopolistic banks or exceedingly powerful corporations. To be sure, this anti-imperialism had its limits, rarely challenged the broader core of US-Latin American relations, and often had to be coaxed by the radical left. But there was nonetheless a substantive current of anti-imperialism through the 1930s.

More than this, a more radical current—white and black, within and outside the labor movement and the communist party—existed within this broader stream, and took inspiration from Latin Americans. Here, not only did actors in both the United States and Latin America recognize how the United States created oppressive conditions across the Americas, they sought to work together in ways that would oppose US imperialism and the political-economic system it supported—collective struggles to build new worlds. This was particularly pronounced in Nicaragua, where the presence of an anti-imperialist rebellion, led by the compelling figure of Sandino, animated and energized many on the US left—that is, in a case where there was a revolutionary movement with which to be in solidarity. This internationalism was an important site for sustaining radicalism during the 1920s and 1930s.[74]

At the same time, it is worth remembering that the core of anti-imperialism, and what really held it together and made it attractive to broad sectors of American society, was a shared opposition to US military occupation. What this tended to mean is that solidarity developed around "campaigns" designed to force the US troops to withdrawal from this or that country—and relied upon exposing the extreme abuses of the US military to fuel solidarity. Consequently, not only did those Latin American countries where US presence was the most conspicuous often capture the most international attention, but once the military left most of the international solidarity dissipated. Solidarity campaigns, in this sense, were designed with the short-term goal of expelling the United States. Once the United States was gone, so too was much of the solidarity.

This tendency, of course, was due in part to the urgent need to expel the US military. The physical presence of troops not only had violent consequences, but instantly raised the profile of the invaded country, which in turned increased the possibility for US-based international solidarity. It also served to unify political actors with quite different ideologies around the common goal of opposing the United States and restoring direct rule. And yet, as effective as the focus on US military aggression was in creating opposition in both Latin America and the United States, it had two interrelated aspects that would shape the contours of solidarity going forward during the Cold War.

First, an internationalism that did not look beyond expelling the physical presence of the US military from Latin American countries was (almost by definition) a project not designed to address the underlying political and economic structures driving an imperialism rooted in global capitalism. Various actors on the left in both the United States and Latin America recognized this limitation, and tried to advance collective struggle aimed at deeper transformation. But the left in the United States simply did not have the critical mass to sustain effective solidarity on its own once the withdrawal of the US military from a particular country deflated the political energy around a given campaign. This was particularly true if those countries also lacked their own revolutionary left to which US-based actors could connect. That a more powerful left—in both the United States and Latin America—might emerge seemed quite possible in the 1930s, but the opportunity would be stifled by the Second World War and then short-circuited in both regions by the Cold War in the late 1940s.

Second, as Sandino's death and the US support for the Guardia Nacional under the Somoza dictatorship indicated, the United States would soon realize that using American troops was a practice that was both problematic and solvable. By finding and/or training

Latin Americans to do the dirty work, the United States could retain a military presence in Latin America without maintaining a military presence in Latin America. The physical absence of US troops from Latin America proved quite effective in blunting US-based anti-imperialism. To be sure, activists would eventually find a counter to this, concentrating on military aid as opposed to the physical presence of troops, but the basic logic—of focusing on the military and not imperialism more broadly—would carry into the Cold War period, as the human rights movement put a premium on high-profile abuses, and organized labor removed itself from the solidarity equation altogether.

3

The Cuban Revolution and the Cold War

With the Good Neighbor policy (1933), the United States announced that it was adopting a foreign policy based on the principles of national sovereignty and self-determination, and henceforth would no longer intervene militarily in the internal affairs of Latin American countries. That such a declaration was necessary is in itself suggestive. US aggression during the first three-plus decades of the twentieth century was routine, brutal, unpopular in Latin America, and scrutinized within the United States. The opposition that US intervention engendered both at home and in Latin America, combined with growing concerns about the US economy and political turmoil in Europe, led to a shift away from direct military intervention in the Americas during the late 1930s and 1940s. This departure from open militarism would lead the United States to rely more heavily on less conspicuous methods for maintaining hegemony in the region, ranging from the strategic use of loans and other financial tools to the support of Latin American "strongmen" and the training of national guards.

The Good Neighbor phase lasted for all of about a decade, and was over by 1945, with the end of the Second World War and the beginning of the Cold War. What is striking about the subsequent period, from 1945 to the mid to late 1960s, is not simply that the United States became more aggressive as the Cold War heated up. It is how quickly the anti-imperialist opposition disappeared from public life in the United States, an opposition that had been unevenly present since the late 1800s.[1] As we have seen, prior to the Cold War, increased US aggression in Latin America routinely produced opposition to US empire among sectors of the liberal establishment and the radical left. The opposition was rarely coherent, consistent, or necessarily effective, but it was a presence that at the very least required US imperialists to look over their shoulders. It placed limits on US empire.

The Second World War and the Cold War challenged and altered this dynamic. During the Second World War, concerns about US empire were necessarily sidelined as liberals and the left joined the fight to defeat fascism. After the war, however, the space for anti-imperialism—or really any progressive challenge to US foreign policy—did not open back up, and was closed after 1947. This was in part because under the guise of anti-totalitarianism the US political establishment refashioned the struggle against fascism into one against communism.[2] The perceived threat of communism was understood as both an internal and external menace, meaning that as the United States began to assert itself on a global level—and justified such aggression in anti-communist terms—there was little space for domestic opposition to empire. Many liberals, including the core of the labor movement, either joined the fight against communism, now often understood as totalitarianism, or distanced themselves from a left that was increasingly persecuted not simply for being "communist," but for advocating the redistribution of wealth or exposing the imperial nature of US foreign policy. In other words, even for liberals who did not entirely embrace the anti-communism of the late 1940s and 1950s (and there were plenty who did), there was sufficient incentive to separate themselves from left projects and organizations, and to narrow their political visions and horizons.

After the war, then, the fight against communism quickly deepened, widened, and became the justification for imperial aggression for the next 40-plus years. The anti-communist crusade targeted not only communists, but a wide spectrum of the liberal left, including fairly conservative socialists, most of the democratic left, union movements, and others on the liberal end of the political spectrum. Even those who were not actively targeted quickly got the message: political dissent was severely circumscribed. This anti-communist campaign did not simply mean rooting out communists at home, "containing" communist countries, or even targeting countries with strong revolutionary movements. It was not simply that progressives were under attack in the United States, Guatemala, or Cuba. It was that they were under attack everywhere, simultaneously. As progressive coalitions struggled to sustain themselves at home, they found it difficult to reach out to international allies who were themselves in a weak position to establish or sustain cross-border alliances. With both ends of the equation in retreat, international solidarity was a tough haul.

The Unravelling of Anti-Imperialism

In the United States, the post-Second World War dismantling of anti-imperialism is perhaps best understood through the history of black internationalism and labor—two core constituents of the anti-imperialist camp which emerged during the first half of the twentieth century. In both cases, the process through which anti-imperialism as a political project unraveled happened swiftly and thoroughly between about 1947 and 1950, and occurred in part by severing the uneasy alliance between liberals and the left that had given anti-imperialism its breadth and force in the United States in the decades leading up to the Second World War. By the end of the 1940s, most liberals had moved firmly into an anti-communist camp that accepted US hegemony as a part of the Cold War order. This necessarily involved separating themselves from a left that was being marginalized and repressed (almost) out of existence.

This process was particularly pronounced within black internationalism, in part because the Cold War offensive afforded African Americans on the left even less room to maneuver. The current of black internationalism that emerged in the first half of the twentieth century—partly through an engagement around US intervention in the Caribbean basin—understood the struggle against Jim Crow and racism at home in relation to the anti-colonial, anti-imperialist struggles taking place in Africa, Asia, and Latin America. In many ways, this political project continued to develop through the Second World War, a global event which amplified the notion that the experiences of black Americans were indelibly linked to anti-colonial struggles throughout Africa and Asia in the 1940s and 1950s. This project seemed hopeful in 1945, even as late as 1946, when the US government's stance towards colonialism was unclear, and it still seemed reasonable to advocate a worldwide New Deal that addressed global

73

inequalities—that economic recovery, anti-colonialism, and even peace might go hand in hand.[3]

The anti-imperialism of black internationalism would not, however, survive the beginning of the Cold War. As Penny M. Von Eschen has shown, the civil rights push by African American liberals in the early years of the Cold War relied on the argument that discrimination at home should be fought because it undermined the legitimate leadership of the United States over the non-communist world—an argument that was not without merit, as Castro himself continually pointed to US racism with great political effect. Once the logic of the Cold War and US hegemony were accepted as the rationale for fighting racism at home, there was little space for a critical internationalism that assumed and opposed US imperialism. The Cold War assumption that the United States was the legitimate leader of the free world meant that the basic tenets of its foreign policy were unassailable—a stance that the Truman Doctrine essentially imposed after 1947. As Von Eschen notes, "after the Truman Doctrine and the Marshall Plan, the criticism of American foreign policy that had been an integral part of the politics of the African diaspora fell beyond the limits of legitimate dissent, and the broad anticolonial alliances of the 1940s were among the earliest casualties of the Cold War."[4] Quite clearly, this was a dramatic departure from the black internationalism that had emerged between the two world wars—and even a sharp break from immediately after the Second World War, when international concerns remained deeply tied to domestic issues such as civil rights.[5]

Moreover, what the acceptance and fact of global US leadership brought, and what liberals of all persuasions were increasingly silent on as the Cold War effectively forced them to accept US hegemony, was the repression of anti-colonial and anti-imperialist struggles throughout the Third World. As African American liberals embraced US Cold War foreign policy (with the hope of receiving domestic civil rights in exchange), and as black leftists were repressed and marginalized, the terms of black internationalism were fundamentally altered, and "effectively severed the black American struggle for civil rights from the issues of anticolonialism and racism abroad."[6] This did not, as Carol Anderson has argued, mean that anti-colonialism was completely off the black liberal political agenda, and some organizations—most notably the NAACP—pursued an anti-colonial project which was narrower in vision and divorced from communism and left politics. Such pragmatic projects were not without merit, and at times proved effective vehicles for promoting anticolonial independence and human rights in a world defined by the Cold War. But they also eschewed anti-imperialism as an analytical framework and political project, and assumed that capitalism and global inequality were fundamental features of the world order.[7]

This was a significant shift. It was not simply that a sector of the black political class abandoned an internationalism that understood global politics through a prism shaped by socialism and anticolonial struggles for a more concentrated focus on domestic civil rights. It was what was lost in a larger sense. As we saw, the black politics that was emerging before (and through) the Second World War had been enriched by the constant exchange between "domestic" and "international" concerns in a way that brought the liberal-left together (into something of a black popular front) around critical understandings of not only inequality and racism, but other big topic issues like democracy, freedom, and justice in the modern world. These understandings certainly pointed to the importance of race, but also encompassed broad visions of a democratic world in which resources were more equitably distributed. The early years of the Cold War went a long way in eradicating this process and tradition.

The dismantling of this politics not only meant that the Third World (temporarily) lost much of its importance within black politics, or rather came to be understood apart from US imperialism during the 1950s and early 1960s, but that even semi-critical understandings of race and racism were increasingly understood apart from their roots in colonialism, slavery, and capitalism (and often reduced to psychological problems peculiar to the United States).[8] In this sense, how anti-colonialism and racism themselves came to be understood shifted as they were increasingly severed from political economy. Worse yet, the very institutions that had nurtured this project—the black press, black churches, trade unions, and so on—would not only distance themselves from anti-imperialism, but would themselves be either destroyed or neutered by the process. It also meant that as

African American liberals distanced themselves from left politics, and in many cases simply adopted anti-communism, they also separated from a left with which they had been in an uneasy, but productive, relationship during the 1920s and 1930s—a relationship that (at its best) had embraced the struggles of colonized peoples, understood all black people as part of the laboring classes of the world, and worked for a more democratic and just world. In fairly short order, the Cold War made great strides towards eradicating this framing and the institutions that had sustained it.[9]

Nor was recovering a critical black internationalism easy during the late 1950s and 1960s. Civil rights activists continued to operate within the confines of a world shaped by the Cold War. Although leaders such as Martin Luther King Jr. and Bayard Rustin had personal interests in anti-colonialism, "it was not a programmatic part of the civil rights movement." Moreover, with the silencing of an earlier generation of leaders such as Du Bois and Paul Robeson, an anti-imperialism that was also anti-capitalist lost its footing within African American political worlds, forcing new generations of activists such as the Black Panthers to "reinvent the wheel as they developed their own critiques of American capitalism and imperialism."[10]

They were not alone. A parallel process occurred throughout the US body politic, and was particularly pronounced within the house of labor, which had profound implications for black liberation since black freedom was so deeply intertwined with the fate of trade unions during this period (in part because the CIO had done so much to organize black workers before and during the Second World War). In the case of labor, it was not simply that its core constituents quietly and unevenly distanced themselves from a left with which they had been working, and of which they had been a key part, throughout the 1930s and early 1940s. It was that for many in the labor movement, solidarity—and particularly international solidarity in the Americas—came to be defined as solidarity against communism. For the mainstream core of organized labor, the enthusiastic embrace of anti-communism effectively ensured that meaningful, effective, international solidarity was off the table for the rest of the twentieth century (notwithstanding some important exceptions). To be sure, we could argue that this was not a huge loss. The mainstream core of organized labor had never gotten behind anti-capitalist, revolutionary labor organizations in Latin America. In the first decades of the twentieth century, Gompers had sought to establish a Latin American labor movement that was moderate, worked with business, and followed the AFL's lead, even if at times it could support progressive causes.

The onset of the Cold War, however, meant that the spaces for radical currents within US labor were effectively shut down, which in turn narrowed the ideological range of the movement as a whole. The left was purged, and with it the liberal-left coalition that had animated labor's gains during the 1930s and early 1940s. This ideological shift was amplified by the fact that Latin American workers were themselves under fierce attack, so that at the same time as US labor was moving to the right, Latin Americans were not in a position to push them to the left. More than this, the Cold War also meant that the core of organized labor in the United States (led by the AFL-CIO after 1955) not only sought to support like-minded, business-friendly unions, but actively and aggressively sought to prevent more militant, anti-capitalist labor movements from emerging in the region. Put another way, during a period when most non-labor solidarity activists were effectively (if temporarily) silenced, the largest and most well-funded form of US solidarity—organized labor—sided with US empire and sought to weaken democratic movements in the region. An important potential link in the solidarity chain was not simply absent or silenced. It was playing for the other team.

This political climate—whose reactionary influence reached far beyond black internationalism and labor—meant that it was very difficult for anti-imperialist activists, or liberal critics of any kind, to reconstitute public opposition to US foreign policy. To be sure, domestic opposition to US empire had always been sporadic and lacking in institutional continuity, but as Van Gosse suggests, "there is almost a total break" during the late 1940s and 1950s. "Once the Cold War closed in, almost all sectors of organized liberalism acquiesced to empire...."[11] As testament to this broader chill, when the United States orchestrated the overthrow of a democratically elected government in Guatemala in 1954 through one of the most blatant acts of imperialism in US history, there would be little US-based opposition.

The US press ignored American involvement in the coup, and rejoiced over how Guatemalans had (by themselves) successfully overthrown communism. Everyone seemed bewildered by the anti-US demonstrations that swept across Latin America in response to the coup, but such protests never really generated much of an oppositional response in the United States.[12]

In other words, the silence was deafening.[13] From the late 1940s through the Cuban revolution, the rhetoric and repression of Cold War anti-communism gave the US government relatively free rein abroad. This was helped by the fact that although the United States was becoming less of a good neighbor, it only rarely intervened directly with the military, preferring instead to operate by covert means or through Latin American proxies.

The Limits of Latin American Solidarity during the Cold War

The Cuban revolution was a global event that had the potential for reviving a broad current of anti-imperialism in the United States. As Van Gosse persuasively argues, it is in the solidarity surrounding the Cuban revolution that we find early cracks in the Cold War consensus. This was partly because the Cuban revolution was momentarily understood in such a way that implicitly challenged this consensus by insisting that the entire world was not defined by the US–Soviet conflict—by American capitalism and Soviet-style communism. There were alternatives. The Cuban revolution was understood, at least initially by a fairly broad swath of Americans, as part of the powerful surge of anti-imperialist nationalism that swept the Third World during the two decades after the Second World War. Drawing from a range of nationalist and internationalist impulses, anti-colonialists led cross-class coalitions that successfully overthrew European rule in dozens of countries in Africa and Asia.

It is hard to overstate the importance of this shift. Prior to the Second World War, although nationalist and internationalist projects came in a range of forms, from the inhumanities of twentieth-century fascism to the struggles of revolutionary socialists, they tended to be defined by two broad features. First, as Perry Anderson notes, prior to the end of the Second World War the dominant thrust of nationalism had always been primarily an "an expression of the propertied classes," whereas internationalism had been "an expression of the labouring classes."[14] This is not to say that the two currents could always be easily distinguished, were always opposed to one another, or that working people could not support or be drawn into nationalist causes. Lower classes played key roles in the French revolution, during independence struggles throughout the Americas, and in the nationalism that drove the horrors of the First World War. Likewise, elites could take on the internationalist cause, as radical allies to socialist struggles, as anti-imperialists, or as advocates for more liberal forms of internationalism. Yet, prior to the Second World War, the most dynamic strands of nationalism had been animated first and foremost by capital, with (the less powerful) internationalism remaining largely within the domain of labor.

Second, because both nationalism and internationalism were products of Western capitalism, and because Western capitalism so decisively shaped world history, the intertwined histories of nationalism and internationalism had been primarily driven by Europe and (to a lesser extent) the United States. There were certainly nationalist and internationalist impulses and contributions outside these regions, but the momentum behind these currents was rooted in the West.

What makes the period following the Second World War, roughly from 1945 to 1965, so remarkable is that not one, but both of these pre-war constants were upended in ways that had profound consequences for how solidarity was understood and practiced. Not only was the historic connection between capital/nationalism and labor/internationalism disrupted, the West ceased to be the primary force driving forms of nationalism and internationalism. The dominant current of nationalism after the Second World War was Third World-based and anti-imperialist, whereby popular sectors engaged in a global revolt against Western colonialism and imperialism. These struggles were, at their core, nationalist struggles of liberation which were led by heterogeneous, cross-class coalitions which varied widely from country to country. And because they took place throughout the Third World, particularly in Africa and Asia, and were primarily and collectively directed against European colonial power, the internationalist current of anti-imperialism running through them was also profoundly shaped by racialized understandings of the world order.

Cuba was understood through this lens, and initially captured the imagination of a broad swath of the liberal left in the United States for that reason. Castro represented himself and the uprising as "revolutionary nationalist," had broad support throughout Cuban society, and—during and immediately after the revolution—was quite popular in the United States. Yet, as the us government took an increasingly hard line, and forced Castro in the direction of the Soviet Union, Cuba slid into the communist camp by the early 1960s. As it did, Cuba's ability to disrupt the Cold War consensus eroded, especially from the perspective of the us government and media. Sectors of the New Left continued to see Cuba as a Third World alternative to both the United States and the Soviet Union, but by the mid-1960s the ideological space for such claims was increasingly small within the us mainstream, as Cuba was slotted firmly into the communist camp. Cuba, in that sense, was immensely important for the us left, but could not be the vehicle through which large numbers of liberals returned to anti-imperialism. Quite the opposite, its embrace by American radicals in some ways ensured that anti-imperialism would remain the province of the left in the United States.

This meant two things. First, despite the best effort of activists, us-based solidarity surrounding the Cuban revolution was marginalized and the Cold War consensus reaffirmed. Solidarity with Cuba remained important for the left, and brought together a number of progressive currents, but such opposition was increasingly marginalized and off the public radar. Second, in part because Cuba loomed so large, and did in fact find its way toward Soviet-led communism, subsequent efforts by Latin Americans to advance reforms of any kind tended to be quickly labelled "communist" by the us government and its reactionary allies in the region. This provided cover for the emergence of a region-wide violence that was so one-sided it produced what would eventually become understood as human rights abuses and victims, while successfully destroying the left throughout much of Latin America.

It also made it very hard for Latin American solidarity to re-emerge beyond Cuba during this transitional period of the early Cold

War. On the one hand, left internationalism was effectively dismantled from both ends, in the United States and Latin America. On the
other hand, although the anti-colonial nationalism of Third World
revolutionaries was taking the world by storm, and had an impact on
US radicalism during the 1950s and 1960s, its ability to become a central way of framing, inspiring, and organizing international solidarity
in the United States was limited by a number of factors. Not only was
it centered in other parts of the world, but anti-colonialism's close
association with communism put it at a considerable disadvantage in
the ideological marketplace of the Cold War United States. This was
especially true as the romance of Third World revolutionaries, which
had appealed to young Americans during the 1960s, started to wane
in the 1970s. The effective end of formal colonialism, marked by
Portugal's withdrawal from its colonies in the mid-1970s, only added
to this tendency. Anti-colonialism not only seemed less urgent, even
outdated, once self-determination had been achieved, it became less
attractive to many Americans as revolutionaries began to govern new
nations beset by poverty and violence.[15]

Consequently, when US-backed Cold War violence swept over
Latin America, the very forms of internationalism that might have
been available to oppose empire were largely absent. Few in the
United States paid much attention to Bolivia during the 1950s, the violence surrounding Stroessner's Paraguay in 1954, the overthrow of
Arbenz in Guatemala in the same year, military rule in Brazil during
the mid-1960s, or the US invasion of the Dominican Republic in 1965.
Even the most robust instance of solidarity—Cuba—was quite limited. More to the point, when Latin Americans sought foreign allies
they had few places to turn. Human rights networks had not yet developed, leaving Latin Americans to appeal for solidarity through the
most familiar of internationalisms, as socialists reaching out to fellow
socialists. Their calls were not completely ignored, especially in the
Soviet Union and Europe, but there was not much to connect to in the
United States.

In the short term, at a time when open support for the revolution was becoming increasingly difficult in the United States, the
fragility of left internationalism set serious limits on the scale and
impact of solidarity with Cuba, while at the same time making its very

presence all the more important. Despite a degree of continuity, US-based Cuban solidarity during this period came in two distinct phases, the early and late 1960s. Solidarity in the early 1960s came from two important sources, African American leftists and the Fair Play for Cuba Committee (FPCC), a multiracial organization that brought together various currents within the broader left.[16]

These efforts, which were severely restricted by the conservative milieu of the early 1960s and then actively crushed by the US government, were then followed by the Venceremos Brigades in the late 1960s. An outgrowth of Students for a Democratic Society (SDS), the Brigades brought hundreds of US citizens to Cuba to support the revolution at a time when anti-imperialism/colonialism, which had been on life support, was once again informing a greatly expanded and diversified US radicalism. During a period when activists were frustrated by the inability to end the Vietnam War, trips to Cuba offered people an opportunity to practice a hands-on solidarity that was aimed at advancing a radical political project. They also served to challenge the Cold War vision of Cuba put forth by the US government, were immensely important for reviving/sustaining left internationalism during a transitional period, and shaped the subsequent trajectory of Latin American solidarity.[17]

Cuban Solidarity in the early 1960s

From the vantage point of today, or pretty much any point after 1961, it hard to imagine that the American public ever held a favorable view of Fidel Castro and his fellow revolutionaries. In the lead-up to the Cuban revolution, however, Castro was portrayed in the respectable media as charismatic, courageous, and heroic. He stood in stark contrast to Batista, a dictator who had run a repressive police state and had turned the country into a mafia-saturated haven for gambling, prostitution, and corruption. Castro represented an opportunity for the United States to shed its reputation of supporting dictators and get on the right side of freedom and liberation in the Third World. As a non-communist intellectual of middle-class origins, Castro was a liberal, revolutionary, and nationalist patriot we could get behind. The news coverage of Castro's jungle adventures was so uniformly positive, so inspiring, that hundreds of young Americans tried to enlist in his Rebel Army.[18] Van Gosse captures the place of Cuba in the mood of period:

> Years before The Port Huron Statement was issued in August 1962, even before black students started sitting down at Southern lunch counters in February 1960, disparate US citizens—gun-toting teenagers, diehard liberals, excited reporters, stray adventurers, even Errol Flynn—had taken up the revolutionary cause championed by CBS News in a primetime May 1957 special called "Rebels of the Sierra Maestra: The Story of Cuba's Jungle Fighters." In contrast to those team-playing organization men who were the fifties' explicit role models, the ragged barbudos led by Fidel Castro, chomping their cigars and darting down green mountains slopes to ambush Batista's garrisons, were every teenage boy's dream of gunfighting, personal heroism and nose-thumbing at received authority. Two years of enthusiastic US press coverage and solidarity both vicarious and practical climaxed when Batista fled Cuba on New Year's Eve, 1958, leaving an entire column of would-be Yankee guerrillas stranded in Miami.[19]

During the late 1950s, Castro momentarily challenged the Cold War straitjacket which framed everything in terms of rigid binaries: East versus West, Soviet Union versus United States, totalitarianism versus freedom, communism versus capitalism. This was part of his appeal. On his first trip to the United States in April, 1959, over 1,000 people greeted him at Washington's National Airport, 2,000 at Penn Station in New York, and some 10,000 came to hear him at Harvard.[20] This is also what made him so threatening. At a moment when left politics seemed off the table, Castro provided an acceptable outlet for radicalism precisely because he was so difficult to categorize in Cold War terms.

This would prove ephemeral. Castro's public image in the United States deteriorated quickly during the second half of 1959. The trial and execution of Batista's secret police alienated much of the US public, and the Eisenhower administration publicly wrote off Castro when he implemented sweeping agrarian reform and expropriated the properties of US companies. By the early 1960s, with Castro turning to the Soviet Union, the failed Bay of Pigs invasion, and the Cuban missile crisis, US policymakers and media all coalesced around a fairly rigid Cold War understanding of Cuba and Castro. The mainstream media in particular felt betrayed by Castro, and goaded the US government to take a harder line.[21]

For US leftists, however, Cuba was a fresh, close-to-home, symbol of anti-colonial struggle and Third World resistance to foreign domination. Complicating Marxist orthodoxies, and emerging at a time when the repressive, authoritarian, and bureaucratic nature of Soviet and Chinese communisms was becoming apparent, the Cuban revolution's inclusion of peasants, workers, students, and intellectuals, its commitment to racial equality, and its innovative brand of socialism all made it extremely appealing to an older generation of leftists, to what was becoming the New Left, and to the US Third World left. For older leftists, like Paul Sweezy, Leo Huberman, and even C. Wright Mills, Cuba was attractive in part because it emerged at a moment when Soviet communism had lost its luster. For globally focused US radicals of color, Cuba allowed them—as it had done for earlier generations of blacks—to see themselves as part of a US Third World Left whose own struggles for racial and economic justice were intimately connected to global struggles against colonialism and imperialism.[22]

The two most important organized challenges to the Cold War framing of Cuba at the start of the 1960s came from African Americans, who "have been the only consistent source of U.S. solidarity with the Cuban Revolution,"[23] and the FPCC. Both groups mobilized support for Cuba just as mainstream opinion had turned against the revolution. They would not shift the broader debate or perception about Cuba, and would eventually be overcome by the powerful wave of anti-communism themselves, but they nonetheless prefigured a multi-racial, anti-imperialist, strand of solidarity which would expand during the Vietnam War.

African American support for the Cuban revolution has ebbed and flowed, but it has been present in some form from the late 1950s through the present day. This support has been periodically renewed and cultivated by Castro himself, who made a very public week-long stay in Harlem in 1960, consistently committed the revolution to racial equality and building relationships with black radicals in the United

States,[24] and seriously supported black liberation in Africa, most notably in Angola where Cuba sent tens of thousands of troops.[25]

Interestingly, however, at the same time as the mainstream press was embracing Castro's efforts leading up to 1959, the black press largely ignored the issue. Along with much of the more radical left, many African American journalists were initially leery of Castro because of his popularity with the respectable media which emanated in part from the vagueness of his political statements. However, in January 1959 hundreds of journalists, including those from important black newspapers, were brought to the island as part of "Operation Truth." At that point, the black press began to report on the racial integration of the Rebel Army and the new government; applauded Castro's powerful call for racial equality in both Cuba and the United States; generally supported Representative Adam Clayton Powell Jr.'s conspicuous support of Castro and the Revolution; and (most interestingly) provided a quite different perspective on the Cuban government's execution of Batista supporters following the triumph of the Revolution.[26]

Black reporters also noted the tendency of white America to loudly denounce the executions in Cuba while quietly tolerating white violence against blacks in the United States. Others compared the execution of Batista supporters with the US North's decision not to punish or disempower Southern elites following the civil war, and what that decision meant for generations of blacks. Above all, black Americans watched with excitement the prospects of Cuban blacks under the new government.[27] Cuba and Castro brought Third World solidarity, already fueled by decolonization in Africa, "closer to home, and in so doing indicated the ways in which the nascent anti-imperialism of African-Americans would surface powerfully a few years later, during the era of 'Black Power,' the Black Panther Party, and the multiracial movement against the war in Vietnam."[28]

Black radicals, many of whom had long watched events on the island, were drawn to Cuba's revolution in the late 1950s. Du Bois and Julian Mayfield were early supporters, and a number of prominent African Americans were founders of the FPCC and central figures in a 1960 trip to Cuba organized by the group, including Leroi Jones (later Amiri Baraka), Robert F. Williams, and Harold Cruse.[29]

Their experience on the island, where they witnessed the revolution's commitment to combatting racism and the central role played by black Cubans in the military and government, was radicalizing, and in many cases led to continued engagement. In 1961, Cuba gave sanctuary to Williams, an NACCP leader who had become famous for organizing armed self-defense against the Ku Klux Klan (KKK) and was being pursued by the FBI. From there, he would broadcast calls to the United States for revolution on "Radio Free Dixie."[30] For black radicals like Williams, Cuba would become—both literally and figuratively—something of a "sanctuary from U.S. racism and an ally in the struggle for full citizenship and black freedom within America."[31] Nor was he alone. Black radicals—from Stokely Carmichael and Eldridge Cleaver to Angela Davis and Assata Shakur—would continue to support the Cuban revolution in broad terms while debating the extent to which it had or had not eradicated racism.[32]

African Americans were also prominently involved in the FPCC, which "brought together the broadest array of constituencies of the early New Left, from old-fashioned liberals to early Black Nationalists."[33] Initially formed by a couple of CBS journalists and a liberal businessman, it was subsequently adopted by the Socialist Workers Party, and given a boost by the publication of *Listen, Yankee!* by C. Wright Mills.[34] It sought to lobby, protest, and otherwise shape public opinion to support Cuba's right to self-determination at a moment when tensions with the United States were high. It included Marxists, black radicals, and well-known individuals on the cultural left such as "James Baldwin, Amiri Baraka, Carleton Beals, Truman Capote, Harold Cruse, Waldo Frank, Allen Ginsberg, Lawrence Ferlinghetti, Norman Mailer, Jean-Paul Sartre, and William Appleman Williams." It constituted "one of the first multiracial, truly anti-imperialist formations of the American sixties era."[35]

In less than six months, the FPCC went from three local chapters with perhaps 2,000 members to a national organization with some 27 chapters and 40 student councils.[36] At its height, the FPCC brought over 300 activists to Cuba during Christmas of 1960, and subsequently became the central force organizing protests after the Bay of Pigs failed invasion (April 1961). Thousands protested across the country, even as public opinion stood firmly behind President Kennedy, and even as "common sense" had determined that standing behind Castro could no longer be dismissed as youthful indiscretion, but was in fact something akin to treason. Such protest may seem small by the standards set later in the decade, but it stands in stark contrast to anything that came before it. That thousands entered the streets to protest US foreign policy at this moment, under considerable pressure from the US government, and in support of a country and leader that posed a much greater threat than Guatemala and Arbenz ever did, was not only remarkable, but was an important early crack in the Cold War consensus.[37] For "a small but measurable number of older liberals, churchpeople and academics, for many younger 'radical-liberals', independent socialists, pacifists, antipolitical Beats and African-Americans fed up with the caution of their elders, Cuba's right to self-determination superseded the US claim to defend a Free World."[38]

Organized solidarity with Cuba declined after 1963, both because many of Fair Play's leaders were persecuted by the FBI and US Congress, but also because it was discovered that Kennedy's assassin, Lee Harvey Oswald, had been a member.[39] Individuals on the US left continued to agitate around Cuba after the FPCC formally disbanded in the mid-1960s, and the Communist Party of the USA (CPUSA) and Progressive Labor party sent various delegations, but consistent organized solidarity around Cuba would have to wait until the broader surge of political activity in the late 1960s.[40] Even so, this early 1960s solidarity with Cuba was an important hit on the largely unchecked nationalism of the period, constituted a crack in the rigidly bipolar Cold War vision of the world, and sustained—however precariously —a left internationalism around Latin America during a bleak period.

The Venceremos Brigades

When US radicalism intensified in the late 1960s Cuba emerged as an ideological compass and magnet for the US left. Unlike in the early 1960s, however, when Cuba's place in the world was not yet settled, Cuba was now formally part of the communist world, meaning that solidarity was largely the province of the radical left. For often different reasons, a wide range of leftists (re)turned to Cuba when looking for outside inspiration, ideas, and guidance, from an older generation of communists and socialists to more recent formations of the New Left and a US Third World Left with ties to black and Chicano power. Cuba became a useful site to think through questions of racial inequality, socialism, radical democracy, women's liberation, revolutionary transformation, and international solidarity (especially as Cuba supported Vietnamese liberation). Its brand of socialism, its youthfulness, and its anti-racism were all attractive to the US left, which pointed to Cuba and its accomplishments as an alternative to both US capitalism and Soviet-style communism.[41] With Cuba, revolutionary change was on the table.

Black radicals remained not only among some of the most consistent supporters of the revolution, but among the most deeply engaged. They were also, at times, a bit less likely to idealize Cuba when thinking through their own struggles. In a prelude to the deeper turn to Cuba in the late 1960s, Stokely Carmichael, the famous Student Nonviolent Coordinating Committee (SNCC) organizer, spoke to a global crowd of over 1,000 in 1967 at the Organization of Latin American Solidarity in Havana, telling the audience that they shared the common enemy of "white Western imperialist society." For his troubles, the US government quickly promised to take away his passport for violating the travel ban; while others called for his citizenship to be revoked completely.[42] Carmichael, who would later break with, and subsequently reaffirm, ties with Cuba over disagreements about how to achieve racial equality, would remain an important supporter and sympathetic critic of Cuba throughout his life. Nor would Carmichael be alone in the turn to Cuba. The SNCC, the Black Panthers, SDS, the Young Lords Party, the Socialist Workers Party, and the CPUSA all sent contingents to the island during this period.[43]

Yet it was the Venceremos Brigades that not only sent the most delegations and activists to Cuba, and in effect became the largest and most prominent expression of Cuban solidarity during the period, but in doing established a model for Latin American solidarity going forward. The Brigades, which in various ways would incorporate most of the era's left expressions, including antiwar, feminism, the SNCC, Black Power, Puerto Rican, Chicano and Asian American activism, were involved in two main activities: hands-on support of the revolution by breaking the travel ban and participating in Cuban economic development, most famously assisting in the sugar harvest; and publicizing the concrete gains associated with the Cuban revolution in order to provide an anti-imperialist grassroots foreign policy that countered the propaganda coming out of Washington. Not surprisingly, given the political climate and the provocative image of hundreds of young people openly disobeying the travel ban to advance socialist revolution, the Brigades found themselves under immediate attack from the us government and mainstream media.[44]

Nevertheless, the very existence of the Venceremos Brigades in 1969 is a testament to how much the political landscape changed between the early and late 1960s. The Civil Rights movement did not simply expand the sphere of political debate and discourse. It cemented a whole range of tactics and strategies into the public imagination that had been barely visible even a decade earlier, including large protests and marches, sit-ins, boycotts, and civil disobedience. Black power and the student movement pushed the political boundaries even further. Above all, the debacle in Vietnam, and the ensuing antiwar movement, meant that us foreign policy came under increasing scrutiny, and that anti-communism could no longer justify any and all actions by the us government overseas (or at home).

The Venceremos Brigades began in much the same way that subsequent solidarity struggles would be forged, with Latin Americans either highlighting the consequences of imperialism (and asking for help) or responding to enquiries by people from the United States about how they could support certain efforts or causes. In this case, delegates from sds were in Havana on January 1, 1969 when Castro announced the goal of harvesting 10 million tons of sugar. Together, Cuban advisors and sds activists settled on a mode of international solidarity which brought groups from the United States to cut sugar cane and otherwise make concrete contributions to the revolution.[45] The notion of bringing a diverse group of Americans to volunteer on behalf of an existing socialist revolution was both novel and compelling.

Activists who went on the brigades tended to be young, and despite the fact that most of the initial organizers were white, the brigades themselves were exceptionally diverse along almost all lines.

Organizers pulled from prisons, gangs, and even the armed forces "to sign up alienated blacks, Chicanos, Puerto Ricans, and working-class whites. Students, Black Panthers, trade union activists, GI organizers, and military veterans swelled the ranks of the Brigades as well, as did many young people with no specific affiliation."[46] In this sense, as Teishan Latner notes, the brigade "is notable as one of the few organizations of the era that prioritized the bridging of the New Left and U.S. Third World Left, white activists with activists of color, as a precondition for a viable politics of North American solidarity with the Third World."[47] Speaking to the diversity, one participant noted that her brigade included "Quakers committed to total nonviolence as well as at least a dozen Weatherman, who viewed their sojourn in Cuba as part of an effort to recruit members for the coming struggle back home."[48]

The brigades occurred during a transitional moment for the New Left. SDS had effectively imploded by the end of 1969 when the first brigade arrived in Cuba. Young activists were flooding into the antiwar movement, and the Cuba trips were seen both in terms of a broader opposition to US foreign policy and as part of a growing solidarity with Third World revolutions. They also served, if temporarily, to semi-unify SDS around a common project, and channel youthful energy at a moment when activists were looking for not only alternatives to capitalism, but new modes of revolutionary praxis. The possibility of contributing "concrete work" in the form of physical labor proved particularly attractive to activists who grappled with the difficulty of "being in solidarity" with Third World peoples while living in an imperialist country. This project was not just about developing revolutionary ideas or political rhetoric, or even about witnessing or observing revolution. It was about productive "action" in support of socialist revolution. It was also appealing because activists hoped to import ideas and practices from revolutionary Cuba to enrich their own struggles in the United States.[49]

In this sense, not unlike Freedom Summer (1964), whereby white college students from the north went to Mississippi in order to register black voters, the Venceremos Brigades benefitted both visitor and visited. According to organizers Sandra Levinson and Carol Brightman, participants would not simply support the revolution by harvesting sugar, but would "gain direct experience with a Third World socialist revolution and a greater understanding of 'revolution' as something which entails much more than guns in the hills, something which means working every day."[50]

In this respect, the Venceremos Brigades offered up a fairly distinct, or at least innovative, model of solidarity.[51] Like solidarity efforts before and after, a central component of the brigades was "witnessing," which in Cuba meant observing both the consequences of US foreign policy and the positive impact of the revolution. An important component of this was political education in the United States, communicating to US audiences that the reality of US foreign policy and the Cuban revolution were far different from what they were hearing from the US government and mainstream media.[52]

The brigades also contributed two innovative twists to Latin American solidarity beyond witnessing and speaking truth to power. First, there was the emphasis on concrete action, in actively supporting Latin Americans not simply in the sense of telling their story to US audiences, or opposing US intervention through political means in the United States, but in working with Latin Americans to advance socialist revolution. This was made possible, of course, by the presence of an actual revolution in which socialists had taken power. Here, solidarity was conceptualized not in humanitarian terms, as privileged northerners helping marginalized allies in the global South, but as socialists working with fellow socialists to advance a shared struggle (in this sense, it was not "development" work as we now normally think of it).[53] We saw a bit of this with radical labor solidarity along the US–Mexican border during the Mexican revolution at the start of the twentieth century, but the brigades represented something fairly novel. Many subsequent efforts would embrace this idea of actively working with Latin Americans as a core feature of solidarity, even if "concrete action" during the 1980s and 1990s tended to take on more of a humanitarian quality—where solidarity is understood less in terms of a shared struggled than as aid.

Second, and related, for US activists the brigades were understood centrally, and perhaps even primarily, in terms of how they could help the US left and struggles in the United States. This may sound self-centered. But many Cubans understood the brigades in these terms as well—as places where Americans could come and learn about revolution in ways that radicalized participants and helped them in their own struggles back home. This is not unrelated to the understanding of a shared struggle in which political comrades advance a common cause and learn from each other. That this revolutionary praxis did not always work perfectly in practice does not lessen its importance. It was also not without considerable impact, as participants in the brigades would go on to play central roles in virtually every social movement in the second half of the twentieth century. However, as we will see, this ideal of engaging in a shared project in Latin America that strengthens struggles in the United States proved difficult to carry forward in subsequent solidarity, in part because the left in both the United States and Latin America found itself in retreat from the 1970s onward. In coming decades, it was often the case that there just was not much to return to in the United States regardless of what people learned in Latin America.

Conclusion

As we saw in Chapter 2, domestic opposition to US empire during the first decades of the twentieth century at times lacked continuity. But this anti-imperialism could nonetheless be counted on to emerge in response to the more overt and egregious expressions of American intervention, and contained within it anti-capitalist threads that understood international solidarity in terms of a collective struggle of laboring people against US empire and capitalism more broadly. This left internationalism was effectively silenced during the early Cold War between 1945 and the Cuban revolution. As an anti-communist wave spread across the Americas, and a Cold War consensus deemed any reformist politics as "communist" with the intention of containing or eliminating them, the left in both Latin America and the United States found itself under attack.

Cuba, in this sense, was something of a bright spot during this otherwise bleak period. In part because Castro occupied a liminal space, the Cuban revolution was initially received quite positively by sectors of American society, especially those who felt uneasy about the political rigidity imposed by the Cold War.

However, as the US government adopted an increasingly hostile position, and as Cuba pivoted towards the Soviet Union, Cuban solidarity struggled to survive at a time when open support for the revolution became difficult. Even these efforts had trouble developing and were eventually silenced.

Still, Cuban solidarity represented an early and important, if limited, challenge to a Cold War consensus which not only silenced radical opposition, but sought to eliminate the very notion that revolutionary-socialist projects should be part of the political imagination. Cuba kept this alive, not only for the American left, but for much of the Americas during this period—even as the anti-communist fear of "many Cubas" was used by the United States and its allies in Latin America to crush the left, including its internationalist expressions.

At the same time, the impact of Cuban solidarity was limited, not simply in the sense of being unable to shift the broader debate about Cuba, but in being unable to sustain or revive a more vigorous left internationalism during this period—a nearly impossible task. As we will see in the second part of the book, left internationalism would rebound for a variety of reasons, including the broader rise of radicalism and opposition to Vietnam during the late 1960s and early 1970s, but it would remain a minority current within a Latin American solidarity that ultimately became captured by human rights internationalism, a political project that presented an important, but limited, challenge to US Cold War policies and practices.

4

South American Dictatorships and the Rise of Human Rights

As late as 1970 there was little reason to think that either a Latin American solidarity movement or a human rights movement was about to emerge in the United States, or that the two would become deeply intertwined. Interest in Latin America, let alone solidarity, was limited. Although the Cuban revolution had garnered considerable attention in the United States, actual solidarity with Cuba remained on the political margins. Solidarity surrounding US interventions in Brazil and the Dominican Republic in the mid-1960s foreshadowed what was to come, but hardly signaled an impending solidarity boom. If anything, the limited nature of US-based opposition to imperialism, as well the general lack of concern for Latin Americans on the wrong end of intervention, confirmed the region's marginal place in US political life, the chilling effect of the Cold War, and the largely free rein that the US government continued to enjoy with respect to foreign policy in the Americas.

Likewise, although the language and practice of human rights was beginning to register on the public's radar, there was nothing resembling a movement, and what existed was not firmly connected to Latin America. Human rights were barely on the map and most commonly understood as a rough equivalent to civil rights, and thus associated with domestic issues. For the broader public, international human rights were largely connected with conservatives and the Cold War fight against Soviet-style communism. They were not something that liberals had yet captured in order to confront right-wing military dictatorships supported by the United States.[1]

And yet, within less than a decade, by the mid to late 1970s, not only were Latin American solidarity and international human rights recognizable as political projects, they were so deeply intertwined that it was hard to imagine one without the other. It was not simply that the two blossomed during the 1970s, but that these largely independent political currents became deeply connected and fueled each other's ascent. Just as it is hard to imagine that Latin American solidarity would have emerged with such force without human rights, it is also difficult to see how the human rights movement would have taken shape without Latin American solidarity. How do we understand this?[2]

Quite clearly, the intensity of repression in Latin America, and the fact that it was heavily supported by the United States, contributed to the emergence of international solidarity and human rights during the 1970s. The conspicuous, brutal, and widespread nature of repression served to capture global attention, and created an ideal situation for human rights intervention. With the example of Cuba looming over the hemisphere, and a broad swath of reformers and revolutionaries demanding social change, military regimes responded by falsely imprisoning, torturing, exiling, and murdering thousands of their own citizens. That they did so quite publicly, and under the guise of an anti-communism that could be traced to the doorstep of the US government, made the call for human rights action all the more compelling.

Yet repression alone does not create a human rights movement. That one would emerge only seems obvious in retrospect. Human rights violations had been, and would continue to be, routinely ignored across the globe. They did not automatically generate human rights movements or campaigns, especially because much of what came to be associated with human rights practice simply was not in place at the start of the decade. The sharp focus on torture and false imprisonment, for example, had not yet been become an effective part of the arsenal of human rights organizations for mobilizing public opinion. Even more basic, it was not yet widely accepted that foreign governments, let alone non-aligned international actors, had the right to interfere in another country's internal affairs to prevent human rights violations. At the same time, as we will see, the language, practice, and profile of human rights had developed just sufficiently by the early 1970s, through cases both outside and inside the Americas (in Greece, Vietnam, Brazil, the Dominican Republic, and elsewhere), that when military repression swept the region, and the Pinochet government offered up a particularly compelling case of human rights violations in Chile, the embryonic movement was poised to take action.[3]

The rise of human rights was, however, made possible not simply by the fact that the level of violence was so intense that it captured media/public attention, but because repression was relatively effective in extinguishing the left throughout much of South America. The importance of this for shaping the future of solidarity cannot be overestimated. The dismantling of the Latin American left did not automatically ensure that human rights would carry the solidarity banner, but it made it more difficult, and in most cases nearly impossible, for a robust left internationalism to emerge. It effectively eradicated the Latin American side of left internationalism—the more radical and vibrant end—while significantly limiting the avenues for subsequent political expression. The array of Latin American actors, organizations, and political currents that US progressives were able to connect with was severely circumscribed, in effect limiting the boundaries within which the future of international solidarity would flow.

The violent assault by the military, then, insured that Latin Americans would require and request solidarity, but it also meant that such solidarity could not follow traditional left channels and forms. This opened up space for alternative internationalisms to emerge which could operate in a context where political activity was severely circumscribed and the left in disarray. This does not, of course, explain how or why this space was eventually filled, and begs the question: Why did repression in Latin America during the 1970s capture the attention of so many people in the United States, and why did they channel solidarity through the language and practice of human rights? How do we understand the solidarity boom of the 1970s?

In answering this question, the next two chapters suggest that the dramatic ascent of human rights not only profoundly shaped Latin American solidarity during a formative period, but assumed and facilitated the marginalization of other forms of internationalism. Human rights became the dominant way to think about and practice internationalism, a process that drew unprecedented human and financial resources to international activism, while at the same time working to detach such solidarity from an identifiably left politics.[4] Nor was this uneven process without long-term consequences. Subsequent generations of international solidarity activists not only inherited a narrowed political vision from the human rights movement, but acquired an organizational infrastructure and analysis that has been ill equipped to deal with the central concern of solidarity since the 1990s: neoliberal capitalism.

An International Turn

To say that there was relatively little interest in Latin America (beyond Cuba) among progressives prior to the Chilean coup in 1973 is not to suggest that there was no interest at all, or that the 1960s was not a period of intense activity for the left as a whole. Global and domestic political currents blossomed during this period, energized one another, and opened up space in the United States for social movements and political-cultural radicalism. Of particular importance for our story was the growing interest in both the "Third World" and US foreign policy during the 1950s and 1960s. Although this attention was not heavily focused on Latin America, it nonetheless shaped the possible futures of internationalism, and amplified the political currents that progressives could draw upon once global interest returned to Latin America in the 1970s.

As we have seen, at the heart of this international turn was the explosion of anti-colonial movements throughout Asia and Africa during the two decades after the Second World War. The global force of these movements not only brought European colonialism to an end, but shifted the center of progressive internationalism to the Third World. More than 40 countries threw off colonial rule and became independent nation-states during this period,[5] reducing the number of people living under colonialism from some 750 million to less than 40 million.[6] In this global pursuit for self-determination and the nation-state, anti-colonialists drew from a range of leftish projects that were both nationalist and internationalist in scope, including most notably communism, but also pan-Arabism and black internationalism. This collective struggle against empire rarely drew on human rights for inspiration, and when it did so, it conceptualized them not in terms of individual protection against the state, but as part of a collective struggle for self-determination against imperial rule.[7]

In this sense, "Third World" movements, and the growing identification with them—a sense of solidarity with the likes of Che Guevara, Ho Chi Minh, and Kwame Nkrumah—would not only transform the globe, but shape how the us left thought about and engaged in both domestic and international struggles. As the us left blossomed in the 1960s, more and more African-Americans, Chicanos, Native Americans, and progressives in general came to see "domestic" struggles in global, anti-colonial, terms—loosely coalescing into the us Third World left. Likewise, Third World revolution ensured that us-based internationalism would be heavily informed by anti-colonialism, self-determination, and (at times) socialism. There were, as noted earlier, political limits to what us actors would or could draw from Third World "revolution," in part because many of these overseas movements were not as radical as they were understood in the United States, and in part because the anti-communism of the Cold War period constrained the ideological arena. But the influence of Third World rebellion on internationalism emanating from the United States was undeniable.

Vietnam was of course central to this process. The protracted failure of the United States in Southeast Asia and the emergence of the anti-war movement dealt a serious blow to the hegemony of Cold War foreign policy. This did not mean that us policymakers suddenly renounced anti-communism as a guiding principle. To the contrary, the zenith of us Cold War aggression in the Americas was still to come, and would define Latin America during the 1970s and 1980s. However, the imperial blunder in Vietnam meant that the us government could no longer assume free rein abroad. Broader cross-sections of the American public were both interested in and willing to question the motives and practices of us foreign policy.

The political energy surrounding Vietnam was also integral to the emergence of a broad array of social movements. Along with the anti-war movement, Black Power, student, women's, and farm worker movements not only contributed to the unraveling of the domestic political order, but helped create a climate that allowed for the broader questioning of US global hegemony. This happened in large part because Vietnam and Third World liberation movements led many within these domestic movements to see the connections between US imperialism abroad and systems of oppression at home.

The timing of all this was particularly important for Latin America and human rights in two senses. First, when US progressives turned their attention to Latin America in the mid-1970s after the Chilean coup, they would do so in a climate that looked quite different from even the late 1960s. The Latin American left, especially in South America, had been decimated or was being dismantled, the US left was imploding after a period of intense activity, and the allure of Third World revolution had faded. The conditions, then, were not particularly conducive for building left internationalism with Latin America. And yet, the level of repression and pleas for solidarity that came from Latin America with increasing force in the 1970s required an internationalist response, one that human rights would prove ideally suited to provide.

Second, although the debacle in Vietnam meant that was there not much appetite in the United States for an ambitious foreign agenda, the official end of the war in January 1973—just months before the Chilean coup—meant that Washington was ready to once again start lecturing the rest of the world. The only real question was when the sermon would resume and what form it would take. Once the United States stopped slaughtering people in Asia, it became plausible for US policymakers to adopt the language of human rights as a way of restoring the place of the United States on the global stage. Liberals in Washington soon realized that human rights was useful for challenging the moral bankruptcy of the Nixon administration, carving out a virtuous space for the United States on a global level, and confronting the horror of military dictatorships. It was ideal precisely because human rights was a limited, but important, project that allowed policymakers to capture the moral high ground without investing much at all.[8]

A Religious Turn

This international turn, however, and particularly the move to human rights, would not have been possible, nor particularly meaningful in

Latin America, were it not for the simultaneous rise of a progressive religiosity. A large part of why solidarity with Latin America was able to take off so quickly in the 1970s was not simply because US progressives were increasingly critical of US foreign policy, or vaguely attracted to Third World revolution, but because thousands of US-based religious actors established significant commitments to the region in the 1950s and 1960s. They had been laying the groundwork and were there. They traveled to Latin America in record numbers following the Second World War, where they not only came into contact with poverty and political repression, but developed deeper and more sustained relationships with a Latin American religious community which was undergoing a significant political transformation. This would ultimately provide the grounding for Latin American solidarity as that physical presence became increasingly politicized during the late 1960s and 1970s.

It started in the 1950s, however, as the Catholic church in Latin America not only began to encourage its followers to participate more actively in the here and now, but trained tens of thousands of lay people to engage in social action. This initial uptick in activity often took rather apolitical forms, but as the political winds moved leftward during the 1960s, and as Pope John XXIII (1958–63), the Vatican Council (1962–65), and the Latin American bishops (Medellin, 1968) promoted a "popular church" whose purpose was to "liberate" the poor, religious and lay activists in Latin America were politicized, becoming a dominant force in progressive activism in Latin America.[9] This Latin American embrace of liberation theology, in turn, fueled an ongoing and related process of politicization among US religious actors, a process which was stimulated by both anti-colonial movements and the broader questioning of US foreign policy surrounding Vietnam. It subsequently intensified as increased repression brought greater numbers of Latin American refugees to the United States (where they were often hosted by people of faith).

Indeed, the subsequent, forceful, emergence of Latin American solidarity during the 1970s and 1980s can be explained in large part by the thousands of US churchgoers who began traveling and working in the region in the 1950s and 1960s. Their first-hand experience with US-sponsored repression in Latin America—at a time when

Americans were starting to question foreign policy more broadly—coincided with a deeper and often politicizing engagement with Latin Americans.[10] Together with an increased emphasis on social commitment in religious communities, this lived experience of US foreign policy, and its often devastating impact on Latin American allies, provided the basis for a growing collective awareness in faith-based communities about the role of the United States and the presence of social movements in the region.

In this respect, President Johnson's 1965 invasion of the Dominican Republic was particularly important, and "had a profound impact on a cluster of radicalized missionaries and former volunteers who had served"[11] in the country and returned to the United States "committed to turning their own religious institutions away from complicity in dominating the hemisphere."[12] Methodist missionaries quickly questioned the wisdom of the intervention, along with a number of foreign governments, and eventually mainstream US politicians such as William Fulbright. The African American press was noticeably silent initially, in part because of the fear that the conflict would distract from civil rights at home. But more radical African Americans such as those in SNCC connected the intervention to US racism and imperialism more broadly, particularly in Vietnam. The opposition to intervention would never be particularly large, in part because armed resistance in the Dominican Republic was quickly squashed, and also because about three-quarters of Americans initially supported the US presence (even if those numbers would fade over time).[13] Nevertheless, certain aspects of solidarity, such as the phenomenon of religious actors returning from Latin America and energizing the movement, as well as the broader notion of a grassroots, citizen-driven diplomacy, can be seen in efforts around the Dominican Republic in the mid-1960s.[14] More than this, the 1965 invasion itself would become one of the foundational events that over time formed part of a shared knowledge and consciousness among growing numbers of progressives. Solidarity's most important research center, the North American Congress on Latin America (NACLA, 1966), and its oldest activist group, the Ecumenical Program for Inter-American Communication and Action (EPICA, 1968), were both byproducts of the Dominican experience.[15]

The occupation of the Dominican Republic, then, along with the unraveling of Vietnam, the emergence of anti-colonial movements, the civil rights movement, liberation theology, and the broader presence of the New Left, were all part of a leftward shift that led faith-based groups to view US foreign policy more critically at the exact moment when they were developing sustained connections with Latin Americans. To be sure, the long-term consequences of this process were far from clear in the mid to late 1960s. It would take years to attract significant numbers to the embryonic movement, build institutions, and develop visions and strategies. Yet it was this diverse religious community that would provide the human, financial, and organizational core of Latin American solidarity as it developed during the 1970s and 1980s.

This religious community would also spearhead the turn to human rights within Latin American solidarity. The two were in many ways a natural fit. Religious institutions, and particularly the Catholic Church, had formally committed to greater social engagement, and some in the church were clearly on the left. This left sector—as we will see in both Brazil and Chile—pushed for a relatively expansive understanding of human rights which included broader socio-economic issues such as land reform, poverty, and inequality. Although influential, neither they nor this expansive vision would carry the day, with both losing influence as the 1970s wore on (especially after Pope John Paul II was inaugurated in 1978). Yet even for more moderate sectors in the Church, including those who generally remained opposed to taking any sort of "political" stance, human rights was both compelling and a challenge. In the human rights movement's insistence on remaining bipartisan and above politics, human rights provided a platform for social engagement that was difficult for conservative sectors in the church to completely oppose without appearing to openly support atrocity. In this sense, it allowed for broad cross-sections in the church to support a limited type of political intervention. This space, in turn, allowed more progressive sectors in the church to go all in on human rights. It is important to note, however, that although religious actors have invoked human rights (in some sense) for centuries, the "full-throated theological and activist embrace" of human rights as an ideology and set of practices did not take place in religious circles until the early to mid-1970s.[16] In this sense, Brazil in the late 1960s and early 1970s was something of a testing ground.

Brazil

There is probably no clearer evidence of the limited nature of US-based internationalism during this period, as well as the energy, promise, and tensions embodied in early solidarity efforts, than in Brazil, starting in the mid-1960s. When the Brazilian military, with the blessing of the US government, staged a coup in 1964, with the goal of restoring the domestic political order by eliminating all forms of dissent, there was little in the way of opposition from groups in the United States. Vietnam had not sufficiently unraveled to allow for the broader questioning of US foreign policy, and few Americans were interested in, let alone challenged, US policies toward Latin America (outside of the left's ongoing interest in Cuba).

However, by 1968 when the Brazilian military regime renewed its commitment to violence, the political winds had shifted sufficiently to produce a small, but energetic, solidarity campaign between Brazilians, made up largely of exiles, and Americans, made up largely of academics, clergy, and other progressives with experience and expertise in Brazil.[17] They established the American Committee for Information on Brazil in February 1970, and published *Terror in Brazil* several months later, based on testimony from Brazilian exiles. As Patrick William Kelly notes, the report reflected how new and un-familiar human rights was during this period, in that it "was rather informal and amateurish ... when compared to the more robust human rights reports" that would come just a few years later. But the document was nonetheless "a harbinger of human rights inves-tigative reports to come" and paved the way for subsequent efforts.[18] More immediately, it led both the National Council of Churches and the World Council of Churches to call out the military government, demanding that it stop torturing Brazilian citizens. Prominent civil rights activists such as Ralph Abernathy and Andrew Young even-tually became involved, and in 1972 Amnesty International released its compelling *Report on Allegations in Brazil*, which signaled the

SOLIDARITY

organization's turn to torture as a major focus of its work. By the early 1970s, then, what started as a very small campaign had succeeded in shaming the Brazilian regime internationally.[19]

Its emergence was due in part to the fact that activists began to unevenly and tentatively frame the Brazilian cause in the language and practices of human rights. In what would become routine within a decade, Latin Americans asked international allies to publicize the crimes of the Brazilian military government. Human rights would prove to be a particularly effective way of doing this, in part by separating the violence itself from the messiness of political agendas, and doing so in a way that the "international community" could understand, connect with, and rally around. Although this shaming strategy would not prove particularly effective in lessening the repression or removing Brazil's military government, the campaign did succeed in turning the Brazilian government into an international pariah defined by human rights violations. This public relations success began to ensure that the tactic of shaming military governments by exposing human rights abuses would become a central part of the solidarity toolkit.

It is important to note, however, that the small numbers of activists who were most actively involved in the initial efforts, including both Brazilians and their US allies, articulated a fairly expansive version of human rights which made connections between repression and the broader political projects of both the military regime and its opposition. It was by no means common sense during this period to understand repression as "human rights violations," or to disconnect such violations from a larger politics aimed at limiting reforms and ensuring wealth remained concentrated in a few hands. As James Green notes, activists worked to help people make connections between, on the one hand, the horror of human rights abuses and, on the other, the military's war on the poor; on US backing for repressive regimes in Latin America, support for similar governments in other parts of the world, and regressive economic policies; on the relationship between repression and the Brazilian government's treatment of indigenous people in the Amazon basin.[20] Indeed, Brazilian religious figures in particular worked from an expansive understanding of human rights which moved well beyond political and civil rights to include issues of land reform and poverty.[21] This stance reflected the growing influence of liberation theology, whose broad social vision led towards a more expansive understanding of human rights than the more narrowed version around which liberal-religious sectors would eventually cohere as the decade wore on.

These efforts at education, at making connections, met with some success as the mainstream media in the United States caught on to some of these themes and issues, especially as they resonated with the war in Vietnam. Yet torture and brutal prison conditions, particularly when disconnected from politics, were always an easier sell than economic inequality, especially in a climate where such discussions could quickly be labeled communist. The broader effort to link the "human rights" cause to leftist programs for social change, to understand and support the political projects of those being targeted by state violence, did not find much traction in the United States. Not only was there not much to connect to in the United States, but what there was tended to focus narrowly on torture, leaving aside the question of broader collective political projects and solidarity. James Green captures the complexity of this early campaign, including not only its inability to produce a fundamental shift in the policies and practices of the Brazilian dictatorship, but also the ambiguous nature of "solidarity" itself.

> The campaigns against torture won international support, and linked the Brazilian government to repressive actions, but did not seem to have a palpable effect on the military's policies. The regime was not about to introduce political liberalization, and the opposition was still reeling from aftershocks of the previous four years. In the United States, torture in Brazil had been denounced, and then men and women of good will had moved on. Even the phrase "Brazilian solidarity group" has a clumsy, inauthentic ring to it, because many signatories of petitions against Brazilian torture and repression were reacting against an inhumane situation and not necessarily in favor of a program or political current in Brazil.[22]

Brazil provided a hint of solidarity's future, and many of the main players would become central to efforts in Chile just a few years later, but international solidarity movements around human rights in the

Americas were in their infancy in the late 1960s. Latin Americans were much more comfortable with other internationalisms, particularly socialism, and were often skeptical or simply unclear about human rights as a concept or tool. On the US side, both Cuba and Brazil demonstrated the political limits of US-based internationalism, and although activists found human rights to be useful in the case of Brazil, the campaign remained quite small and the concept itself had limited traction.

Even as late as the 1973 coup in Uruguay, where intense repression seemed ideally suited for a human rights framing, Uruguayan activists were slow and reluctant to adopt the language, instead understanding "torture and death as part of the risks of leading a proper revolutionary life. In the years immediately before the coup, denunciations of abuses by the police, the military, and paramilitary forces adopted a revolutionary language in which local ruling elites and u.s. imperialism were to blame." This was no doubt common sense to many Latin American leftists, who had long struggled with how to combat state violence while simultaneously fighting for socialism. Many activists assumed that occasional arrests, brief stays in prison, periodic exile, and certain levels of state violence were fundamental features of being active in the left. The primary question was how to "advance the popular cause" by overcoming repression and persecution.[23]

As Vania Markarian notes, even with respect to political prisoners—the very issue that would animate the human rights movement for the rest of the decade—Uruguayan leftists clearly situated repression within a broader context of class struggle. As the Committees for the Defense of Political Prisoners of Uruguay powerful noted in 1974:

> Neither humanitarian laments nor purely informative activity will advance our objectives .... The problem of the political prisoners should be confronted politically, positioned in terms of class struggle .... We ... believe that the prisoners will be freed the day that the revolutionary fight ... forces the bourgeoisie and its armed tool to do so, or when, sweeping them away together with their exploitative system, those who are exploited open the doors of the jails.[24]

Such a framing by no means precluded international solidarity, and

Uruguayans found some like-minded allies in Europe, but it was not intended to (nor could) attract an emerging human rights movement, much less appeal to us policymakers. The potential audience for a revolutionary framing of repression remained relatively small in the United States.[25]

Nevertheless, although Latin Americans were unclear and/or skeptical about human rights as a form of engagement, by the early to mid-1970s the emerging international movement was difficult to ignore. The level of repression in many countries had intensified so dramatically that it had become increasingly difficult even to be a leftist. The struggle for socialism, many reasoned, could not be advanced without first securing basic civil and political rights. More than this, initial indications suggested that human rights possessed the potential for attracting a wider range of allies both at home and abroad, in part because even people who agreed on little, who shared no political project, could agree that governments should not falsely imprison and torture their citizens. Human rights was also difficult for Latin Americans to ignore because other internationalisms were bringing relatively few allies (especially from the United States) to the table at a time when they were so desperately needed. And, as the growing presence of organizations like Amnesty suggested, the international human rights movement seemed poised to provide support from around the world at a time when allies were scarce. It was a potentially useful tool.

Amnesty International and the Mainstreaming of Human Rights

The rise of Amnesty International captures most clearly the sudden and powerful emergence of human rights during the 1960s and early 1970s, as well as the long-term impact of its brand of solidarity. Founded in 1961, Amnesty barely survived the 1960s. It almost collapsed in 1967 because of internal disputes, and the us section, which emerged in 1965, nearly folded under financial pressure in 1970. The organization's fortunes changed dramatically in the 1970s. The number of dues-paying members skyrocketed during the first half of the decade, allowing it to hire staff and establish offices through the United States. By 1977, it had won the Nobel peace prize.[26] Within a decade, then, Amnesty went from near collapse to become the world's foremost human rights organization.

Timing was clearly part of its success. Human rights activism exploded during the 1970s. Organizations formed, governments took note, and the term itself became part of mainstream public discourse. By the end the decade there were more than 200 groups working on human rights in the United States. The Ford Foundation and other funding agencies made human rights a focus, channeling millions of dollars toward the cause. The US Congress held hearings, eventually tying foreign aid to a country's human rights record. President Carter made it a cornerstone of US foreign policy. Human rights had arrived. It had become respectable.[27]

Amnesty's success was due to more than good timing, however. It did not simply benefit from the human rights boom. It propelled it, an achievement that was due in part to strategic decisions by the organization's staff. In 1970, AIUSA committed resources to organizing local branches around the country, a tactic that worked remarkably well in expanding its base, and helped bring human rights out of the hallways and offices of the United Nations and into the public arena. This emphasis on building at the grassroots, especially on college campuses, was common sense among many who came to Amnesty; "nearly all of the 1970s AIUSA staff had done antiwar and civil rights work," and assumed mass mobilization was a fundamental feature of progressive politics and social change.[28]

With Amnesty, however, the tactic was not about mass mobilization in the sense of taking to the streets, but mass membership to support well-orchestrated letter-writing campaigns. This was Amnesty's central tactic during the early years. Each affiliate, or adoption group, was assigned a political prisoner. Members then wrote letters to offending governments, journalists, politicians, and international organizations. Done with increasing sophistication, and in large enough numbers, this tactic proved relatively effective in securing the release of prisoners.[29] What this also meant, however, was that Amnesty had to devote more and more resources to identifying worthy prisoners in order to satisfy the demand of growing numbers of local affiliates.

As a result, Amnesty leaders discovered fairly quickly that not only did the organization not need the masses for street mobilizations, but they did not need a membership to adopt prisoners and write letters. Professional human rights organizations could do the work themselves, saving prisoners in Latin America by lobbying politicians in Washintgon DC. Gathering information ceased to be a means to an end, a way of building a mass base. It became the end in itself. Amnesty became a professional organization that gathered facts and then directly lobbied journalists and politicians in an effort to put pressure on human rights violators.[30] In short, it became a modern human rights organization. Whatever its virtues, this was a different type of politics, one that relied on insider access to political elites and a mass membership whose central purpose was not taking to the streets or writing letters, but writing a check to support Amnesty's efforts.

As Kenneth Cmiel outlines, the question of what path of political engagement to pursue, whether to be a grassroots type organization or a professional lobby (or a bit of both), was one that Amnesty leadership debated quite intensely during the 1970s.[31] The leaders had, after all, come from a tradition of grassroots organizing. However, for other human rights organizations, which were emerging almost on a daily basis during the 1970s, and in many ways became the path within US-Latin American solidarity, the question was increasingly off the radar. A new political formula, supported in part by the innovation of direct-mail fundraising and the largesse of philanthropic foundations, had emerged. If a network of professional activists, lawyers, and academics could influence elites, get results, and be financially sustainable through grant writing and fundraising, why bother building a mass base? And Amnesty was hardly alone. Its rival, Human Rights Watch, was a product of Ford Foundation funding, and created as an "independent" human rights monitor focusing on abuses in the Soviet Union.[32]

This was a professional form of politics that increasingly required being divorced from a politics rooted in mass mobilization. As the central task of human rights organizations became the professional gathering and public dissemination of accurate information about human rights violations, the legitimacy of human rights organizations in the eyes of governments, the United Nations, and the broader public became crucial. Human rights organizations came to deal in information, and that information had to be reliable. This legitimacy rested, at least partly, on insuring that human rights organizations were themselves not only professionally run, but neutral and nonpartisan, and that their activities were independent of politics, particularly the (transformative) political projects of human rights victims, violators, and their supporters.

Like most human rights organizations of the period, then, Amnesty not only "traded on its claim to be above and beyond politics," but "defined itself against the left," even when it targeted the victims of right-wing dictatorships.[33] As it developed, the heart of human rights activism did not simply forget or postpone a larger political vision. It actively separated itself from broader political agendas.[34] As Patrick William Kelly notes, "human rights organizations such as Amnesty … shunned any overt mention of politics. They donned a depoliticized cape as if it immediately bestowed upon them an invincibility of objectivity. By self-consciously trumpeting a depoliticized message, Amnesty saw itself as trading in a moral message that transcended the political quagmires of the past."[35]

In this sense, the meteoric rise of this brand of human rights did not simply serve to further marginalize a range of left internationalisms, to replace one internationalism with another. Its rise altered the very nature of internationalism itself, of solidarity, by displacing a range of internationalisms that assumed a collective politics of liberation with a form of internationalism that was openly antithetical to political projects or visions rooted in notions of collective emancipation. This was solidarity without politics as the left had traditionally understood—whereby politics assumes collectively struggling for an alternative way of ordering the world. It treats "political problems as moral ones, thereby eliding the deeper political changes that social justice often required."[36] For many activists, human rights became a "new foundational creed" and "ideology that rose above politics."[37]

Many activists recognized this tension, with some reasoning that in order for the human rights movement to be effective its organizations had to be seen as legitimate, and this required a strict separation from partisan politics. This was a strategic decision. The torture had to be stopped, and that required a pragmatic, whatever works, act-now-think-later, approach. Some adopted the non-partisan practice and language of human rights quite consciously as a way to attract larger numbers of people into political activism, and as a tool for gaining access to policymakers and the mainstream media (even as they tried to tie human rights work to a larger politics by maintaining relationships with movements in Latin America). For many, then, human rights remained contested terrain, particularly with respect to whether it should or should not be openly connected to a larger politics. Regardless, however, when the left in both Latin America and the United States began to resist and frame their opposition to repression through human rights, they not only helped elevate human rights—a remarkably vague and elastic concept—to new heights. They also embraced a concept and set of practices whose broad contours and uses the left would ultimately not control—a "decision" that generated a range of short and long-term consequences that were not immediately transparent at the time.

To get ahead of our story a bit, what is perhaps even more important than the open tensions within solidarity circles is the fact that this distinction itself, between human rights and various forms of left internationalism, became increasingly invisible to a generation that came of age after the 1980s—especially in the United States, where the left was disappearing from public life.[38] For many activists, who had limited connection with left internationalism, took it for granted that socialism was dead, or "became political" when human rights out-shadowed other forms of solidarity, human rights was simply a "progressive" way of engaging the world in a meaningful way. Human rights became the beginning and end of political work. The goal was to end human rights abuses, a supremely worthy cause, and other projects were deemed too complicated, impractical, or (more often) simply not part of a narrowed political imagination.

To be sure, there was always a portion of activists for whom human rights served as a gateway towards a more radical politics. As we will see in the next chapter, this was especially true with Central American solidarity, which by reinvigorating a left internationalism inspired by Third World revolutionary politics, provided viable avenues for those looking to advance a transformational politics. Currents of left internationalism certainly persisted, pushing the human rights movement and attracting activists who were inspired by the urgency of human rights, but ultimately frustrated by its limited political project.

Yet over time, and especially after the Central American revolutions had been defeated, the political avenues for left internationalism faded from public view and became increasingly hard to find for new generations of US progressives. Equally important, this broader shift towards a solidarity divorced from politics was stimulated by, and brought with it, a very different method of political engagement, one that relied much more heavily on professional staff, lobbying, insider access to political and media elites, and so on. This professionalization of solidarity work, which emerged very unevenly during the coming decades, and would never become completely hegemonic, nevertheless became a defining form for much of international solidarity in the coming decades.

Chile

Chile made human rights, and human rights made Chile. Chile, including the 1973 overthrow of Allende, the intense repression that followed, and the global debate that emerged, was central to the development of the broader human rights movement. Human rights came of age in part through Chile, a process that not only encompassed the left, liberals, religious communities, the media, policymakers, and broad swaths of the US population, but also ensured that human rights would be a dominant political current within US solidarity from the 1970s onward. The growing presence of human rights during this period also made "Chile" a subject of global interest and a site for political engagement through the 1970s. Chile would not have garnered so much sustained interest, especially in the United States, had it not emerged through a blossoming human rights movement.[39]

At the time of the coup, however, it was far from clear that human rights would become a vehicle through which the coup was understood and political activity channeled. Chile itself was home to a powerful left which, although caught off-guard by the level of repression following the coup, understood Pinochet's assault as part of a broader class war. Intense debates and divisions emerged within the Chilean left over how and when to respond to the coup, but the broader goal was to forge a political opposition that could regain political power and build a better future.

On a global level, there was very little assurance that human rights would become the primary way through which international actors would understand Chile. The million-plus people throughout Latin America, Europe, and to a lesser extent the United States who took to the streets after the coup did so not because Chile was understood as a human rights cause, but because it had inspired as a socialist democracy.[40] In the United States, despite some inroads by Amnesty, human rights was a largely unfamiliar term that was most commonly associated with (domestic) civil rights. International human rights were still part of the conservative-led fight against Soviet-style communism, and not yet an established component of the liberal battle against right-wing military dictatorships.[41] More than this, Chile itself was not of great interest to the US mainstream. On the eve of the coup, Chile was the domain of a left that opposed US intervention in order to advance a democratic socialist revolution.

In this sense, given that the left had such a head start and there was little or no human rights movement at the time of the coup, how and why did human rights become so central, so quickly, to understanding and engaging with Chile? And how did the rise of human rights shape the potential of other internationalisms to frame Chile and solidarity efforts in general?

Events in Chile played a decisive role in elevating human rights. The repression on and after September 11 was so intense that it essentially wiped out pre-existing political actors on the left. Virtually all forms of political activity were curtailed, and churches quickly emerged as almost the only actors that still possessed a relatively intact organizational infrastructure.[42] Chileans who wanted to remain politically active flocked to the relative protection of church-led organizations. The turn to human rights also happened very quickly because other political avenues were cut off. The international spotlight gave churches limited room to maneuver, but they could not criticize the regime on most matters or be seen as taking a "political" stance.[43] Yet, as a moral authority, religious institutions could cautiously criticize the regime for actions that were simply "beyond the pale." Human rights provided both the language and practice for such an intervention. It became the preferred path for political activity in part because it was one of the only ones that remained.

Within three weeks of the takeover, Chilean religious leaders founded the Comité de Cooperación para la Paz en Chile. COPACHI, or the Comité Pro Paz, was not actively or formally opposed to the military regime, and initially saw itself as an apolitical human rights office, but it quickly developed an expansive social agenda.[44] COPACHI's human rights reports, documenting hundreds of cases, became the raw material for groups like Amnesty, the Red Cross, Americas Watch, and the United Nations.[45] COPACHI's successor, Vicaría de la Solidaridad, would also stress that it was a humanitarian (and not political) organization, both for safety reasons and to win more conservative supporters in and outside the church.[46] At the same time, the lines between economic aid, charity, and more political work were inevitably blurred, and sectors in the Chilean religious-based human rights community urged international actors to expose the regime's regressive economic policies.[47]

Even so, in the United States it was far from clear that Chile would be framed through human rights. What interest and solidarity there was prior to the coup came from small groups of academics, independent journalists, religious actors, radicals, and others who were broadly influenced by or actively part of the New Left, and in some cases had lived in Chile. They understood Chile primarily in the anti-imperialist terms of a promising socialist revolution that was under attack by the US government and American business. They sought to support the Allende government and (subsequently) Chilean opposition to the coup. Consequently, much of the work focused on educating Americans about the truth regarding Allende, the military regime, and US government/corporate intervention. Most of the pre-coup efforts did not reach mainstream audiences, but journalist Jack Anderson's 1972 report, followed by Senator Frank Church's (March 1973) investigation into ITT,[48] represented high water marks that both energized solidarity and led sectors of the media and political establishment to view events in Chile more critically.[49]

Anti-interventionist solidarity expanded dramatically following Allende's overthrow. Significant numbers of prominent academics and other professionals quickly "labeled the coup as beyond the pale." Such a consistent and immediate reaction from members of the intelligentsia proved decisive in forcing media outlets to provide more critical coverage of the coup and US involvement. Academics also led the first national protests after the coup.[50] Denunciations came from broad cross-sections of the liberal-left, including labor unions such as the United Auto Workers, fairly militant groups like the Black Panther Party, and religious organizations such as the Quakers.[51]

Sustained solidarity subsequently went in a variety of directions, reflecting the diversity of the left. US communists established local solidarity organizations throughout the country while establishing the National Coordinating Center in Solidarity with Chile. Anti-imperialists cohered in the form of Non-Intervention in Chile, were committed to a fairly militant style of protest, and stressed connections between US corporate capitalism at home and abroad. They would eventually have chapters throughout the country. The National Chile Center took a more moderate stance, and stressed a pragmatic emphasis on legislation and working with liberals.[52] The broader solidarity movement was remarkably diverse, including feminist organizations, "countless unions, academic associations, churches, synagogues, and city councils that formally endorsed solidarity actions, wrote letters, and showed up at rallies."[53] There were eventually somewhere between 50 and 100 solidarity groups working throughout the country in large cities and college towns, holding events, distributing newsletters, and otherwise trying to get the message out. Cultural icons of the liberal left, such as Joan Baez and Pete Seeger, also lent support.[54]

Numerous unions, such as the UFW and UAW, also quickly passed resolutions against the coup, and joined the growing call for a consumer and trade boycott designed to halt US trade with Chile and encourage consumers to stop purchasing Chilean grapes, wine, and vegetables. The International Longshore and Warehouse Union even refused to load or unload Chilean goods until the military government restored basic rights to labor unions. Major international union federations also condemned the regime and called for sanctions. Even the AFL-CIO tentatively joined the cause, calling out the regime for imprisoning and executing labor leaders. Although the AFL-CIO would ultimately fail to endorse the boycott after Pinochet committed to improving labor rights, the broader push in the labor movement signaled a willingness of sectors in organized labor to break from the federation's Cold War stance.[55]

It was around the boycott that left internationalism would come closest to cohering. Consumer and trade boycotts would never have an economic impact on the Chilean economy, but the tactic was primarily designed to mobilize and bring attention to the broader cause. In that respect, it experienced some success, though it was deeply tied to and shaped by the emerging human rights movement. For many on the left, the point of the boycott was to isolate the Pinochet regime by connecting human rights abuses to its regressive economic policies, or to what would become known as neoliberalism.[56] However, for the most part this was not how the boycott would (or could) be understood, or catch on, outside the left. That is, despite efforts by solidarity activists to connect the regime's violence to its commitment to neoliberalism, the call for boycotts was most easily interpreted and adopted as: the United States should not do business with a regime that commits human rights atrocities.

This may seem like a subtle difference. But seeing the boycott through a human rights lens effectively diminished the left's attempt to insert a deeper discussion and analysis of economics into the solidarity equation. The human rights-infused understanding of the boycott implied that all the Pinochet regime had to do was stop committing gross human rights abuses in order for business to return to normal. Put another way, as long as the military government stopped torturing and imprisoning its opponents it could continue with a set of economic policies that were exacerbating inequality and devastating the working class. Some solidarity activists pushed a more radical line, but the space for this was relatively limited. as human rights had taken off and critiques of neoliberalism were just gaining traction.[57]

Nevertheless, the left's (albeit limited) success in promoting and framing Chile was made possible by the strong anti-interventionist current running through American society following Vietnam. Opposition to US foreign policy was now mainstream, producing a liberal-left bloc that rejected the basic premises of the Cold War and was willing to contest US efforts to contain popular movements overseas.[58] As a minority partner, the left's challenge was to push anti-interventionism towards a deeper left internationalism, in effect making the case that US intervention was not apolitical or well-intentioned, but supported repressive regimes that undermined democratic movements and sustained wealthy interests at home and abroad.

This would have been an uphill battle under any circumstances, but human rights certainly complicated the terrain. Liberal versions of human rights offered an anti-interventionism that was politically soft, one whose central requirement was that the US government not support military regimes that committed the grossest of human rights violations (in itself a worthy goal). The politics and policies of these regimes, as well as the politics of their opponents, were essentially irrelevant, as were the deeper motivations and practices of the US government and corporations in other parts of the world. This is an anti-interventionism that moves beyond the politics of the Cold War by ignoring it, in effect declaring traditional politics irrelevant and left solidarity obsolete, undesirable, or anachronistic.

This soft anti-interventionism was also central to the success of human rights as a movement. The human rights movement allowed for a diverse range of anti-interventionists to work under its broad umbrella, to oppose US policy, in part because the vagueness of the human rights concept allowed people who had quite different under-standings of what "it" meant to work together. The net result was that the rise of human rights during the second half of the 1970s made it easier to disconnect anti-interventionism from a left politics. Human rights did not simply marginalize other internationalisms, it also defined the outer limits of opposition to US foreign policy in politically neutral terms.

Nevertheless, it was by no means given that human rights would capture and energize Chilean solidarity at the time of the coup. As noted, it had been effectively captured by conservatives in order to reinvigorate anti-communism through a focus on Soviet repression. Most of what Americans would come to associate with international human rights, including its affiliation with liberals, its principal institutions, and its tight focus on torture and political prisoners, either did not exist or was barely off the ground in 1973. The US section of Amnesty International had a total of 3,000 members in 1974, and struggled to find meeting space in Washington D.C. Human Rights

Watch did not exist, nor did the Lawyers Committee for Human Rights, the Human Rights Law Group, or the hundreds of other rights groups that would emerge in the second half of the 1970s. There was one international human rights organization headquartered in the United States at the time.[59]

And yet, between religious groups, secular non-governmental organizations, and sympathetic policymakers—the three core constituencies of what would eventually become the human rights movement—there was a sufficient presence to respond to calls for solidarity from Chile. Of the three groups, religious actors were in the best position to respond at the time of the coup. From the end of the Second World War until the late 1960s, the most consistent source of human rights discourse emanated from small groups of religious actors and international lawyers. They toiled away in relative obscurity, often working with largely unknown and impotent sections of the United Nations.[60] The relative readiness of church groups was heightened by the growing emphasis on social commitment within religious circles, along with increasing distrust of US foreign policy, two trends brought about by a decade of civil rights organizing, the rise of liberation theology, and the broader disenchantment surrounding Vietnam. A growing sector of the religious community was, in a sense, ready for Chile.

The religious response to Chile was immediate, global, included a wide range of denominations, and had support from the highest levels of church hierarchy. Pope Paul IV immediately expressed concern, as did church leaders from around the world. Calls for restraint quickly turned to concrete action, including direct support for Chilean human rights organizations, the development of a sophisticated lobbying campaign in the United States, and active aid to refugees/exiles. The World Council of Churches (WCC) immediately established the Emergency Task Force on the Chilean Situation, promising to commit over $500,000 to the cause, a fundraising goal that was immediately surpassed. The WCC, along with Catholic, Presbyterian, and Lutheran churches, helped COPACHI get off the ground, and foreign sources would provide the organization with almost all its budget. Between 1974 and 1979, international actors, with churches taking the lead, would funnel more than $100 million to Chilean churches and their human rights organizations.[61]

The Latin American Strategy Committee, an ecumenical collection of North American church groups that had coalesced in connection to Brazil in 1968, quickly formed the Washington Office on Latin America.[62] The Washington Office on Latin America (WOLA) would become a significant force on Capitol Hill with respect to Latin American policy. Efforts steamrolled, and by the mid-1970s, groups like WOLA, the US Catholic Conference, and the (Quaker) American Friends Service Committee had established what came to be known as "the religious lobby," a relatively small number of faith-based activists, numbering probably less than 150 people at the end of the decade, who were well resourced, well informed, and had strong connections with sympathetic policymakers. With close ties to human right organizations in Chile, they became an important information source for the media, decision makers, and the broader public.[63] They were also, by and large, quite sophisticated in their analysis of repression in Latin America, including the role of the United States,[64] and very committed to the region in a way that emphasized building pragmatic, strategic, non-sectarian alliances aimed at addressing an urgent situation.

The collective efforts of this very diverse religious community were predicated on and stimulated by the broader rise of secular-liberal human rights in the United States. Within a very short period of time, it was liberals, both in the US government and outside in organizations like Amnesty, who would take the lead, defining the broad contours and orientation of the movement. The liberal turn to human rights happened slowly and unevenly during the late 1960s and early 1970s, shaped by events in Greece and Brazil, as well as growing awareness about the Holocaust and political prisoners in South Vietnam. International human rights attracted liberals in part because its limited aspirations fit so well into a moment when there was little appetite for a more ambitious US foreign policy; in part because dictatorships were a very real problem; in part because human rights allowed the US government to reclaim the moral upper hand on the global stage without investing much at all; and in part because human rights was proving effective at garnering public attention.[65] The increasingly sharp focus on torture and prisoners propelled this process by defining human rights and foreign policy aspirations in narrow terms while framing the issue in a way that captured the public's attention and confirmed America's moral superiority.

The liberal embrace of human rights could not gain full momentum until after the Vietnam War finally ended in January 1973, in part because it was difficult to lecture the rest of the world about human rights abuses when the US government was committing massive atrocities in Asia. In this respect, the September coup in Chile was timely, and was "the watershed event that would grab headlines and bring liberal human rights concerns—political imprisonment and torture above all—into mainstream public consciousness."[66] Amnesty International and the International Commission of Jurists responded immediately after the coup, cabling the Inter-American Commission on Human Rights to insist that refugees be allowed to leave the country and that the new government respect human rights.[67] In the next two years, virtually every major human rights organization would send delegations to Chile and/or issue reports. Sectors in the United Nations did all they could to keep up.

Indeed, Amnesty's investigation and subsequent report, coming just two months after the coup, was a watershed not only because it was the first in-depth account of human rights abuses in Chile, but because of "its credibility, objectivity, and breadth of its sweeping conclusions."[68] It helped shaped the broad contours for human rights work going forward, in part by stimulating the process through which human rights organizations became the places to which governments, the news media, and intergovernmental organizations went for information about human rights abuses. This happened remarkably quickly, and rested on an objectivity rooted in the active separation of human rights from politics. As one of the report's authors noted, "the revolutionary cause, either before or after the revolution, was none of our business."[69] This objectivity, and depoliticized discourse, would become a defining feature of mainstream human rights activism.

So too would the emphasis on torture, which defined the report and shaped its reception. By helping the report capture public attention, the focus ensured that torture would remain a central concern of human rights investigations. And by elevating human rights in general, the spotlight on torture in turn helped to undermine the doctrine of state sovereignty, which prior to the 1970s allowed governments to claim that violations fell exclusively under domestic jurisdiction—that foreign governments and organizations had little or no jurisdiction over human rights abuses. This was no doubt a positive development, but the relatively narrow focus on torture and false imprisonment also set a fairly high bar for political intervention, and contributed to a growing fixation in solidarity circles on cases of extreme abuse.[70]

Nevertheless, it was the efforts of both religious actors and secular-liberal human rights organizations such as Amnesty that eventually put the issue firmly on the radar of members of the US Congress. The elevation of human rights in Congress was also the product of political sparring in the United States as well as genuine concern about human rights abuses in Chile. Human rights activists pushed policymakers with increasing intensity and sophistication, providing information, talking points, and even wholesale legislation. More than this, human rights and Chile—followed by Argentina in the latter half of the 1970s[71]—provided liberal congresspersons with a compelling avenue for challenging the Nixon administration. Kissinger's intransigence and hostility, his initial unwillingness to give an inch on congressional human rights proposals, created an energetic backlash at a time when the Nixon administration was vulnerable and increasingly seen as morally bankrupt. Subsequent revelations that the United States, under Kissinger's direction, had actively undermined the democratically elected government of Allende provided congressional opposition with powerful ammunition and elevated Chile to *cause célèbre*.

Supported by human rights organizations, leading liberal congressional democrats such as Donald Fraser, Edward Kennedy, and Tom Harkin adopted human rights as a liberal tool for pursuing a foreign policy project that was at once remarkably limited and profoundly important: to make sure the US government did not aid dictators who torture and imprison their own people. On the one hand, ceasing to pay for dictatorship did not require even modest change to a country's political or economic system, or necessarily imply a more democratic vision for the future. It could simply be "an outlet for moral indignation and a program for virtue without cost."[72] On the other hand, the withdrawal of military aid could—in certain countries at particular moments—have profound consequences for Third World social movements. This possibility would be a central concern as solidarity activists turned their attention to Central America beginning in the late 1970s, a region that contained not only repressive military dictatorships backed by the United States, but armed revolutionary movements pursuing radical political agendas.

Conclusion

By the late 1970s, the broad contours of US–Latin American solidarity were set on a shifting ground defined by two differentiated and intertwined currents, left internationalism and liberal human rights, with the latter coming to occupy a dominant place in the movement as a whole. The rapid rise of human rights was attributable to a number of factors, but Chile was quite clearly at the heart of the process. As Patrick William Kelly puts it, "Chile, more so than any other country, remapped the terrain of human rights activism, especially on the transnational plane." Hundreds of human rights organizations formed after the coup, and intergovernmental bodies such as United Nations began to devote considerably more resources to the issue. "The very cause of human rights became a raison d'être for many social activists. To Tom Quigley of the US Catholic Conference, human rights were 'the air we breathed'; and the Chilean coup was 'the event that catalyzed everything else'."[73]

Indeed, when President Carter embraced human rights in the late 1970s, it seemed quite plausible that it would thoroughly capture, and in effect become, progressive internationalism in the United States. Then came Reagan. He reinvigorated US foreign policy with an anti-communism that had horrific consequences in Central America and was never particularly popular at home. This not only ensured that human rights would remain relevant as a tool for disrupting US support for military dictatorships, but served to breathe new life into left internationalism. As the remnants of a broader US left based in the civil rights, labor, and antiwar movements evaporated in the late 1970s and 1980s, activists turned their attention to Reagan's foreign policy with such energy that it is only a slight exaggeration to suggest that the progressive wing of the peace movement became the left in the United States. As we will see, however, they were increasingly isolated, and the resurgence itself was tied to the broader rise of the right and decline of the left.

Moreover, the broad parameters of US–Latin American solidarity that had been established around South America in the 1970s would largely hold through the 1980s in relation to Central America. That is, as dynamic as left internationalism would be during the 1980s, the dominant current of international solidarity was a human rights/ peace movement based in church groups, liberal human rights organizations, and Washington D.C.-based policymakers.[74] As Latin American solidarity developed in the 1980s, then, it cohered around a fairly narrow, but important, political project that was in large part a legacy of 1970s solidarity work—namely opposition to human rights abuses and US support for military regimes. To be sure, a significant and important minority saw solidarity in terms of more radical transformation, and worked directly with revolutionary movements to advance socialism in Central America. This was possible in large part because, in contrast to South America, Central America possessed viable revolutionary movements that actively sought international solidarity.

Yet, as we will see, the core of a heavily faith-based movement, supported by liberal human rights organizations and sympathetic policymakers, saw solidarity not in terms of a long-term struggle to build a new world, but as an urgent call for help to end human rights atrocities and military repression (or protect its victims). The uneven gravitation towards this limited political project came from a now familiar set of sources. Many people shied away from taking sides, either because they did not support the revolutionary movements themselves, did not see it as their place to intervene, or simply felt that being "political" would empower anti-communist rhetoric and otherwise undermine a fragile movement that was struggling against a popular President in an increasingly conservative climate. The tendency to cohere around a soft anti-interventionism that avoided connections with broader political projects was also embraced because it was a useful way for communicating with political-media elites and attracting larger numbers to the movement. Human rights was particularly effective at bringing relatively large numbers of people into a progressive movement at a time when the left was slowly disappearing from public life.

The movement's limited political project attracted human resources, financial support, and media attention, but also represented a form of internationalism that was never designed to outlive its short-term goal of stopping human rights atrocities and the US policies that supported them. It was not simply that a portion of the movement lacked a larger political vision, that activists failed to make connections between human rights abuses and the regressive economic policies being implemented by military regimes; or between repression and the political projects being pursued by "human rights victims." It is that much of the movement pursued a form of internationalism that actively dissociated itself from politics, offering up instead a form of solidarity whose noble aspiration worked to obscure a limited goal that was to be pursued through an organizational infrastructure that was not built for sustained international solidarity. This tendency, emergent in human rights solidarity around South America during the 1970s, would continue to develop, and be challenged, through the Central American peace movement of the 1980s.

5

Central American Solidarity
in Reagan's America

The Central American peace movement of the 1980s represents a watershed moment in the history of Latin American solidarity. Although it shared much with earlier solidarity efforts around Chile and Argentina, including many of the same actors, organizations, strategies, and issues, the movement was exponentially larger in terms of the human, financial, and organizational resources involved. It was also rooted in much broader and more sustained connections between people in the United States and Latin America. Within a relatively short period of time, tens of thousands of people were participating in a range of solidarity campaigns and organizations. At its peak, more than 100,000 US citizens mobilized against US intervention in Central America.[1] Some 80,000 signed the Pledge of Resistance, committing to civil disobedience in the event of a US invasion of Nicaragua, and thousands more supported the Nicaraguan revolution in one way or another and/or mobilized against US aid to El Salvador.[2]

In this respect, it is worth remembering how much the political landscape had changed during the course of the Cold War. Few in the United States had paid much attention to the planning, implementation, and subsequent repression associated with the US-sponsored coup in Guatemala in 1954. Even a decade later, in 1964, the military takeover in Brazil garnered little interest despite US involvement. It took several years of repression, and appeals from Brazilian exiles, to generate even a modest campaign from progressives in the United States. Chile represented something of a break, but the extent of this shift can be easily overstated. In the lead-up to the coup, the Nixon administration was relatively free to demonize and sabotage the Allende government. It was only after the intense repression following the 1973 coup, and desperate pleas from Chileans, that Chile inspired a significant progressive response in the United States. This solidarity was vitally important, but in many ways came too late for democracy or the left in Chile.

Central America, however, was something of a different beast. Solidarity emerged quickly on a much larger scale, and would be sustained over a decade-long period. Reagan's ongoing obsession with stopping communism in Central America, combined with the horrific consequences of US policies, ensured that the region would remain a highly visible source of political conflict throughout the 1980s. In a very real sense, Reagan created the peace movement, or at least ensured that some sort of significant opposition would emerge and endure.

More than this, Central America in the 1980s was not South America of the 1970s. In South America the armed forces seized power, eliminated democratic governments, and largely destroyed the left. US-based campaigns then emerged in solidarity with the victims of repression. In Central America, there were armed revolutionary movements throughout the decade which not only challenged for state power, but had a fairly significant and sustained presence in the United States. In Nicaragua, the Sandinistas (Frente Sandinista de Liberación Nacional, FSLN) successfully carried out an armed insurrection, overthrew a US-backed dictator, and were implementing a socialist revolution while battling the Contras. For many US progressives, the revolution had to be defended, or at least allowed to develop on its own. In El Salvador, the Farabundo Martí National Liberation Front (FMLN) had a legitimate shot at overthrowing a repressive dictatorship which was financially dependent on the United States. Guatemala was similar, though after President Carter cut off military aid the US connection was less explicit (even as the Reagan administration found ways to funnel aid). More than this, refugees, exiles, and representatives from various groups in Nicaragua, Guatemala, and (especially) El Salvador had a significant, organized, and sustained presence in the United States. Central Americans, both in their home countries and in the United States, worked closely with North American allies.[3]

Put another way, Reagan's aggressive anti-communism, combined with the existence of a revolutionary left in Central America—one that was engaged in ongoing struggles whose outcomes were far from determined—altered the solidarity equation. Operating in a context defined by revolutionary movements and ongoing civil wars, Central American solidarity could never focus on something as discrete as a military coup and its victims. This ensured that us-based solidarity would be less centrally rooted in human rights, that the conditions would be relatively conducive for the development of left internationalism, and that the peace movement would be housed under a broad and diverse umbrella of anti-interventionism that loosely coalesced around the goal of cutting off us military aid.

Indeed, despite a shared commitment to stopping military aid, activists were animated by a wide range of goals, agendas, and political visions. Central American solidarity would include leftists who saw the struggle against us military aid as part of a broader solidarity with the Sandinistas or the FMLN, a project that included educating Americans, sending material aid, taking to the streets, and lobbying Congress. It would also have room for activists who understood the fight against us militarism as part of a more general solidarity with "the Central America people," but who distanced themselves from any particular political group. And it even allowed for those who were openly opposed to the Sandinistas or the FMLN, but nonetheless stood against us foreign policy because they believed in Central America's right to self-determination or were simply opposed to the economic costs associated with us adventurism. Human rights was clearly a central part of this discussion, especially as violations were used to bolster arguments for stopping military aid, but the breadth of debate, alliances, and forms of organization was impressive in what was always a very decentralized movement.

If the movement was organizationally decentralized, it was nonetheless held together by shared opposition to a us military aid that fueled human rights abuses and supported repressive dictatorships in Central America. It was the urgency of the human toll, and the prominent role played by the Reagan administration, that drew so many to the movement. This meant that once the civil wars were over, us military aid slowed, human rights abuses diminished, and Central

America left the front pages, the movement lost the urgency that had drawn so many human, financial, and organizational resources to it in the first place. This was to an extent inevitable. Yet what was left was a multiplicity of relatively small, professionally run organizations that by and large had not been built for, nor were equipped to engage in, a long-term struggle for political power and economic equality as neoliberalism descended over Central America during the 1990s.

The Peace and Solidarity Movement

In the 1970s, Nicaragua, El Salvador, and Guatemala were all home to long-standing, US-backed military regimes that were becoming increasingly repressive toward popular movements which threatened a status quo defined by poverty, massive inequality, and a general lack of political freedom. The military governments that ruled the region had suppressed traditional forms of political participation so thoroughly that opponents were turning to the only option left—armed insurrection. However, despite the seemingly inevitable march towards civil war, and an associated uptick in violence and human rights abuses, solidarity with Central America would remain relatively limited throughout the 1970s. To be sure, small groups of progressives, many with connections to Latin American (and particularly Chilean) solidarity, were becoming more involved in Central America and responding to the political situation in the region. In much larger numbers, these were the very same actors—religious groups, human rights activists, labor unions, and the left—who would eventually form the core of the peace movement less than a decade later. But even at the very end of the 1970s, despite some important initiatives,[4] solidarity efforts were relatively small and received little attention. There was no reason to believe that activism around Central America was about to take Latin American solidarity to unprecedented heights.

Nevertheless, by the mid-1970s the political situation in El Salvador and Nicaragua had captured the attention of some US progressives and Salvadorans/Nicaraguans living in the United States. By 1975, for example, Salvadoran and American activists had formed one of the earliest solidarity organizations in San Francisco in response to a massacre of Salvadoran college students. And at roughly the same time,

Nicaraguan exiles and North American allies organized early mobilizations in San Francisco, Los Angeles, and Washington D.C.[5] Small solidarity committees, in some cases prompted by Nicaraguans who had fled Somoza's rule, formed in New York, Chicago, Boston, Los Angeles, San Francisco, Washington D.C., and New Orleans. Seeking to educate Americans, organize opposition to Somoza, and support the Sandinistas, these efforts had just begun to coalesce in the form of the National Network in Solidarity with the Nicaraguan People (NNSNP) when the Sandinistas successfully overthrew Somoza.[6]

Despite these early initiatives, however, solidarity with the Nicaraguan Revolution during the 1970s was relatively limited and late in developing, especially when we consider that the Sandinistas were leading an inspirational revolution to overthrow a repressive dictator supported by the United States. Likewise, there was little reason to believe that solidarity with El Salvador or Guatemala was about to take off in the late 1970s, even as human rights abuses piled up.

In this sense, it is all the more remarkable how quickly and forcefully the peace movement emerged. The upsurge in solidarity was tied to a variety of broader forces, including the rise of the human rights movement, the legacy of South American solidarity, the deepening presence of religious actors in the region, and ongoing skepticism about US foreign policy. More than this, however, three immediate factors were central to the peace movement's rapid emergence in the early 1980s: the Sandinista victory in Nicaragua in 1979, the assassination of archbishop Oscar Romero and four American churchwomen in El Salvador in 1980, and the election of Ronald Reagan, whose obsession with fighting communism not only kept the region on the front pages, but upped the ante by funneling millions of dollars of military aid into a region that was sliding into civil war.

The success of the Nicaraguan revolution in July 1979 changed the nature of solidarity. The NNSNP had formed just months before, facilitated in large part by church activists, but also supported by the United Auto Workers, numerous religious denominations, and sympathetic congresspersons. Nor were they alone. With the Sandinista victory, "numerous local Chile or Latin America committees reoriented themselves towards Nicaragua in 1978-79."[7] Once the revolution was victorious, it became a "friendship association between the two countries," supporting literacy campaigns and speaker tours.[8] Exiles returned to Nicaragua to support the revolution, and the NNSNP got to work, funneling humanitarian aid while educating the American public and pressuring the US government to "grant generous and unconditional aid to Nicaragua."[9]

However, even during "Sandinismo's first hopeful glow, there were no large national campaigns to promote solidarity." Beyond pushing for US aid, it was difficult to generate support for a successful revolution or create a sufficient sense of urgency in the absence of crisis. The revolution had been won, the civil war was over, and thousands of US citizens were visiting Nicaragua on their own.[10] More than that, although the Carter administration was sending mixed signals, it was not waging an all-out war against Nicaragua. Reagan's 1980 presidential campaign suggested an ominous future, but his election remained a distant prospect, as did the likelihood that his policies would be as awful as his campaign rhetoric. It was only after Reagan's election, and his active support of the Contras beginning in 1982, that Nicaraguan solidarity would become re-energized and expand beyond the relatively small groups of progressives who continued to actively support Nicaragua in the immediate aftermath of the revolution.

More importantly, just as activists were figuring out how to support a successful (though ongoing) revolution in Nicaragua, reports about the deteriorating political situation in El Salvador led many to change focus. This solidarity turn towards El Salvador really took off with the assassination of Archbishop Romero in March 1980 and the brutal murder of four American churchwomen later in the year. Their deaths were a defining moment for both El Salvador and US solidarity. Violence against religious figures signaled that the Salvadoran military would stop at nothing, that normal political activity was no longer possible, and that civil war was all but inevitable. The murders were a call to action for many in the United States, stimulating a broader solidarity which encompassed human rights organizations, peace groups, the left, and a range of other groups.

Nowhere was the impact of this violence against religious leaders felt more greatly than in the faith-based community, or what would become the heart of the emerging peace movement. The assassinations of Oscar Romero and the churchwomen introduced the crisis in Central America to a much broader audience. By 1980, US religious communities had more than a decade of exposure to liberation theology and extensive experience with Latin America. There were over 2,000 missionaries in Central America alone by the end of the 1970s.[11] They were spending a lot of time in the region, had developed a critical perspective with respect to US involvement, and were returning to the United States in large numbers with the express goal of educating the American public. As a result, when the brutal murders put a spotlight on both the region and US foreign policy, there was already a progressive foundation of faith-based peace and human rights organizations with expertise in Latin America. Religious groups in particular were poised to mobilize.

It is worth noting, however, that this progressive faith-based community did not have the deepest of political roots. The oldest Latin American solidarity group, the Ecumenical Program for Inter-American Communication and Action (EPICA), was started only in 1968 by an Episcopal missionary who served in the Dominican Republic during the lead up to the US invasion in 1965. EPICA would play a particularly key role in early solidarity efforts with Nicaragua, and would remain an important actor throughout the period. At around the same time, the US Catholic Conference and the National Council of Churches were working to bring together US and Latin American academics, religious activists, and progressives.[12]

This continued through the 1970s. Nationally, the Washington Office on Latin America (WOLA) was created in 1974 by major churches to act as a coordinated lobbying arm in Congress to stop US intervention. Soon after, the Coalition for a New Foreign and Military Policy (CNFMP) and the associated Human Rights Working Group (HRWG) emerged as principal sites for policy work. More than this, solidarity organizations were forming throughout the 1970s and developing a model of solidarity rooted in "people-to-people" interaction. Most were local in nature, generally located on the East or West coasts, had few resources, and remained active for as long as particular events required.[13]

In this sense, Romero's assassination mobilized and greatly

expanded a (heavily faith-based) solidarity infrastructure that had been taking form since the late 1960s. US-based religious actors immediately began to organize Salvadoran solidarity chapters throughout the United States. On a national level, the Religious Task Force on El Salvador was formed by Catholic activists in early 1980 just prior to Romero's assassination. Two months later Protestants followed suit, establishing the Inter-Religious Task Force on El Salvador (which would later morph into the Inter-Religious Task Force on Central America). These two institutions would become a key part of the national infrastructure that connected local faith-based organizations by educating members, lobbying Congress, and holding demonstrations.[14]

Other national-level organizations, such as Salvadoran Humanitarian Aid, Research and Education Foundation for Peace in El Salvador (SHARE), New El Salvador Today (NEST), Christians for Peace in El Salvador (CRISPAZ), all formed during the early and mid-1980s and joined existing organizations such as WOLA, the National Council of Churches, and the US Catholic Conference in coordinating solidarity with El Salvador. Solidarity with refugees, through the Central American Refugee Centers (CARECEN) and especially the Sanctuary Movement, also came to occupy a central place in Salvadoran solidarity work.[15]

The secular left was drawn to El Salvador for similar reasons. The US Committee in Solidarity with the People of El Salvador (CISPES) was formed in October 1980, the same month that five Salvadoran guerilla movements united to form the FMLN. CISPES was powered mainly by leftists who were motivated both by atrocities in El Salvador and were inspired by the FMLN's struggle for revolutionary change. By the end of the decade CISPES was a truly national organization, with considerable staff, chapters throughout the country, conferences, and the capacity to lobby, organize protests, and send material aid. Openly supporting the FMLN, CISPES was at the heart of grassroots mobilization and demonstrations within the movement, but also worked with religious, peace, and human rights organizations on lobbying, aid, and a broad range of outreach efforts. There was some tension between CISPES and the faith-based core of the movement, but in general activists were so focused on the issues at hand—human rights abuses, violence, and stopping military aid—that ideological differences remained submerged.[16]

Key to all of these efforts, but especially to Salvadoran solidarity, were Central Americans who visited or fled to the United States. Central Americans not only brought heart-wrenching accounts of trauma, hunger, torture, and mass murder, which spurred US citizens to take action, but played key roles in developing the solidarity infrastructure. They arrived in large numbers at an opportune moment. Half a million Salvadorans came into the United States between 1979 and 1982. By 1982 almost 10 per cent of Nicaraguans, or about 250,000 people, were living in the United States. Guatemala's civil war would displace even more by 1983.[17] The rapid arrival of so many Central Americans not only undermined Reagan's propaganda, it put a human face on US foreign policy.

And yet, as important as the Sandinista victory and the assassination of Romero were for mobilizing Central American solidarity, it is impossible to imagine the movement reaching the scale it did without the election of Reagan in 1980. It was not simply that his policies contributed significantly to human rights abuses, ongoing violence, and the decade-long civil wars in Central America. This alone would have produced a progressive response. But Reagan aggressively pushed these policies as part of a highly visible anti-communist foreign agenda. His rhetoric and policies would keep Central America front and center, in effect sustaining and animating the emerging opposition.

In 1981, just weeks after Reagan was inaugurated, Jeanne Kirkpatrick, the President's ambassador to the United Nations, famously declared that "Central America is the most important place in the world for the United States today." Such a statement, coming on the heels of the Iran hostage crisis, must have seemed a bit odd to Americans. Yet the Reagan administration, indeed Reagan himself, made it his mission to convince the US public that it was absolutely crucial to stop communism in this region of the world. As he stated (without irony) in 1983, or exactly when US-supported atrocities were at their peak throughout the region, the "national security of all the Americas is at stake in Central America. If we cannot defend ourselves there ... the safety of our homeland would be in jeopardy

.... If Central America were to fall ... our credibility would collapse, our alliances would crumble."[18]

After laying the public relations groundwork, Reagan promoted a variety of policies to roll back communism in the region, including crippling the Nicaraguan economy, funding and training the Salvadoran military, restoring aid to the Guatemalan army, and developing a commando force of Cuban exiles to attack Nicaragua. The public backlash against these early initiatives was so quick and so intense that it caught the Reagan administration by surprise. Confident that the election had provided a mandate to roll back communism, Reagan now found himself associated with a set of unpopular foreign policies that had the potential to undermine his domestic political agenda.[19]

The President briefly backpedaled, but events in Central America soon forced the administration's hand. The war was not going well for the Salvadoran army, and—despite tentative support for the Contras[20]—the Sandinistas were firmly in control. Reagan's inner circle of advisors insisted that force was needed and could produce the desired results if used immediately and decisively. The Sandinistas could be overthrown and the Salvadoran army saved. Reagan again took the case to the public, selling the need for forceful intervention while implementing it on the ground.[21]

Reagan's myopia put Central America into the national and international spotlight. By 1981 there were more foreign journalists in El Salvador than in Vietnam during the height of the war. The *New York Times*, which hardly mentioned Central America during the 1970s, published "an average of 3.4 articles and editorials a day during the eight years of the Reagan presidency."[22] TV news coverage exploded and publishers cranked out books about the region. And yet despite the fact that much of the media was largely uncritical of Reagan's broader mission, such attention never delivered the mandate Reagan was hoping for. According to Gallup polls during the early 1980s, about two-thirds of those who were paying attention felt El Salvador could likely turn into another Vietnam, and "the majority of Americans simply believed the U.S. should steer clear of Central American military conflicts." Reagan was never able to convince a majority of Americans that the United States should financially support the Contras or the Salvadoran military.[23]

This opposition to Reagan's agenda was due in large part to the peace movement, which quickly developed into a counter-propaganda machine. Solidarity groups became incredibly good at combatting Reagan's distorted version of events through research, first-hand experience, and testimonials. These efforts were aided by a larger context of post-Vietnam apprehensions about military intervention, a chorus of negative world opinion, a domestic opposition to Reagan that sought to exploit any weakness in an otherwise popular President, and a general unease about Reagan's obsession with Central America in respected foreign policy circles, think tanks, and academia. Reagan's over-the-top rhetoric and his administration's penchant for ignoring Congress and violating US law also bolstered opposition. A series of unsavory undertakings, including the CIA's mining of Nicaraguan harbors, the distribution of manuals to teach Nicaraguans how to sabotage their own government, and of course Iran-Contra,[24] all caused considerable scandal, fueled the opposition, and ultimately limited the US government's ability to pursue even more aggressive policies in Central America.[25]

Reagan's continual efforts to undermine the Sandinista government, and especially the first Contra attacks in March of 1982, took the peace movement to new heights. Nicaraguan solidarity had waned after the Sandinista victory in 1979, when many activists turned to the crisis in El Salvador. By contrast, once it developed, Salvadoran solidarity became so well established that the re-emergence of interest in Nicaragua around the Contra war did not so much signal a shift in focus as it announced the arrival of a full-blown peace movement with a number of distinct, yet deeply intertwined, currents that fed off of each other.[26] The Contra war brought the formation of two of the most important solidarity organizations of the period, Witness for Peace and the Pledge of Resistance, and stimulated the rapid expansion of the sister city movement. The focus of congressional lobbying shifted decisively towards Nicaragua and the debate over Contra funding, but El Salvador remained an important concern inside the beltway, and was always at the heart of grassroots mobilization in the movement (in part because it was more centralized and very well organized through CISPES).[27]

The movement as a whole found a certain unity in opposing US foreign policy, particularly with respect to military aid, the US embargo of Nicaragua (after 1985), and the threat of a full-scale US invasion of Nicaragua. Not only did opposition to US intervention come in a range of forms, from street mobilization and civil disobedience to lobbying and educational outreach, the movement embraced a diversity of tactics, projects, and goals. In addition to opposing US policy, solidarity groups supported Central Americans in almost every imaginable way, including close alliances with the FSLN/FMLN, pushing for the release of political prisoners, harvesting/selling coffee, participating in peace brigades, and sending hundreds of millions of dollars worth of humanitarian aid.

This was a period of continual, intense, and often quite militant political activity. The movement was, in a sense, both large and small. It was large by the historical standards of Latin American solidarity, and in terms of its public presence and staying power. A number of national marches drew close to 100,000 people, numerous others fell in the 5,000 to 10,000 person range, and hundreds, even thousands, of smaller protests, vigils, and actions took place throughout the country for the better part of a decade. The movement combined street-level mobilizations with one of the most dedicated, competent, and consistent lobbying campaigns in the history of progressive activism. It was, in this sense, a movement that felt like it was everywhere all the time.[28]

More than this, some 80,000 people signed the Pledge of Resistance, committing to civil disobedience in the event of a US invasion of Nicaragua. Witness for Peace brought over 4,000 US citizens to Nicaragua to learn about the revolution, witness the disastrous impact of US foreign policy, and protect communities against Contra attacks. Thousands more travelled on their own and with other groups to pick coffee and support the revolution.[29] Likewise, by the late 1980s, the Sanctuary Movement, led by a broad range of religious denominations, and actively supported by students, human rights organizations, and entire cities, had established more than 500 declared Sanctuaries throughout the United States. In defiance of US immigration law, US citizens working in the Sanctuary movement provided a safe haven for thousands of Central Americans who were forced to flee the conflict, but were nonetheless denied refugee status by the US government.

At the same time, as Van Gosse also points out, "this was always a very small movement, trying to mobilize the left when it seemed that the country had embraced the right." There were probably fewer than 20,000 activists involved at any one time, and even some of the larger national organizations such as CISPES, Witness for Peace, and Neighbor to Neighbor were relatively small compared with the millions supporting organizations like Greenpeace and the Nuclear Freeze.[30]

The limited size of the movement, combined with an astounding degree of diversity and organizational fragmentation, placed serious limits on a progressive movement that was operating in an increasingly hostile political climate. In the end, the peace movement could not achieve its largest, most conspicuous goals. It operated in a context of decimated social movements, entrenched oligarchies, and repressive militaries in Central America, and a US political system characterized by a popular right-wing President, a weakened labor movement still enmeshed in Cold War ideology, and a public with limited knowledge or interest in foreign policy. It also did not help that Reagan was ideologically driven, fixated on Central America, and willing to "stop communism" and restore US global hegemony by any means. The movement did not bring a quick end to the civil wars, military regimes, or human rights abuses, let alone (consistently) stop military aid or ensure the long-term survival of revolutionary movements. Indeed, although the movement transformed the routine passage of military aid into full-scale congressional battles, and even managed to periodically slow/stop aid, the Contras—a group created out of thin air with no real base of support in Nicaragua—were nonetheless able to acquire more than $1 billion in US aid. This assistance flowed while the US government waged an all-out war against the Nicaraguan economy. For its part, the Salvadoran military government received somewhere around $4 billion in aid.[31]

The human costs of all this were hardly surprising, if nonetheless staggering. Central American economies were largely destroyed, millions of people were displaced, and hundreds of thousands were killed. By the end of 1985, the Contra war had effectively accomplished US policy objectives in Nicaragua. It cost the Nicaraguan economy more than $1 billion, a figure that climbed to close to $10 billion by the end of the decade, while killing, terrorizing, and displacing thousands of Nicaraguans. It destroyed the Sandinista project. In El Salvador tens of thousands died in the civil war, including 40,000 at the hands of death squads alone by 1985. The Salvadoran economy was left in even worse shape. Guatemala experienced the worst of the brutality, with hundreds of indigenous villages literally wiped from the map, over 100,000 people either killed or disappeared, and over a million displaced. Altogether, more than 200,000 Central Americans lost their lives during the 1980s, over 2 million were displaced, and the region's economy was largely destroyed.[32]

And yet, without irony, we can say that it would have been worse in the absence of the peace movement. The movement set limits on US intervention, which in turn lessened the violence and created limited political space for Central Americans to fight for democracy, even revolution. At a time when congressional Democrats were retreating in virtually every other policy realm, the movement provided them with the backbone to confront Reagan over an important issue. In many ways, the movement produced Iran-Contra and eventually stopped military aid explicitly directed at overthrowing the Nicaraguan government (in the Boland Amendment of 1984). It bought the Sandinistas time, prevented the Contras from winning, and may have even stopped the full-scale invasion of Nicaragua. These were important victories.

Conclusion

As Van Gosse has noted, the Central American peace movement was a movement that everyone knew "was there, but few, even among its supporters, knew where it came from or how it operated."[33] Activism came in a variety of forms, from candlelight vigils, street marches, and travelling to Central American war zones to illegally housing refugees, committing civil disobedience, and pressuring political representatives. National-level entities such as Sanctuary, Witness for Peace, Pledge of Resistance, Neighbor to Neighbor and CISPES gave the movement a certain coherence, and long-standing peace organizations provided some stability and experience. Yet in many ways the movement was characterized by the proliferation of local solidarity organizations, most of which were sharply focused in one way or another, working on a particular country/city, organized by or around a particular group (such as nuns or students), or limited to particular type of solidarity (such as lobbying).

This decentralization allowed for broad and varied participation which gave a relatively small movement the appearance of being everywhere at all times. It was a strength. As Gosse puts it:

> This pluralism was the source of a remarkable enthusiasm and tolerance, since people generally went where their instincts and talents led them and found their natural bedfellows. It was also an excellent antidote to the kind of sectarianism that on occasion plagued the antiwar movement and earlier solidarity efforts with Latin America. There was little or no space for bitter maneuvering over the grand strategy of "the movement," since the regionalized war required several simultaneous strategies.[34]

At the same time, it also seems worth noting that the lack of a mass-oriented organization limited the movement's capacity to act with coherence, with focus, or with the kind of political power necessary for changing the fundamentals of US–Latin American relations. It also had the effect of spreading human, financial, and organizational resources thinly across hundreds of small organizations.

The consequences of this tendency towards fragmentation were not entirely apparent as long as Central America remained a site of intense interest and thousands of progressives poured their time, energy, and money into the movement. However, once the civil wars ended and progressive interest shifted to other causes, this lack of organizational coherence meant that what was left was a multiplicity of relatively small organizations with few resources, committed professional staff, and little in the way of a popular base. As we will see in coming chapters, activists shifted the focus of their work to address the range of crises generated by neoliberalism. Yet a solidarity infrastructure defined by NGOs that had become particularly good at highlighting human tragedy in order to shame the US government and mobilize supporters was not equipped to help rebuild social movements in Central America, or oppose a Washington Consensus that was imposing neoliberal policies throughout the region—

perhaps too tall an order for international solidarity operating in a political climate defined by a declining left and ascendant right.

The difficulty of maintaining the intensity of solidarity after the civil wars was no doubt partly inevitable, but it was also the product of a solidarity that had relied on crisis as its fuel. For many in the movement, Central American solidarity was a response to an urgent plea for help. Refugees, exiles, and Americans returning from the region educated people in the United States about the reality of Central America, a reality that differed fundamentally from Reagan propaganda, and that was absolutely horrific in its human consequences. When confronted with the violent impact of US foreign policy, a wide spectrum of Americans—already leery of US adventures abroad—concluded that military aid had to be cut off and its impact countered through material aid, sending human witnesses, and providing sanctuary for refugees. This urgency was precisely what gave the movement its force, passion, commitment, and energy. It may also have stopped a full-scale US invasion of Nicaragua or even deeper involvement in El Salvador.

At the same time, such urgency produced an act-now-think-later approach that gravitated around positions and strategies that could quickly mobilize as many people as possible around campaigns with relatively short-term goals. In many ways, this lowest common denominator approach—borrowed in part from the human rights movement—was necessary to bring together as many people as possible and produce a forceful response to intense levels of violence. But it also tended to reduce Central America's problems, as well as role of the United States, to military aid and US foreign policy. It made it difficult to develop solidarity that pursued immediate goals in order to advance longer-term objectives such as transforming the fundamentals of US–Latin American relations. To be sure, there were actors (such as CISPES) that attempted to push the movement in such directions, but the urgency of the Central American situation, combined with the broader decline of the US left, the dramatic ascendancy of the right, and the continued conservatism of labor during this period, meant that this project was continually kicked down the road. Urgency and crisis had a way of undermining, if not derailing, efforts to link short-term goals with longer-term projects of collective liberation.

This tendency was further reinforced by the fact that by and large the Central American peace movement "never [had] any deep concern for whether or not it would or could change the United States."[35] The movement's lack of interest in broader US politics was a byproduct of both a deep commitment to Central America[36] and a domestic climate in which conservatives had seized the momentum in virtually all spheres. In this sense, this was not Cuban solidarity of the 1960s, which had operated in a climate characterized by a relatively vibrant US left that was engaging in international solidarity at least in part in order to advance its own struggles at home. Such a project no doubt made little sense in the 1980s, at a moment when left currents in the United States were submerged and/or in retreat.

Indeed, with labor and 1960s-era social movements playing defense, it is not entirely surprising that many of the most prominent progressive initiatives of late 1970s and 1980s revolved around foreign policy, including anti-apartheid, the nuclear freeze campaign, and the Central American peace movement. In the context of a dismal domestic political scene, looking outside the nation's borders had a certain appeal. In contrast to the United States where progressives were largely in retreat, Central America was a region where revolution was actually on the table, and where US allies could play a key role in advancing significant change simply by altering their own country's foreign policy.

The problem, however, was that because foreign policy is not divorced from the domestic political realm, and in some ways follows broader political trends, it was hard for a small, and politically isolated, movement to have a dramatic impact on US foreign policy. Put another way, it is hard to change US foreign policy—let alone US economic presence within the Americas—in a significant way if there is no capacity to transform the balance of forces in the United States that produced that policy in the first place. This responsibility, of course, did not all fall entirely on the peace movement. There were real limits to what a movement could accomplish that was politically isolated, largely disconnected from domestically oriented progressive initiatives, and unconcerned with the larger US political economy. Perhaps more importantly, solidarity that focuses narrowly on stopping military aid or altering US foreign policy, and is not concerned with really "changing the United States," may not be designed for a long-term solidarity aimed at ushering in a deeper transformation of US–Latin American relations, including policies and practices that reproduce inequality at both home and abroad. It is also not a left movement in the traditional sense.

6

NAFTA, Fair Trade, and Globalization

At the start of the 1990s the left in both Latin America and the United States was at a twentieth-century nadir. The Soviet Union had collapsed, socialism had been declared dead, and the United States had claimed victory in the Cold War. Military regimes had wiped out much of the left in South America during the 1970s and 1980s, and counterinsurgency had finished the job in Central America by 1990. Nor was there much reason for hope. Cuba was isolated and on the brink of collapse, and the Sandinistas—once a beacon of hope—had been soundly defeated. To be sure, military regimes were withdrawing from presidential offices throughout the region, but their departures were not the result of popular rebellion or the resurgence of the left. Militaries were not so much defeated as exhausted. They lost considerable legitimacy and were partially discredited, but Latin American armed forces remained a powerful presence that served to narrow the boundaries of acceptable political behavior, and inhibited the return of the left. In short, the arrival of democracy in Latin America was tenuous, ambiguous, and partial throughout the 1980s and 1990s.

More than this, democracy was predicated on the continued implementation of neoliberalism. Elites consolidated power under democratic rule, paving the way for structural adjustment and the rapid redistribution of wealth upwards. Such a project was made possible by, and contributed to, a severely debilitated left. Opposition forces were in no position to shift political debate, let alone advance a more progressive agenda. Human rights abuses had diminished, but civilian rule rested on continued violence and the intensification of inequality in Latin America during the 1980s and 1990s. Nor was there much reason to think that the Latin American left would rebound less than a decade later.

Once in power, neoliberal civilian regimes not only failed to resolve the economic problems that had plagued military dictatorships, they facilitated privatization, the pillaging of public enterprises, and the further concentration of wealth, all of which intensified the exploitation and impoverishment of working people. Structural adjustment decimated labor unions, peasant organizations, and working-class power, continuing the destruction of left institutions while undermining the capacity of popular groups to forge solidarity. It also bestowed a "lost decade" upon the region in which overall productivity stagnated while inequality worsened. The political assault and the broader economic war were, in fact, part of a single process.

Not surprisingly, the one-sided nature of class war in Latin America did not create an ideal climate for the development of left internationalism at the start of the 1990s. It is not as if labor unions, peasant organizations, social movements, and revolutionary actors disappeared from the Latin American scene, but traditional institutions of the left were significantly compromised even in countries that had escaped the worst of the violence. They, along with the hundreds of NGOs that emerged throughout the region during this period, were drawn into relatively local, largely defensive, struggles aimed at lessening the worst effects of neoliberalism. As larger numbers of Latin Americans found themselves politically and economically marginalized, these struggles eventually led to a broader challenge to the entire system in the form of the so-called "pink tide." In the short term, however, the situation was bleak. The 1989 Caracazo, a wave of protests against structural adjustment reforms in Venezuela, foreshadowed the anti-neoliberal backlash that was to come, and peasant-indigenous groups were beginning to contest neoliberalism with more consistency and ferocity by the early 1990s, but the prospects for a more sustained and large-scale opposition were not promising.

The progressive landscape was no brighter in the United States at the start of the 1990s. It is highly unlikely that a more vibrant US left would have tilted the political scales in Latin America, but the weakness of the US left, combined with the decline of the Central American peace movement, did little to improve the situation or give much hope for the development of internationalism. The number of people and amount of resources devoted to solidarity not only declined dramatically after the end of the peace movement, the overall focus shifted. After a difficult period of transition, many of the remaining/smaller solidarity organizations reoriented themselves towards economic issues related to neoliberalism and a global economic system that was delivering greater poverty and inequality to the region.

To be sure, solidarity rooted in opposition to US military aid persisted, now turning to Colombia as massive amounts of aid flowed there, but it did not reach the intensity or scale of the Central American peace movement. Likewise, although human rights solidarity remained prominent in Colombia,[1] as well as in Central America, Mexico, and much of the region as violence was refashioned under democratic rule, it did not preside over solidarity to the degree that it had in the 1980s. Human rights organizations proliferated as they professionalized in the 1990s, but human rights activism itself became more diffuse as the sources of violence became more dispersed under neoliberalism. In this respect, human rights followed the broader flow of solidarity towards the neoliberal crisis more than it propelled it.

This reorientation of solidarity during the 1990s coincided with the uneven entrance of US labor to the world of progressive internationalism. Having spent the Cold War undermining labor organizing in Latin America, the AFL-CIO finally emerged from the Cold War fog and became part of the solidarity equation. Labor's turn towards a progressive internationalism was further stimulated by neoliberalism and globalization, a process that saw the welfare state dismantled as much of US manufacturing moved overseas. The safety net was being destroyed at the precise moment when sectors of the US working class were reeling from the effects of globalization, and needed support the most. This opened up more of the labor movement to internationalism, but with the Cold War lingering and labor in retreat domestically, the turn towards a progressive internationalism remained slow, uneven, and half-hearted at the start of the 1990s.

In this broader context, Latin American solidarity as a whole nevertheless retained a certain urgency as the economic situation grew increasingly desperate throughout the region. Existing solidarity groups refocused and new ones emerged, concentrating their efforts on a range of groups and issues related to the neoliberal crisis. Indeed, notwithstanding the reduced amount of people/resources engaged in solidarity, the challenge facing internationalism was as much about fragmentation as it was about sheer numbers, resources, and energy.

The tendency for solidarity to be defined by the proliferation of relatively small and isolated organizations only intensified after the Central American peace movement dissipated. With the civil wars over and dictatorships fading from the scene, the shared opposition to something as identifiable and discrete as US military aid no longer held together what had always been a decentralized movement. And although most of the issues taken up by solidarity groups in the 1990s could be tied to neoliberalism in one way or another, it proved difficult to forge or unify a broader opposition around something as large and ill-defined as neoliberalism (much less capitalism). Neoliberalism produced a seemingly endless number of crises and causes, each demanding immediate attention and a new NGO.

The broad and hegemonic nature of neoliberalism—"There Is No Alternative" (TINA) in the words of Margaret Thatcher—not only made it difficult to analytically connect seemingly disparate issues to a single "cause," but impeded the ability of the left to name the problem, shape the contours of the debate, and forge an anti-neoliberal bloc. This was true in both Latin America and the United States at the start of the 1990s. The task of developing a progressive project that recognized the connections between seemingly distinct tragedies was, of course, impeded by the fact that social movements and the left had been dismantled over a decades-long period. These were the very sites where alternative visions could be articulated, brought to wider audiences, and mobilized around—where the inevitability of neoliberalism could be challenged both intellectually and organizationally. This project was also inhibited by the widespread disillusionment with the state as a potentially positive force in people's lives. Working to influence or capture state power seemed not only far-fetched in the absence of viable social movements, but pointless in a context where neoliberalism retained an air of inevitability and the state had lost much of its capacity to intervene on behalf of working people.

What the next three chapters trace, then, is a transition towards a Latin American solidarity that focused heavily (though not exclusively) in the 1990s and early 2000s on labor-economic issues tied to neoliberal capitalism. Chapter 6 starts with the growing focus on trade in progressive circles in the late 1980s and 1990s, beginning with opposition to NAFTA as well as the ongoing development of "fair trade." Chapters 7 and 8 then explore solidarity efforts around the Zapatistas, the global justice movement, anti-corporate campaigns, and the anti-sweatshop movement.

In different ways, all these initiatives responded to—and tried to address—the horrific consequences of neoliberalism for working people. They all emerged in a neoliberal context defined by the decline, retreat, or disappearance of large-scale oppositional movements, which in turn both provided opportunities and placed limits on internationalism. And they all opposed neoliberalism while embracing an anti-statism that moved away from the state as a key site of political activity and struggle.

On this later point, the battle over NAFTA represented something of a turning point. As we will see, although the mainstream of the NAFTA opposition forged little in the way of international solidarity, and in fact embraced a nationalism that made it more difficult to build cross-border alliances, the intensity of the conflict pointed to a growing concern on the left with global trade. This was particularly true in solidarity circles, in large part because global trade connected and impacted working people throughout the hemisphere. After NAFTA, wider and wider sections of the public no longer assumed "free trade" to be a neutral phenomenon whose expansion would lift all boats. Such critiques have a long history, but they were largely outside the mainstream until the 1990s. From NAFTA onwards, virtually all proposed trade agreements, policies, and frameworks became sites of intense conflict. Free trade—an important pillar of neoliberalism which had previously gone largely unquestioned—was losing its ideological grip, even as its advocates still had the power to impose it.

At the same time, although the struggle around NAFTA served to erode the sanctity of free trade, it did little to undermine the most basic tenet of neoliberalism—its anti-statism. The power of neoliberalism was rooted in its ideological and material assault on a kind of state that—at least in theory—protected working people from the vagaries of the market while redistributing wealth downwards. The idea that the state should play such a role had been unevenly eroded during the post-Second World War period, but neoliberalism stimulated the process and made it seem natural and inevitable. Ideologically, it defined the state as an entity that undermined growth and prosperity by restricting free trade, overspending on social programs, and otherwise interfering with the natural workings of the market. Materially, neoliberal policies dismantled the public sector and undermined the capacity of governments to intervene on behalf of working people, a decades-long assault that ensured the ideological claims became something of a self-fulfilling prophecy. The more neoliberalism's architects let free trade reign, shifted resources from public goods to corporate coffers, and reduced spending on social programs that protected working people from the vagaries of the market, the more ineffectual governments in fact became as a positive force in the daily life of most people (in many cases, they actually became more repressive). The ongoing destruction of the state bolstered neoliberal claims that government was in fact the problem, making it all the more difficult to imagine a state that had the capacity (let alone will) to serve the interests of the nation. This, in turn, made the left's traditional political project of constructing broad-based movements designed to acquire state power seem pointless or outdated.

Even as it took on trade, then, the opposition to NAFTA did little to undermine the anti-state core of neoliberalism. In fact, the enduring anti-statism of the period partially explains why forces opposed to NAFTA, although quite capable of mobilizing against the US government in order to stop the trade deal, were unable to develop an alternative model of economic integration that resonated with wider publics and served to mobilize a more effective opposition. Such a project requires a positive vision of the state as something that can be influenced by, and serve the interests of, working people—a state that in this case cannot only shape a more equitable system of global trade, but redistribute wealth downwards and limit corporate power while protecting workers from any range of dislocations associated with not only trade, but automation, unemployment, market trends, technological change, and so on. This was a hard sell at the start of the 1990s, and partially explains why critiques of global trade could lead people in a variety of political directions.

The growing common sense anti-statism of the period also helps us understand the post-NAFTA trajectory of Latin American solidarity. Some of the most conspicuous expressions of solidarity from the period, including efforts as disparate as the internationalism surrounding the Zapatistas, the ongoing development of fair trade, and the anti-sweatshop movement, were both reactions to, and products of, neoliberalism. It was not simply that they tried to address the growing inequality and poverty associated with its implementation. It was that, despite deep and distinct historical origins, they were all— by the 1990s—the product of a broader climate that was defined by the absence of large-scale oppositional movements that possessed the capacity to influence public debate and policy. They were innovative, experimental, and creative expressions of progressive activism, but they both reflected, and were a product of, the left's overall weakness. Each, in turn, also embodied and embraced a politics that assumed the anti-statism of the neoliberal moment, pursuing a form of politics that no longer saw the state as a central site of struggle.

NAFTA

The struggle to defeat NAFTA was not US labor's first effort to address the impact of global trade on working people or to engage in international solidarity. Yet, at least in terms of solidarity in the post-Second World War era, the pre-NAFTA track record of the AFL-CIO was neither deep nor particularly commendable. In part because international affairs had not been a high priority for most US labor unions, internationalism tended to be under the control of a handful of high-level union leaders who conducted labor foreign policy outside the purview of rank and file members. For most of the twentieth century this meant that the senior leadership of the AFL-CIO practiced a deeply nationalist form of internationalism, effectively taking their cue from the US government. This generally entailed supporting policies that favored US corporations at the expense of working people in Latin America. Meaningful international solidarity was, in effect, jettisoned in the hope that support for US business interests abroad would translate into benefits for American workers at home.[2]

With the onset of the Cold War, this tendency was infused with anti-communism. The AFL-CIO helped the US government and its allies suppress militant labor movements, undermine democracy in Latin America, and ensure that US capital had access to raw materials and expanding markets at the expense of Latin American workers.[3] There were always dissident sectors in US labor, but these were minority currents in a labor movement otherwise defined by Cold War foreign policy.

However, as US–Soviet relations thawed in the 1970s, and Vietnam unraveled, more rank and file union members began to question their leadership's own reactionary brand of Cold War imperialism. This questioning opened up new spaces in the labor movement for more meaningful forms of internationalism. Dissident sectors, at times in open opposition to the AFL-CIO, but more often simply acting on their own, began to engage in solidarity with Latin America. Such efforts developed something of a critical mass and degree of coherence through Central American solidarity during the 1980s, but labor solidarity nonetheless remained targeted, limited, and above all sporadic.[4] Nevertheless, by the 1980s and early 1990s, powerful unions such as the Teamsters, the United Automobile Workers (UAW), the Communications Workers of American (CWA), and the United Electrical, Radio and Machine Workers (UE) were all engaging in an internationalism which in some way challenged the Cold War stance of the AFL-CIO.

It was not until the Soviet Union finally collapsed, however, that the ideological straitjacket that had locked the AFL-CIO into a Cold War internationalism finally began to loosen. It is hard to overemphasize the importance of this shift. The Cold War had not simply turned the core of the labor movement against communism, it had served to remove radicalism, militancy, and internationalism from the table altogether. The end of the Cold War opened up the possibility of a progressive internationalism spearheaded by the leadership of organized labor's largest confederation. More than this, the turn towards internationalism during the 1980s and 1990s was further facilitated by a series of factors, including deindustrialization, overseas outsourcing, stagnating wages, and an eroding safety net, that came home to roost during the 1980s and contributed to a growing sense in the labor movement that new directions had to be explored. The AFL-CIO's traditional endorsement of free trade and support of US capital abroad came under increasing scrutiny from within the house of labor as US corporations began outsourcing production while working standards, wages, and labor rights eroded at home.

And yet, in part because this rethinking took place at a moment when US workers were extremely vulnerable, the turn towards internationalism in the US labor movement was uneven and contradictory. Defensive strategies aimed at helping unionized workers hold on to what they had, such as industrial protectionism or anti-immigration, were just as likely to resonate as were more innovative forms of international solidarity. Put another way, although the labor movement and working people increasingly recognized that their futures were deeply tied to global currents, this realization did not provide a clear direction at the start of the 1990s.

All of these tensions and contradictions came out in the battle over NAFTA. The agreement was controversial from the moment it was proposed, precisely because it emerged in a context of intensifying neoliberalism and globalization which made the lives of working people increasingly precarious. By creating a trade bloc that insured the relatively free flow of capital, NAFTA was an agreement whose primary beneficiaries were large banks and multinational corporations. Leaving working people and the environment exposed, the agreement revealed how rigged the system was and how much worse it could become. It was not designed to integrate the three countries (the United States, Mexico, and Canada) in ways that actually benefited the majority of people.[5] Consequently, opposition in the United States emerged almost immediately from a variety of sources, ultimately cohering around two broad coalitions: the smaller, and slightly more progressive, Alliance for Responsible Trade, and the larger and more influential, AFL-CIO-backed Citizens Trade Campaign.

The Alliance for Responsible Trade included unions with a deeper history of, and commitment to, grassroots international solidarity, such as UAW, UE, International Brotherhood of Teamsters (IBT), and the Union of Needletrades, Industrial and Textile Employees (UNITE), as well as a range of progressive NGOs and think tanks. It focused more on building cross-border relationships and developing a fair-trade alternative to NAFTA. The Alliance had far fewer resources and less ability to mobilize large numbers of people than did the Citizens Trade Campaign.[6] And although the expansion of tri-national initiatives and worker exchanges may have laid the groundwork for deeper labor solidarity down the road, and in some cases produced innovative models of cross-border organizing,[7] they generated relatively few short-term political wins and remained "marginal in relation to the mainstream of labour and politics in the three countries."[8] This was partly because, despite the formation of an anti-NAFTA coalition in Mexico (the Red Mexicana de Acción Frente al Libre Comercio), the Institutional Revolutionary Party (PRI)-affiliated labor movement represented around 80 percent of all workers and openly supported NAFTA.[9] The possibility of constructing meaningful (labor-based) opposition to NAFTA in Mexico was limited.

The Citizens Trade Campaign, which included the leadership of the AFL-CIO as well as some of its unions, various lobbying organizations, and mainstream environmental groups, focused its efforts on the US Congress. International solidarity was not central to its NAFTA strategy. In fact, although the AFL-CIO mounted an extensive campaign, energized a moribund labor movement, and made the vote considerably closer than observers initially anticipated, it is hard to characterize the efforts as being particularly internationalist.[10] If anything, it was a nationalist response to a global issue that did little to facilitate solidarity between working people in Mexico and the United States.

This is not entirely surprising. NAFTA drew a strong response from rank and file workers because it put a face on much of what they had been experiencing for the previous 20 years, including global restructuring and capital mobility, deindustrialization, a concerted assault on labor unions, declining real wages, downward mobility, and job insecurity. However, although the debate around NAFTA seemed ideal for reminding workers that a nationalist go-it-alone strategy was no longer viable, much of the discussion got quickly bogged down in debates about the exact number of "American" jobs that would be "lost" to Mexicans. Debate also reduced Mexico to a country where lax labor codes served to undermine US jobs. The emphasis on job losses, although effective in generating considerable anger and energy, did not represent a long-term strategy and had the effect of turning Mexicans into enemies of US workers.[11]

Even when organized labor was able to move beyond the defensive protection of "American" jobs, it was largely unable to articulate—in a way that resonated with broad cross-sections of Americans—what an alternative path of economic integration, development, trade, and industry might look like. NAFTA helped renew debates about trade and solidarity in the mainstream labor movement, but overall the discussions came too late, failed to push far enough, and often did not move much beyond lofty rhetoric about international solidarity. As Jefferson Cowie notes:

> [the] mainstream of organized labor in the United States created only the most incipient and fragile of political spaces for progressive alternatives to the trade deal. The tone and content of the campaign did not work to build strong and useful forms of transnational politics in North America, and, equally as troubling, the nation-based social identities which continued to be marshaled by organized labor did not address the fundamental issues presented by the ongoing dilemma of global economic integration.[12]

At the same time, without a left, and in a context where job insecurity made it increasingly difficult for working people to think long term, the path towards a more meaningful international solidarity was by no means clear.

The battle around NAFTA, then, was a contradictory moment for labor, the left, and international solidarity. On the one hand, it energized the mainstream of organized labor, which had been in steady decline and retreat in the face of neoliberalism. The AFL-CIO and its rank and file mobilized and almost successfully stopped an important piece of government policy which was supported by a Democratic president. More than that, workers in all three countries developed cross-border coalitions, increased efforts to connect with one another, experimented with new strategies, and spent more time thinking critically about the connections they had with each other and the nature of economic integration in a global world. To an extent, these positive developments informed and stimulated subsequent solidarity efforts.

On the other hand, while the mainstream of organized labor in Mexico remained under the tutelage of the ruling party and supported NAFTA, the mainstream of the labor movement in the United States framed its opposition to NAFTA largely in terms of job losses and substandard Mexican labor and environmental codes. This framing ultimately proved to be a "nationalistic diversion" that turned Mexicans into enemies and did little to facilitate a broader debate about alternative models of trade and economic integration.[13] More radical discussions took place largely outside the mainstream of the Mexican and US labor movements, in insurgent union spaces as well as more radical NGOs, solidarity groups, and intellectual circles. They never gained adequate momentum to move from the periphery to the mainstream of labor (or environmental) movements in either country.

Nevertheless, the unexpectedly intense opposition to NAFTA put a significant dent in one of neoliberalism's key pillars: free trade. Faced with the devastating consequences of unrestrained capital, growing numbers of people throughout the Americas were rejecting the assumption that free trade was neutral, and that its expansion automatically benefited everyone. After NAFTA, free trade agreements and policies could no longer be imposed without a battle. For those who opposed the treaty, NAFTA reaffirmed (as it imposed) the fact that the system of trade opened up markets for the benefit of large corporations and banks, while weakening or destroying national sovereignty, environmental regulations, wages, working conditions, and labor rights. It contributed to and embodied the so-called race to the bottom that promised to worsen conditions in both the South and North. The interrogation of free trade had gone mainstream. Opponents did not defeat NAFTA, but the success in mobilizing against it was an important moment in the larger push to place social questions at the center of public debates about trade and the economy. More and more people began to ask some version of "What would a trade regime with people and the environment as core concerns look like?" This was a significant development.

In fact, by the mid-1990s, even the World Bank and the Organisation for Economic Co-operation and Development (OECD) were wondering out loud whether increased global integration was good for workers around the world.[14] It was increasingly hard for those who managed the world economy to assert that trade was strictly a commercial interaction devoid of social concerns or costs. When the World Trade Organization (WTO) tried to do just that, in effect dismissing social questions as irrelevant to its mission, it faced a public backlash in what came to be known as the "Battle in Seattle," a popular uprising that prevented the WTO from holdings its 1999 meetings, captured the world's attention, and effectively forced the labor question into the center of deliberations about trade.

At the same time, although the battle over NAFTA and other trade agreements, policies, and frameworks served to undermine one of the hegemonic pillars of neoliberalism, it was limited in a number of important respects. To begin, aside from failing to prevent the passage of most trade agreements or alter the conventional trading regime more broadly, these struggles did not create and mobilize a large-scale opposition movement, or lead to the development of an alternative model of economic integration that resonated with broader publics. In fact, given the tenor of the debate and the rhetoric of the AFL-CIO, it is hard to say this broader project was advanced much at all.

In addition, the most important elements of neoliberalism were left firmly intact. The problems faced by most working people in the United States had less to do with trade—the impact of which on workers could be greatly exaggerated—than with the ongoing assault by capital more generally. This assault restricted the capacity of working people to meaningfully influence state power in ways that strengthened their organizations, distributed wealth downward, limited the power of corporations, and otherwise implemented policies that served their interests. The narrow focus on trade, particularly in the context of neoliberalism's broader denigration of a progressive state, served to obscure this larger assault while stoking unhelpful strands of nationalism.

As we already saw, and as became even clearer with the election of Donald Trump a couple of decades later, a politics that fixates on trade does not necessarily lead us down a progressive path. Workers from other countries, or global competition more generally, became "the problem" during the debates around NAFTA when in fact the broader issue was the inability of working people to construct and develop a state that could advance their interests. Bad trade deals were, in this sense, better understood as indicators of how little power the left in the United States had over state power and policies, than as the source of all evil. Indeed, this partly explains why the anti-NAFTA opposition failed to produce an alternative model of economic integration. To do so it would have been necessary to interrogate and effectively challenge neoliberalism's anti-statist ideology, and insist on a government that is committed to addressing inequality and that protects working people from economic dislocations associated with global trade, technological change, consumer demand, or whatever. This proved a far harder task, one that the US left continues to struggle with.

Fair Trade: The Alternative to Free Trade

For opponents of NAFTA, the free-trade regime embodied in the agreement was unacceptable. But what was the alternative? What form of trade or economic integration did opponents to free trade envision? This "alternative" question was important for the left not simply because the capacity to answer it implies a certain degree of imagination and vision, but because successful opposition to free trade required mobilizing people around the possibility that better forms of economy exist, and could be achieved through collective action. It was not enough to simply say "No" to trade as it currently existed. Effective opposition required not only imagining a new economic model, but developing the political capacity to mobilize people around the development of a different social order. Opponents to NAFTA were never able to achieve this.

Others would try. The struggle to define and create a more equitable system of trade was central to what came to be known as the "fair trade" movement. Fair trade sought to replace the conventional trading regime with a system that returned a larger portion of the trade dollar to producers in the global South. As we will see, the irony—and perhaps the reason why fair trade and the struggle against NAFTA never connected—was that fair trade advocates doubled down on anti-statism. Fair trade not only abandoned the state as a site of political struggle, but embraced a strategy that never really confronted the conventional trading regime. This was a politics that demanded very little of government and left the corporate-controlled system of trade largely untouched. Advocates were not demanding that the state regulate conventional trade, or even that government policy create space for fair trade to develop. Rather, the fair trade solution was located almost entirely in the market. The argument was that a more equitable system of trade would eventually emerge, become large enough to displace the conventional system, and do so largely through third-party regulators and enlightened consumers. The fact that this political project, and model of solidarity, blossomed in the 1980s and 1990s is explained by a range of factors, including the extent to which neoliberalism had limited the political vision and capacity of what remained of the US left.

The fair trade project itself predates the neoliberal heyday by several decades. Religious activists initiated the first era of fair trade just after the Second World War by marketing handicrafts from European regions that had been devastated by the war. Then, as the crisis in Europe faded, the focus turned to the Third World, with a fairly straightforward goal: eradicate poverty by helping communities in the South gain access to Northern markets. Early on, the intent was not so much to challenge the existing system of conventional trade as to create alternative trade networks by purchasing handicrafts directly from poor producers and then selling those products to conscientious consumers in the North through catalogues or small "world shops" such as Ten Thousand Villages. Trade would increase employment and income, bring development to the Third World, and educate northern consumers about global poverty. Poverty, in short, could be eliminated through creative solutions rooted in the market.[15] This system of fair trade, which came to be known as the Alternative Trading Organization (ATO) model, experienced considerable success. During the 1960s and 1970s, the direct sale of Third World handicrafts expanded dramatically, so much so that by the 1980s there was an established movement that shared basic values, practices, and institutional organizations.

The ATO model still exists, and has been key to the development of the movement as a whole, but fair trade in the modern sense is very much a product of the neoliberal period of the 1980s and 1990s. Increasing globalization, and a growing awareness about it, made the case for fair trade while exposing its limitations. Globalization laid bare the fact that "we" in the North were not only purchasing more and more from "them" in the South, but that our lifestyle, our access to cheap food, cloths, electronics, and so on, was increasingly dependent on the exploitation of working people in the Third World. The inherent inequality and devastating impact of this system of trade on people and environments of the global South became ever more apparent to growing numbers of Northern consumers. Equally important, globalization also demonstrated that despite over 30 years (of the ATO model) of fair trade there had been little progress towards the ambitious goal of eradicating poverty through alternative trade networks. Fair trade had to be rethought.

This rethinking took place within and was shaped by neoliberalism. Beginning in the 1980s, some in the movement sought to expand fair trade by pushing it beyond handicrafts and the small retail world of nonprofit shops and catalogs. Handicrafts worked well as educational tools, and because they were visibly distinct from mass-produced items they were easily identifiable and attractive to conscientious consumers. The problem, however, is that the movement could only sell so many colorful rugs, handmade baskets, and intricate tapestries to sympathetic consumers in the United States and Europe. If fair trade was going to extend its reach and help large numbers of producers, it had to expand into everyday products that were produced by Third World communities and bought by First World consumers in large quantities.[16] Or such was the thinking.

It was in this context that European ATOs introduced the idea of certifying and labeling food commodities, beginning in the 1980s. These commodities, once they had been certified and labeled as "fair trade," could be sold in conventional supermarkets and other mainstream outlets. In theory, this labeling/certifying sector of fair trade is committed to the same broad goals as ATO: fostering egalitarian relations between Northern consumers and Southern producers while campaigning to transform conventional trade practices. Yet it pursues them through different institutional forms and with a business-like focus on expanding sales. Whereas "fairness" in the ATO model

comes from the political commitment of Northern advocates and pur-
chasers, the labeling model of fair trade ensures fairness by creating
more precise, standardized, and formalized measurements of what
exactly constitutes fair trade. By substantiating and specifying that a
product is "fair trade," the label assures the consumer that this cup of
coffee benefits the producers in certain ways. The guarantee of fairness comes not from the reputation of the retailer but from the label,
which theoretically allows fair trade products to be sold anywhere by
anyone.[17]

Initially, for example, fair trade coffee in the United States was
sold through progressive roasters, churches, consumer groups, and
ATO retail shops. With labelling/certification, however, NGOs in the
movement were able to push fair trade coffee into more mainstream
venues like university campuses and mainstream retailers. The big
breakthrough came in April 2000 when, after a year-long campaign
spearheaded by Global Exchange, Starbucks agreed to offer certified
coffee in all 2,700 of its cafes in the United States. Other corporations,
from Proctor & Gamble, Sam's Club, and Kraft to Dunkin' Donuts
and McDonald's, subsequently committed to fair trade in some form.
For mainstream corporations, fair trade might simply be one flavor
among many, but because of their size even a tiny percentage of total
sales allowed for a significant increase in overall fair trade sales.[18]

As fair trade has grown through labeling and certification, it has
become ever more embedded in, and subject to the pressures of, the
very market that many within the movement had sought to avoid or
transform from within. The labeling model of fair trade has become
largely focused on promoting its market position, with the idea that
the more fair trade sales there are, the more producers are helped.
How we interpret this development depends on our vision of fair
trade. Is the goal to increase market share, with the idea of bringing
a perhaps compromised, and narrowed, version of fair trade to as
many people as possible? And can this be done without fair trade ultimately being absorbed, or too severely deformed, by the market?
Or is the point to empower workers and/or transform the unequal
nature of trade relations? Or both? What types of change will expand
producers' access to the market, thereby furthering their integration
into the very market that the movement is working against, while at

the same time deepening the movement's core values, empowering producer organizations, improving the economic situation of small producers, and transforming the conventional system of trade? More concretely, what does it mean when Nestlé is granted use of the fair trade seal, or when Starbucks starts to sell fair trade coffee? Is it a sign that fair trade has made it, and is now able to help many more small producers, or does it signal that fair trade has been emptied of all meaningful political content?

In this sense, most debates about alternative trade, or alternative models of development more broadly, tend to revolve around two interrelated sets of questions regarding (a) the depth of the challenge to conventional systems that a particular alternative represents, and (b) the capacity to "scale up" and become something more than a niche. These debates are not unimportant, or unrelated, since the distinction is often between a vision that favors growth at any cost versus one that balances growth with some commitment to core principles (of equality, fairness, smallness, and so on). Indeed, the growth-first version of fair trade that has won the day allowed for large corporations to enter the game and (minimally) expand the reach of a handful of fair trade commodities. It also meant that what came to constitute fair trade neither generated extensive benefits for producers nor challenged the global trade regime.

At the same time, without dismissing the importance of these debates, and the struggles around them, such discussions tend to miss the broader point. The track record for political projects that "challenge" dominant economic systems by trying to create alternatives to (or outside of) those systems is not particularly strong. The fact that a version of fair trade that provides producers with very limited benefits carried the day is not coincidence, but indicative of a broader balance of power that ensures only watered-down alternatives will survive. It is extremely difficult to create alternative space in a larger capitalist system, but it is virtually impossible with something as central to the economy as food, where powerful interests fiercely protect the status quo, and where emerging alternatives have to compete with an already established food system dominated by some of the largest corporations in the world. It is also why efforts to expand necessarily require that the alternative, in order to be successful, has to look more and more like the conventional system it is trying to replace.

It is not simply that alternative systems have to compete with conventional ones, but that they must do so within broader systems of banking, trade, marketing, production, and transportation, which are hostile to alternative logics and are thoroughly supported by state power. The idea that we can (on a relatively large scale) produce, process, market, distribute, and consume a single commodity in a way that is equitable and sustainable within a system in which every other commodity operates around a logic that is profit-driven, hyper competitive, and destructive is problematic. In this sense, it is difficult to change how we "do" coffee, or food more generally, in isolation because it is thoroughly embedded within capitalism.

Market-based alternatives tend to get watered down partly because market-based activism largely avoids what we might typically think of as a left politics—one that attempts to confront and shape state policies and corporate power. In this sense, although it is not insignificant that alternatives such as fair trade get "co-opted" or "captured" by corporations and regulators, or certain whether such co-optation or capturing is in fact inevitable, the broader point is that market-based politics are not designed to bring about meaningful political change in the first place. This is significant given that these problems are, at their core, political—requiring political movements directed at state power.

And yet it is not hard to understand why a politics rooted in the market was so attractive in the 1990s. With large-scale oppositional movements trying to regain footing in both Latin America and the United States, and with neoliberalism decimating governments to the point of undermining a politics rooted in acquiring state power, the turn to market-based politics had a certain logic, or at least appeal. Traditional politics had not delivered much, many of its organizations were decimated or discredited, and the state itself hardly seemed worth the effort.

As a form of solidarity, however, the results of fair trade have not surprisingly been mixed. For the global South, although the benefits to producers have been fairly minimal, fair trade has nonetheless had a positive impact on small groups in particular regions. That it has done little to combat global poverty, or alter the balance of power between the North and the South, simply puts it in a large group.

For the global North, fair trade reinforced the idea—prominent during the period—that social change could be brought about by individual consumers acting alone on the supermarket aisle. If we, as Northern consumers, simply make the right purchases we could both change the world and go about living our lives as we always have. Aside from reinforcing neoliberal notions of the depoliticized consumer, there is little empirical evidence to suggest that this represents a model for meaningful and sustained social change. In the absence of social movements demanding (for example) international agreements that regulate prices, or national governments that enforce laws and regulations, it is hard to see how conscientious consumers in the North, acting alone and paying slightly higher prices for a handful of products, represent a viable path to social justice.

Conclusion

The start of the 1990s was defined by the ongoing decline of the left throughout the Americas, and the intensified implementation of neoliberalism by civilian governments. These two processes were not unrelated. The dismantling of the left in both Latin America and the United States during the 1970s and 1980s allowed the right to impose an increasingly draconian version of neoliberalism, which exposed working people to the vagaries of the market and furthered weakened their political capacity to shape state power and policies. By the start of the 1990s, the left throughout the region had reached a twentieth-century nadir, a process that both allowed for the deepening of neoliberalism and had disastrous consequences for working people throughout the hemisphere.

This also had profound implications for Latin American solidarity. The Central American peace movement had brought unprecedented human, financial, and organizational resources to Latin American solidarity during the 1980s. The end of the civil wars and the decline of US military aid to the region removed Central America from the front pages, and contributed to the decline of the peace movement during the late 1980s and early 1990s. Not only would fewer human and financial resources flow into Latin American solidarity, the central issues that had energized and unified solidarity during the 1980s—US military aid, the civil wars, and human rights abuses—had lost their force by the start of the 1990s.

However, in addition to the alliances, relationships, and organizations built through decades of political work, the decimation wrought by neoliberalism ensured that Latin American solidarity did not disappear. Activists shifted their attention to a host of economic issues and crises associated with neoliberal capitalism. This repackaging of activism never unified Latin American solidarity in quite the same way as did opposition to US military aid and repressive dictatorships. It did not produce an "anti-neoliberal bloc," in part because neoliberal policies produced an endless supply of seemingly disconnected fires that needed to be put out; and in part because in the absence of a broader US left it was difficult to "name" neoliberalism, let alone mobilize around it on larger scales from the United States. This led to the further fragmentation and NGOization of solidarity work, as well as the tendency—borrowed from human rights—for activists to focus on extreme cases that capture media attention (explored more fully in Chapters 7 and 8).

Nevertheless, as we have seen, a current of this more economically inclined solidarity not only targeted the inequalities produced by (and inherent in) the conventional system of global trade, but tried to move this challenge beyond the local in a way that addressed the national and international frameworks governing trade. Prior to the struggle around NAFTA, opposition to the global rules of trade was not part of mainstream public discussion in the United States. The labor movement, along with the left, shifted the debate. After NAFTA, trade was understood by growing numbers of progressives no longer as neutral or inherently positive, but as a system whose rules were deeply political and tended to benefit the wealthy and powerful at the expense of working people. This critique was important, and continued to develop through the Battle for Seattle and the emergence of the global justice movement (see Chapter 7).

And yet the fact that NAFTA was on the table in the first place reflected the weakness of the left. The labor movement was remarkably successful in turning the trade agreement into a fight, but it was not capable of preventing its passage. Nor was it capable of articulating an alternative system of economic integration that would benefit workers in all three countries and resonate with broader publics in a way that mobilized people behind a different vision of the social order. The fixation on trade, and particularly the tendency to pit American workers against their counterparts in other countries, also made it difficult to build international solidarity while ignoring the broader neoliberal assault.

For their part, fair trade advocates tried to create a system of trade whose expansion not only benefited small farmers from around the world, but (in theory) slowly overtook the conventional system of trade. The results have been extremely limited, and the project as a whole has been part of a broader push towards market-based politics that eschew traditional forms of mass mobilization that target state power. As we will see in the next two chapters on Zapatismo, global justice, and corporate campaigns, this shift deepened and in many ways came to define progressive politics during the 1990s and 2000s. What this meant is that although Latin American solidarity centered its attention more firmly on "economic" issues after the decline of the peace movement, and hence addressed a common critique of human rights work, it did so in a way that was not equipped to deal with a more structural set of problems.

7

Zapatistas and Global Justice

The defeat around NAFTA did little to stimulate a broader renewal of the labor movement or the left in the United States. Labor and its allies fought the good fight, but Congress passed NAFTA, and President Clinton signed the trade agreement in December 1993. Its passage was one in a series of defeats for a left that was losing the capacity to influence public policy and debate. These included the elections of Reagan and Bush, the ongoing assault on labor, the civil wars in Central America, the Gulf War, the passage of NAFTA, and so on. There were few bright spots. Indeed, although hardly anyone on the US left supported Soviet-style socialism by the time the wall came down, its demise nonetheless represented something of a blow to the broader socialist project.[1] Likewise, the electoral defeat of the Sandinistas in 1990 was a disheartening milestone for a generation of activists working on Latin America, and furthered the notion that the left was in crisis, lacked focus or direction, and needed to be reconstituted.

Enter the Zapatistas. The uprising by the Ejército Zapatista de Liberación Nacional (EZLN) on January 1, 1994 immediately captured the attention of the left around the world. It was not simply that the rebellion was cleverly scheduled for the first day of NAFTA's implementation, but that the Zapatistas announced their arrival at a time when progressives in the United States, Europe, and Latin America were in need of a hopeful alternative. The Zapatistas filled this void. They were at once familiar and "revolutionary." On the one hand, they were an armed peasantry from the Latin American countryside. This may have seemed a bit dated by 1994, but it could nonetheless be placed neatly within a longer tradition. On the other hand, they were indigenous, openly committed to gender equality, and skillfully used the internet to communicate with a global audience. And despite the weapons, they advocated democratic inclusiveness and fairly quickly dropped references to socialism and armed revolution. The Zapatistas and their black masks also seemingly appeared out of nowhere, offering hope to global leftists. The situation was bleak, but there was now a path forward articulated by indigenous people.

Most importantly, the Zapatistas not only named neoliberalism as the problem, and deftly articulated how a common set of forces, processes, and actors were oppressing people throughout the world, but offered a solution that was at once global and local, rhetorically grand and yet realizable. They promoted an internationalism that was to be constructed from the ground up by relatively autonomous groups working independently against neoliberalism in particular locales. In this respect, the Zapatistas, as well as their political offspring, the Global Justice Movement, elevated the anti-statism which was percolating through progressive circles to new heights. At the level of rhetoric, the Zapatistas offered an anti-neoliberal, anti-imperialist internationalism that presented itself as a global project, and railed convincingly against the neoliberal state. To get to the promised land in practice, however, they embraced and advocated a kind of politics that was not centrally about building national movements aimed at capturing state power.

Zapatistas, in and Beyond Mexico

At first glance, the armed occupation of Chiapas harkened back to a familiar path for pursuing social change. Was it possible that Latin American peasants were still taking up arms and advocating socialism in 1994? Initial interviews with some of the insurgents as well as early communiques from the EZLN itself suggested that the Zapatistas were in fact fighting for socialism, or at least broad social transformation, and believed that their example would either inspire a national uprising or be ignored altogether. Had either of these predictions come to pass it is possible that the rebellion would have been understood as part of a long history of rural uprisings in Latin America, either as a failed effort relegated to the dustbin of history or as a spark that started a wildfire across Mexico. Neither proved true.[2]

The uprising in Chiapas did not ignite a nationwide rebellion. Mexican labor unions, the peasantry, and the left in general were weak, divided, and in no position to follow the Zapatistas into revolution. Yet even if there was little stomach or capacity for a national-level confrontation with the Mexican state or for taking up arms, the Zapatistas—who quickly put down their weapons and dropped any references to socialism—were also not ignored, and came to occupy a moral high ground both in and outside Mexico. In Mexico, this provided the local uprising with some protection from the army, and put the Zapatistas in something of a privileged place with respect to other social movements. The black masks and rudimentary weaponry served to capture national attention, and the Zapatistas' willingness to lay down their arms and begin a dialogue, combined with their indigeneity, democratic inclusiveness, and a powerful critique of the Mexican state, garnered both sympathy and respect. Indigenous peoples in Chiapas had been hit exceptionally hard by neoliberalism, but their experience and struggle was not unique, and therefore resonated more broadly.

And yet the Zapatistas would never lead—or seriously attempt to lead—a broader opposition to neoliberalism in Mexico as a whole. This was for a variety of reasons beyond the scope of this chapter, but was tied at least partly to the Zapatistas' strategy for confronting neoliberalism. On the one hand, the Zapatistas were quite effective in hitching their horse to anti-neoliberalism, and played a crucial role in naming the problem and elevating the anti-neoliberal cause on regional, national, and global levels. On the other hand, the Zapatistas' political strategy was ill-equipped for actually addressing neoliberalism in Mexico (or anywhere else). Although they recognized that neoliberal policies were being implemented by the Mexican state and required a national (even international) response, the Zapatistas seemed impatient, uninterested in, and/or unwilling to make the kinds of compromises necessary for forging the alliances needed to build a national political bloc capable of confronting neoliberalism and the Mexican state.[3]

Instead the Zapatistas ultimately turned inward, focusing on the creation of democratically run liberated spaces in Chiapas that would possess cultural and political autonomy. The Zapatistas talked, often in global terms (and quite compellingly) about broad aspirations such as democracy, freedom, and social justice, but their concrete path in Mexico for achieving these universalist objectives was a relatively local one. Society would be reconstituted one village at a time. The Zapatista answer to a Mexican state that had ignored Chiapas for decades, and intensified the region's isolation under neoliberalism, was to demand near-complete independence from the Mexican government. On some level, such a position was perfectly understandable, even heroic. The Mexican state had never delivered much in the way of useful economic development to Chiapas, let alone basic services such as decent schools, healthcare, and roads.[4] This only worsened under neoliberalism. When President Salinas modified Article 27 of the Mexican constitution in 1992 to essentially end land reform, he also effectively confirmed that the Mexican state had nothing to offer rural people, except perhaps the intensified exploitation of their land or complete dispossession.[5]

Worse yet, in the aftermath of the uprising, the presence of the Mexican government in Chiapas was largely reduced to the military. In such a context, where the Mexican state delivered little but repression, the strategy of creating stateless-autonomous zones free of neoliberalism had some appeal. Why struggle to reform or revolutionize a state that was simultaneously bankrupt and repressive? This was only reinforced by the fact that building a nationwide antineoliberal coalition out of a compromised labor movement, a debilitated peasantry, a decimated left, and a corrupt party system was no easy haul. The national road was by no means clear, even if ultimately it was the only viable path for confronting neoliberalism in both Chiapas and Mexico more broadly. To oppose neoliberalism in any region of Mexico required at the very least a national strategy. The Zapatistas never seriously or consistently pursued one.

This played well with an emerging "global left." The absence of a national strategy mattered little to international activists, most of whom knew little about the nuts and bolts of Mexican politics, and were drawn symbolically and inspirationally to a Zapatista project that was rhetorically grand, strategically simple, and easy to grasp. It was the strategy of creating local, liberated, inclusive democratic spaces that existed outside of neoliberalism (and the messiness of national politics) that made the Zapatistas so popular with the left beyond Mexico. When combined with a commitment to gender equality, the draw of indigeneity, the black ski masks, and skillful use of the internet, it is not surprising that the Zapatista strategy of challenging the existing system by creating an alternative space outside that system was so popular beyond the borders of Mexico. It was the same political space/strategy that many on the global left in the United States and elsewhere were beginning to occupy—precisely because, like the Zapatistas, activists in the United States found themselves in a political context that made conceptualizing and mobilizing a national struggle seem particularly daunting. The Zapatistas would help define and justify an anti-neoliberal struggle that was rooted in the retreat to the local.

In this sense, the fact that the Zapatista uprising proved to be a primarily symbolic one outside of Chiapas was really only problematic in Mexico for social movements that were looking to build a concrete challenge to neoliberalism. The Mexican left was never, or least not for as long, as uncritically infatuated with the Zapatistas as their international counterparts, who were desperately in need of a progressive glimmer of hope and a place to deposit their political aspirations. The Zapatistas filled this void. Internationally, the fact that the Zapatistas occupied a largely symbolic-inspirational space was not a problem, but in fact a virtue for internationalists who were also inclined towards a vague politics of building a new world one space at a time and confronting neoliberalism wherever they happened to be. As the left disappeared from public life, and progressives in the United States had trouble envisioning (let alone building) a national movement with the capacity for shaping public debate and state power, the Zapatista-led turn towards a far more limited politics of local autonomy peppered with a globalized rhetoric proved seductive. Enveloped by the cachet of Third World indigeneity, the Zapatistas affirmed, stimulated, and took this internationalist tendency to the next level.

It was also a politics that was in many ways ideally suited for international solidarity—or least the currents of solidarity that were available at the time. With Central America no longer capturing as much attention, the Zapatistas became the dominant and most dynamic focus of solidarity activism. Thousands of US activists were drawn to the Zapatistas during the 1990s, and typically channeled their efforts in two complementary, though distinct, currents. First, there were "connected" internationalists who were tied quite directly to the Zapatistas, taking their cues from the needs, events, and attacks on communities in Chiapas and the EZLN. This solidarity came in many forms, and to a large extent built on previous efforts in Central America and elsewhere. Internationalists provided protection against military repression through a constant presence in Chiapas, formal human rights investigations, and engaged in education and outreach. They kept the Zapatistas in the spotlight, could mobilize rapidly when a crisis demanded, and thus helped keep repression by the military and paramilitaries in check.[6]

Within this connected current, there was also a large (and loose) network of organizations that provided the Zapatistas and Chiapas with material aid, including shipments of clothing, computers, and medical supplies, physical labor on irrigation and infrastructure projects, the establishment of clinics and schools, and support for international encuentros. This material aid, which might otherwise have been dubbed charity, took on political meaning as it was part of the broader project of creating spaces in Chiapas that were free from neoliberalism and state presence. Indeed, such aid was central to a Zapatista project which was unique in terms of how it envisioned its relationship with the state. Instead of centering its strategy on trying to increase state investment in the poorest province of Mexico, the Zapatistas were essentially demanding that the state withdraw from the region. Schools, healthcare, and other functions normally assumed by government entities would be taken over by the Zapatistas—and in large part funded by international allies—as part of a political project to eradicate neoliberalism from the region.[7]

Granted such a prominent role in the creation of neoliberal-free Chiapas, it is not surprising that relatively few in the international community questioned this as a strategy. Was it fiscally or practically possible for the Zapatistas, backed by international allies, to build and run schools and clinics, and otherwise take on the role of government? Would such a strategy—even if relatively successful—create an "autonomous" zone that was livable and viable in the short or long term? Was such an approach capable of confronting or exorcizing neoliberalism in Chiapas, let alone Mexico as a whole? These sorts of impertinent, even imperious, questions were difficult to raise.

To be sure, there was debate about international solidarity aid, but it focused not on the relationship between that aid and a broader political strategy, but on the extent to which the various parties—the Zapatistas and their northern allies—should have control over the flow, nature, and delivery of assistance. These were no doubt important discussions, eventually revealing that obsolete computers and expired medicines were not particularly helpful to the cause, and leading the Zapatistas (in 2003) to rethink and restructure the how, what, and where of international solidarity aid.[8] A more "mutual" form of solidarity subsequently emerged, giving the Zapatistas more control. But the basic thrust of the larger Zapatista strategy for Chiapas was assumed sound, or at least went largely unquestioned.

Thoughts indicative of this general sentiment, and where it came from, can be found in the words of Marcos himself:

> If the Zapatista communities wanted, they could have the best standard of living in Latin America. Imagine how much the government would be willing to invest in order to secure our surrender .... The Zapatistas have received many offers to buy their consciences, and they keep their resistance nonetheless. Here, now, poverty is a weapon chosen by our peoples for two reasons: in order to bear witness that it is not welfare that we are seeking, and in order to demonstrate, with our own example, that it is possible to govern and to govern ourselves without the parasite that calls itself government .... Whoever helps one or several Zapatista communities is helping not just to improve a collective's material situation ... but is helping a much simpler, but more demanding, project: the building of a new world, one where many worlds fit, one where charity and pity for another are the stuff of science fiction novels, or of a forgettable or expendable past.[9]

It is hard to know how literally to take such statements, though we might suspect that some people who live in the poorest communities in Mexico might trade a bit of ideological purity for a slightly higher standard of living. The powerful refusal to sell out, the anti-modernism, and the anti-development current are undeniable. Here, the efficacy of material aid from internationalists, or development more broadly, is less important than the compelling (if slightly vague) notion of creating "a new world" that is free of the parasitic state.

The second, or "inspired," current of international solidarity surrounding the Zapatistas was much less directly tied to the EZLN or Chiapas. Here, the ties were largely inspirational or symbolic, and involved taking Zapatismo beyond Chiapas in two complementary directions. Both were global in the sense of taking place outside of Mexico, but the first was local in its strategy of confronting neoliberalism one locale at a time, while the second tried to forge a global network. Hundreds of activists visited Chiapas, participated in the international *encuentros*, and then returned home to practice Zapatismo in their own backyards. This activism took many disparate forms and included a wide range of issues, from food and the environment to affordable housing and prison reform. Its diversity makes it hard to determine the broader impact, but suffice it to say that for many young people the experience of Chiapas was life-changing and led down a multiplicity of political paths. They returned from Chiapas committed to confronting neoliberalism in communities across the United States and elsewhere. Beyond even this, the very example of the Zapatistas, and particularly the anti-neoliberal commitment that they articulated and elevated, inspired activists who never even visited Mexico to take action at home.[10]

This inspirational effect has been quite real. Given how the Zapatistas defined their own project, it made sense that people need not work directly with the EZLN or communities in Chiapas to be "in solidarity." This inspired solidarity is hardly without precedent. The United Farm Workers, for example, trained and inspired a generation of activists whose work went well beyond the fields of California— who took the farm worker spirit, analysis, and commitment to political work for decades. As we saw earlier, a similar process occurred around the Cuban revolution in the 1960s. Political work, or even just knowledge of other people's activism, around Chile, Cuba, and Central America stirred activists whose subsequent interventions might not even be related to Latin America.

At the same time, by the mid to late 1990s, the solidarity equation was looking different at both ends. On the Latin America side, the Zapatistas were pursuing a different brand of politics, one that privileged the development of liberated, autonomous zones that were free of neoliberalism and corrupt states. This was not so much about building a national coalition to dismantle neoliberalism, or overthrow the Mexican state, as it revealed resignation that such a project was no longer viable and the only alternative was to turn inwards. National-level movements in Ecuador, Bolivia, Brazil, Venezuela, and elsewhere would soon challenge this brand, but at the time the Zapatistas were not alone in the local turn.

On the US side, the local-inward nature of the project was not only a virtue, but a strategy that reinforced and reaffirmed an ascendant form of NGO politics that was grounded in the proliferation of small, poorly resourced organizations and affinity groups that were operating largely independently and in isolation from one another. What did fighting neoliberalism "wherever you are" really mean? What constituted an autonomous zone? How did "liberated" spaces present a challenge to neoliberalism? And how would they ever amount to something larger, let alone overturn class power? This organizational infrastructure, nurtured by the human rights movement, characteristic of the Central American peace movement, and generally widespread in progressive activism more generally, went hand-in-hand with the local turn, and away from a broader politics that sought to shape state power and policies on a national level. It was something of a perfect storm.

The second current of "inspired" Zapatismo departed Mexico in a global sense, helping start what came to be known first as the antiglobalization movement and subsequently the Global Justice Movement. To a certain extent, it responded to the limitations of the local turn by attempting to provide—in a loose, inclusive, and decentered way—a network for challenging neoliberalism on a global level. It is to that "movement" that we now turn.

The Global Justice Movement, or A Movement of Movements

Although all large-scale movements contain diverse political ideologies and tendencies within the larger whole, the Global Justice Movement celebrated and embraced internal differentiation. It was, after all, the "movement of movements." "It" included coalitions, networks, groups, and organizations that worked from a wide range of political perspectives. Different actors held quite distinct ideas about what strategies and tactics to utilize, with some advocating for forms of direct action or large-scale marches, while others stressed the importance of localized initiatives and legislative activities. Organizations themselves came in all shapes and sizes, ranging from large labor unions and movement-oriented NGOs to small affinity groups and human rights institutions.[11]

More than this, although the movement was loosely held together by a broadly shared opposition to neoliberalism, not only did understandings of neoliberalism vary considerably, but such opposition was pursued through an almost endless array of issues. Groups challenged neoliberalism by working on the environment, workers' rights, debt, global trade, health, housing, food sovereignty, and a whole host of other local, national, and international concerns. Indeed, even when the movement of movements came together, most conspicuously through the networking encounters known as World Social Forums, the Global Justice Movement explicitly rejected many of the ideas and practices that are often associated with promoting movement coherence—such as spokespeople, manifestos, a unifying political line, and an overarching organizational infrastructure. As a movement, it was always quite hard to pin down, a feature that proved both a strength and limitation.

Nevertheless, although internal differentiation has led observers to locate the origins of the Global Justice Movement in a multiplicity of political currents, most commentators point to the Zapatistas as the most immediate and prominent precursor to the broader movement. With good messaging, media savvy, and a compelling cause, the Zapatistas were able to both name the problem (neoliberalism) and posit a sufficiently broad (some might say vague) solution that activists around the world could connect with, get behind, and even practice in their own backyards. The Zapatistas provided hope at a moment when history, or at least the left, seemed to be coming to an end. They rejected much of what was perceived as stale and outdated with the old left, retained a healthy suspicion of NGOs, embraced cultural autonomy and diversity, and offered a local-global political project that seemed both radical and realizable.[12]

It also did not hurt, especially from the perspective of attracting international supporters, that the Zapatistas were not only indigenous, but seemingly appeared out of nowhere. This dropped-from-the-sky quality contributed to the notion that significant change, or at least global media attention and the sensation of revolution, could not only be achieved relatively quickly, but accomplished in the absence of a broader movement. This model fit nicely into a US context where the left had all but disappeared and the challenge of building a large-scale movement seemed insurmountable. It was a political formula made of and for this particular moment, one that idealized the local as a site of activism while nonetheless retaining global aspirations and visibility through World Social Forums and high-profile protests at the meetings of global financial institutions such as the WTO.[13]

The immediate origins of what came to be the Global Justice Movement can be located in the Zapatistas' own global turn, which combined with the flow of international activists from around the world into Chiapas, led to the First International Encuentro for Humanity and Against Neoliberalism in 1996. The Encuentro, which was followed up by another one in Spain about a year later, welcomed around 5,000 people from 40 different countries, and provided an important building block for the Global Justice Movement. These international gatherings helped establish and/or solidify over 100 Zapatista solidarity groups throughout the United States and Europe, some of which would work directly with communities in Chiapas while others would focus on a range of political initiatives outside Mexico. The Encuentros also led directly to the formation of Peoples Global Action in February 1998, a loose coalition established in large part to facilitate communication and coordination between the variety of social movements, grassroots campaigns, direct action networks, and other groups that fell under the broad umbrella of what at the time was understood as the emerging anti-globalization movement.[14]

It was not, however, until November 1999, when some 20,000 protestors disrupted the WTO meetings in Seattle, that the global justice movement really arrived on the public radar. Although "it didn't start in Seattle," the protests were nonetheless a defining moment. The fact that the meetings of a relatively unknown global financial institution could be the source of fairly militant protests in the United States caught most observers by surprise. This was especially true in the global North, where the Seattle protests reignited discussions about trade and globalization that had emerged around NAFTA, deepened the debate to include more critical dialog about development and North–South relations, and fueled the hope that a global justice movement would not only emerge, but serve to forge a broad-based coalition that included labor unions, environmentalists, students, people of color, seniors, immigrants, anarchists, and so on.[15]

The hope that a large-scale movement would subsequently burst onto the scene was based at least in part on the visible presence in Seattle of both organized labor and a highly differentiated (and embryonic) Global Justice Movement. Seeing steelworkers, Teamsters, autoworkers, and Wobblies alongside environmental organizations like the Sierra Club, Greenpeace, and the Rainforest Action Network, as well as social justice groups such as Global Exchange and Public Citizen, and umbrella organizations like the Direct Action Network, created considerable optimism. The spontaneous decision by more radical sectors in the labor movement to break from the AFL-CIO's planned rally and join global justice activists only fueled the hope that shared concerns about globalization and trade would provide the basis for a labor-left alliance. As it turned out, the potential place of labor in the broader Global Justice Movement was never sufficiently fostered, let alone realized, and largely disappeared after 2001 when global justice activists shifted to an antiwar politics, with organized labor predictably distancing itself from any opposition to US imperialism.[16]

Nevertheless, although US labor largely stood on the sidelines, the Global Justice Movement took off after 1999. Protest after protest followed the summits, talks, and meetings of global institutions such as the International Monetary Fund (IMF), European Union (EU), World Bank, G8, and World Economic Forum. Likewise, the World Social Forums not only began to take place on an annual basis in different locations around the world, but were on an upward trajectory in the early 2000s, with some 150,000 activists attending the gathering in Porto Alegre, Brazil in 2005. This upsurge clearly generated a broader and more critical awareness and discussion about globalization and trade, served to connect activists from around the world, and opened debate within a number of the global financial institutions.[17]

At the same time, the movement's own limitations were apparent early on. Targeting institutions such as the WTO and the IMF was clever, and helped reveal the dark side of globalization, while highlighting the role played by particular actors in creating a global economy that was deeply unfair and inequitable. The protests opened up public debate to a more critical understanding of globalization. Yet not only did they eventually lose their novelty, in part because global elites became better at insulating international meetings from external disruptions, it also became clear that the protests themselves were not producing dramatic policy shifts or changes to the global economy.

Likewise, the hope that the World Social Forums would build and coordinate something resembling a movement—which the protests on their own could not do—never really materialized. Although the World Social Forums served to bring activists together and raised the profile of the Global Justice Movement on an international level, the novelty wore off as it became clear that gathering thousands of activists in what essentially was a progressive conference was not leading to the development of a movement that had the capacity to shape political power. Unfortunately, although the limits of protests and meetings became apparent, this recognition did not necessarily lead to a rethinking of how broad-based anti-capitalist projects might be better advanced. Rather, it seemed to further the retreat to a local or issue-based activism that was largely disconnected from larger-scale organizing.

The arrival of the Iraq war disrupted this process, as activists shifted to antiwar activism between 2001 and 2003, simultaneously energizing, unifying, and distracting the movement as a whole. Opposition to US-led aggression gave the movement a compelling alternative focus at a time when it was becoming clear that the broader project could not be sustained by WTO-type protests. At the same time, not only did the transition to antiwar activism undermine the potential alliance with organized labor, in moving away from global financial institutions the shift served to erode perhaps the one issue that provided the movement with some coherence—namely, opposition to a rigged system of globalization and trade. As a result, the ever-present tendency in the movement to pursue a seemingly endless number of targets and causes only deepened. Some people in the movement recognized this as early as the start of the 2000s. As one activist noted, "It's hard to say if there is a global justice movement right now and what it's doing. I know there are a lot of committed activists doing great work, but I'm not sure how or if it all fits together."[18]

The meteoric rise, short-lived climax, and sneaky quick disappearance of the Global Justice Movement all happened so swiftly that it is hard to say precisely when its moment passed. If 9/11 was the beginning of the end, the movement as a whole was certainly over by the 2008 recession.[19] On the international level, neither the World Social Forums nor the WTO-like protests proved capable of significantly changing the policies of the G8, WTO, or other such institutions, let alone stopping the Iraq war or transforming the global economy. On the local level, movement activists were engaged in all sorts of worthy causes, but it was unclear what it all amounted to, or whether all these seemingly independent efforts were connected in any meaningful way. The Zapatista-inspired strategy of confronting neoliberalism wherever you are, often understood in terms of building semi-autonomous spaces, when combined with a global approach rooted in high-profile meetings and protests, was simply not up to the task.

More than that, at roughly the same time as the Global Justice Movement was coming into its own, the left in Latin America experienced a resurgence as social movements in the region cohered against neoliberalism. The revival of the Latin American left was tied to similar (neoliberal) forces to those that gave birth to the Global Justice Movement, and at times the two movements even overlapped. Chavez, for example, attended the World Social Forum in Porto Alegre in 2005.

Yet, as surprising as the rise of the 'new' left in Latin America was during the late 1990s and 2000s, it was nonetheless rooted in an older political model that had been deemed outdated by many in global justice circles. The resurgence was grounded in country-specific movements that sought to develop national-level capacity to not only disrupt business as usual, but shape or capture state power both outside of, and through, electoral processes. By building social movements linked to political parties that sought public office, the left in Latin America re-elevated a strategic path that had fallen out of favor in many progressive circles, and accomplished what the Global Justice Movement had been unable to do—challenge neoliberalism in a meaningful way.

Despite the relative success of the Latin American left, its influence on internationalists or international solidarity in the United States has been limited. This was not entirely surprising given that what had emerged in the United States over the past several decades was a left that was not overly concerned with establishing strategic paths for building effective political movements that could capture state power or develop a meaningful/radical alternative to neoliberal capitalism. The fact that by the late 1990s the Latin American left was confronting these very issues head-on was at times noticed, but less with the idea of extracting any useful lessons than to point out the imperfect compromises inevitably associated with coalition building and electoral politics—that is, with developing a left capable of wielding power and constructing alternatives. Many US progressives had simply moved away from a politics rooted in political parties and acquiring state power, which—along with the fact that the US left had very little to offer—helps explain why there was relatively little solidarity with the powerful social movements that were emerging in places like Venezuela, Bolivia, and Ecuador during this period.

Conclusion

The Zapatistas emerged at a moment when the left, and particularly socialism, appeared to be dead, and neoliberalism was being imposed as the only alternative available. By offering something that was both new and old, fresh and familiar, the Zapatistas captured the attention of (and helped produce) a global left. The Zapatistas not only generated immense hope and enthusiasm among a young generation of progressives, but in so doing brought a critique of neoliberalism and globalization to wider audiences in and beyond Latin America. This energy, in turn, helped stimulate not only the Global Justice Movement, but a culture of activism among a younger generation of progressives who increasingly shared a broadly similar background characterized by a familiarity with certain political writings, an association with particular causes, a decently developed critique of the global economy, and an affinity for counter-cultural currents that often fetishized the local and were understood as providing some autonomy from neoliberalism capitalism.

The next chapter explores more concrete attempts to challenge corporate power through international labor solidarity. What we find in this semi-distinct current of solidarity is not only a similar lack of concern with building large-scale working-class power aimed at shaping state institutions and policies, but the inability of targeted instances of solidarity to enjoy much success in the absence of broader social movements. Put more concretely, what Chapter 8 suggests is that it is difficult to challenge a particular company or support a specific group of workers over a sustained period of time if the broader balance of power is so deeply skewed against working people. Sustained success on the local level is difficult in a broader sea of intense political and economic inequality.

8

Corporate Campaigns and
Sweatshop Activism

Latin American solidarity during the Cold War tended to closely shadow US intervention. Activism emerged around the Dominican Republic and Brazil in the 1960s following US interventions, gathered steam during the 1970s in response to US support for South American dictatorships, and reached its apogee during the 1980s when Ronald Reagan's aggressive backing of military regimes in Central America drew tens of thousands of people into the peace movement. Regardless of whether US activists were engaged in socialist, anti-imperialist, peace, or human rights solidarity, or whether they were working with armed revolutionaries, clergy, or political parties in Latin America, the horrific consequences of US foreign policy played a major role in stimulating and shaping solidarity in the United States during this period.

Once the Cold War ended, civilian rule returned to Latin America, and US military involvement became less conspicuous, Latin American solidarity became difficult to sustain at levels achieved during the Central American peace movement. The departure of dictatorships in South America, the cessation of war in Central America, and the broader end of the Cold War meant that the human rights crisis was "over," and the urgency that had once compelled solidarity had been removed. It also meant that US culpability was much less direct or apparent as US involvement in the region became defined less by military aid and more by the soft power of a Washington Consensus that imposed neoliberal policies through civilian regimes in Latin America. With US military aid no longer fueling repressive dictatorships or civil war, places like El Salvador, Guatemala, and Nicaragua fell off the front pages and many progressives were drawn to other issues.

Regardless of the ebbs and flows of progressive political energy, however, a solidarity infrastructure complete with organizations, institutions, relationships, strategies, and tactics had been established. Consequently, as the economic situation deteriorated in the region, and became intertwined with widespread violence under democratic rule, US-based solidarity activists were ready, turning their attention more directly to a range of economic issues associated with the onslaught of neoliberalism in Latin America. Such solidarity did not cohere organizationally or ideologically into an anti-neoliberal bloc, but tended instead to flow—some might say fragment—into a multiplicity of crises and causes connected to the consequences and symptoms of neoliberalism.

The two previous chapters focused on solidarity related to trade and globalization, in part because these efforts were among the most prominent of the neoliberal period, but also because as forms of internationalism they attempted to move beyond the local and challenge political-economic structures at national and global levels. Opposition to trade deals, including NAFTA, the Central America Free Trade Agreement (CAFTA),[1] the Free Trade Area of the Americas (FTAA), and most recently the United States-Colombia Trade Promotion Agreement (CTPA), reflected defensive efforts to slow down the neoliberal steamroller in the Americas. Changing the terms of trade between entire nations would in theory improve living conditions for millions. Unfortunately, few of the agreements were actually defeated, and the struggles themselves did little to slow down free trade or make the international terms of trade more equitable, even if they did raise awareness about the impact of global trade on working people.[2]

For its part, the fair trade movement came at the issue of global trade from the opposite end. Instead of directly confronting the conventional terms of trade, fair trade advocates sought to create an alternative system that would address global inequality. Despite international aspirations, however, the actual benefits of fair trade have remained local and limited. Likewise, Zapatismo, followed by the rise of the Global Justice Movement, spurred a global activism that targeted not just a particular trade agreement such as NAFTA, or even the terms of trade more broadly, but neoliberalism as a whole. And yet attempts by the movement to cohere on larger levels through World Social Forums and protests at international meetings have proved limited and ultimately unsustainable.

This chapter shifts the discussion to a political current that has targeted the (bad) practices of particular corporations or industries. As with activism around fair trade, free trade, or global justice, there is a long tradition in international solidarity that attempts to hold American corporations accountable for their sins in Latin America. These anti-imperialist efforts have generally worked to educate the US public about American imperialism through a discussion of corporate malfeasance, often with the intention of shaming US corporations in order to get them to change their practices.

This tradition dates back to the early years of US corporate presence in Latin America. Charles Kepner and Jay Soothill's muckraking accounts of the United Fruit Company, which exposed US corporate practices to an American audience during the 1930s, can be seen as part of this broad legacy.[3] It was not really until the Cold War, however, that efforts to expose corporate behavior sought not only to educate people in the United States, but to cultivate enough public pressure that a US corporation would be "shamed" into changing its practices. Such solidarity was, of course, closely connected to efforts—particularly in human right circles—to "name and shame" Latin American governments that abused their citizens, while also foregrounding the role of the US government in funding these regimes.

As an evolving strategy, such campaigns eventually came to rely on, and have been the vehicles for creating, alliances between labor unions, faith-based groups, community organizations, and progressive activists. Such innovation, although indicative of the creativity of the progressive community, also reflects the fact that these campaigns tend to emerge in contexts where labor and the left are particularly weak—where, for example, labor unions are incapable of stopping corporate abuse by themselves and are forced to turn to international actors to pressure companies and/or governments to behave better or enforce regulations.

US Origins of the Corporate Campaign

The two most prominent corporate-related campaigns of the period, and the ones that in many ways fixed the broader strategy within the progressive canon, came from the United Farm Workers (UFW) and the anti-apartheid movement. The UFW put the corporate campaign, complete with a range of evolving tactics, on the progressive map. It raised public awareness about the plight of farm workers and built a movement that, although rooted in a labor union, drew heavily on consumer, religious, and community support to target particular corporations. Many of the tactics developed and popularized by the UFW, including church–labor–community alliances, the effective use of moral and spiritual claims alongside a discourse of labor rights, the farm worker style of political mobilization, and above all the consumer boycott, entered the repertoires of subsequent generations of solidarity activists.[4] Likewise, the anti-apartheid campaign was central to extending and developing the model in the realm of international solidarity. By the mid-1970s, churches were working with labor activists, both in and outside of labor unions, to pressure banks and major corporations to divest from South Africa.[5]

In important respects, however, both anti-apartheid and the farm workers differed from subsequent efforts in this tradition that emerged during the 1980s and 1990s under neoliberalism. Most importantly, the farm workers and anti-apartheid were less campaigns than movements. They were tied to, indelibly wrapped up in, and sought to build movements that had mass rank-and-file support rooted in working-class organizations such as labor unions and political parties. A range of progressive allies would help propel boycotts and pressure corporations, but they did so as part of larger movements in which significant numbers of working people were the central protagonists. Subsequent campaigns in this tradition would not only be much smaller, but de-emphasize or bypass "the base" altogether, often seeing workers as one "stakeholder" among many within broader campaigns that were increasingly run by professionals. Workers would be mobilized to give testimony or appear before the media, but the campaigns were not rooted in, nor did they seek to develop, large-scale working-class organizations with the capacity to force change on their own. Rather, they assumed the absence of such organization.

This tendency could be seen even in relatively early corporate campaigns, though it would not become fully normalized until the 1980s and 1990s. In the United States, campaigns against Farah Manufacturing and J. P. Stevens, and internationally with Nestlé, served to promote the tactic in solidarity circles by providing a model that could be carried out by a handful of groups with substantial, though not extensive, resources. The 1972–73 campaign against Farah Manufacturing, for example, targeted a company that refused to recognize a labor union at its 9,000-worker facility in El Paso. The campaign brought together the ACWU (Clothing Workers Union), the National Council of Churches (NCC), and the Interfaith Center on Corporate Responsibility (ICCR).[6] The NCC, representing more than half of Protestant churches in the United States, pioneered the tactic of using its equity in publicly held companies to pressure corporations as early as 1963. Taking a cue from the UFW, the ACWU called for a consumer boycott of Farah products, and worked with the NCC on a corporate campaign that included pickets at Farah outlets in New York, Cleveland, and other highly visible sites.[7]

The ACWU also brought in Ray Rogers, who would be central to what in many ways was the first full-scale corporate campaign, the all-out assault on the J. P. Stevens Corporation, a giant textile company located in the US South. The late 1970s struggle with Stevens would achieve an iconic status in labor circles, lead to the production of the film *Norma Rae*, and become the subject of numerous books and articles. Rogers, along with many others, including North American Congress on Latin America (NACLA) co-founder Michael Locker, would bring the machinery of political campaigns and the ideas and styles of Saul Alinsky and the New Left into the labor movement while inventing the "corporate campaign." These were professionally run affairs, whereby experts such as Rogers went to great lengths to identify and leverage the weaknesses of particular companies, their board members, and their allies. A range of tactics, from filing unfair labor practices with the National Labor Relations Board (NLRB), an AFL-CIO-led consumer boycott, a labor strike, and the use of proxy challenges at annual corporate meetings (filed by church organizations affiliated with the ICCR), eventually got J. P. Stevens to recognize the union. It was a significant victory which secured the strategy's place in the labor movement and the solidarity left.

However, although the campaign was successful in an immediate sense, the victory came at considerable cost. More than $13 million was spent on the struggle, and union membership in the newly merged Amalgamated Clothing and Textile Workers Union (ACTWU) actually dropped by nearly 20 percent during the height of the campaign in the late 1970s. As Jarol Mannheim notes, although the verdict was still out on whether such campaigns could build long-term union strength, this did not deter Rogers, who quickly formed the consulting firm Corporate Campaign, Inc., and would be hired by numerous unions to target the likes of Hormel, Campbell's Soups, and Texaco.[8] Rogers described this project in quite clear terms:

> Corporate Campaign is set up as a team of professional trouble-shooters. We're experts in all facets of political and community organization, communications, public relations, research, analysis, strategy development. We maintain a database of more than 700,000 organizations, including every labor union, religious, civil rights, and other groups sympathetic to labor and progressive causes.[9]

The challenge with such a project is not so much that these tactics do not have a place within the labor movement, but that the high-profile nature of such campaigns led many to the conclusion that this was the path forward for building working-class power, when in fact it was more a reflection of how far the labor movement and the left had fallen. The broader turn to the campaign as a path forward only deepened as the labor movement got weaker during the 1980s and sought solutions from all corners. More than this, although early campaigns such as Farah and J. P. Stevens never aspired to spark broader movements, they were nonetheless connected to—and concerned with strengthening—labor unions. As this tradition evolved through the neoliberal era, and especially as it translated into international solidarity, where human rights outshone labor solidarity as the dominant current of internationalism, the corporate campaign became increasingly disconnected from the practice and goal of advancing working-class power through mass-based institutions and organizations.

Anti-Corporate Activism in Cold War Latin America

As we have seen, US support for repressive dictatorships in Latin America, and the human rights abuses and civil wars that followed, attracted considerable political interest from progressives. Not surprisingly, some of this attention focused specifically on US corporate involvement in the region. Although anti-corporate activism remained a minority strand in the broader current of Latin American solidarity during the 1970s, academics, the progressive media, and others consistently shone a spotlight on US companies operating in the region.

The NACLA *Report on the Americas*, which began to be published in 1967, focused attention on the impact of US multinationals such as United Fruit in Guatemala and ITT in Chile.[10] Likewise, in 1973, Eduardo Galeano published his widely read *Open Veins of Latin America*, which called for international attention to the role of corporations in Latin America. Similarly, the *Multinational Monitor*, which began publishing in 1978, announced the need to disseminate information for those seeking to "curb corporate excesses and injustice." And these are just a few examples. As the Cold War heated up, and US companies were either involved in or benefitted from military repression, activists intensified the effort to highlight the often nefarious role of US corporations in Latin America.

It was with Chile, however, where Allende's 1970 election captured the attention of the international left, that the effort to expose corporate excess was perhaps most intimately tied to an emerging project of solidarity. In March 1972, columnist Jack Anderson published company documents demonstrating how ITT had made overtures to the CIA in order to help prevent Allende's election, undermine Chile's economy, and if necessary bring about "an internal political crisis requiring military intervention."[11] NACLA's April 1972 issue reprinted the documents, and in December, Allende accused ITT before the United Nations, asserting that the company "has driven its tentacles deep into my country. I accuse the ITT of attempting to bring about civil war."[12] Nascent Chile solidarity groups picked up the banner, though mostly after the 1973 coup when human rights concerns elevated Chile and the human rights movement to new heights (see Chapter 4). Nevertheless, sectors of the left kept the issue of corporate influence alive,[13] with "Church people" harassing "ITT's annual meetings for years, picketing in the hundreds and using their pension-fund holdings" to raise impertinent questions at corporate gatherings.[14]

It was not until the late 1970s and early 1980s, however, with the Guatemala Coke campaign, that the various components of what became anti-corporate labor solidarity in the 1990s and 2000s really came together in relation to Latin America, including the fusion of anti-corporate activism and labor solidarity, the all-important alliance between the left and sectors of organized labor, and the attempt to use consumer power to enhance international labor solidarity. In many ways, the Coke campaign resembled the UFW and J. P. Stevens campaigns in that it answered the call of a beleaguered labor union, and used consumer and shareholder activism to pressure an individual company to recognize union demands.

The conflict itself started simply enough. In 1975, Coca-Cola workers in Guatemala began a union organizing drive in response to persistent problems with managers at the bottling plant where they worked. Although they followed the legal procedures for forming a union, the local franchise's president, John Trotter, a lawyer from Houston, locked the workers out of the plant with the help of friends in the Guatemala military. The workers subsequently engaged in a hunger strike which generated repression, followed by public sympathy and support, and eventually the formation of a national labor confederation. Within two weeks, the Guatemalan government, including the president, intervened, got the bottling plant to rehire the illegally fired workers, and affirmed the workers' right to organize.[15]

Trotter then initiated a reign of terror defined by the constant harassment, false imprisonment, kidnapping, rape, and even murder of union leaders and their allies. The next four years, from 1976 until 1980, were characterized by an all-out assault against the union by Trotter and the bottling company, in uneasy alliance with sectors of the Guatemalan state and Coke-Atlanta. As it became clear that Trotter would not be stopped by either legal rulings or union/ popular pressure, and that his allies within the Guatemalan military and police were willing to intimidate and repress workers almost endlessly, the labor union began to look for international allies to level the playing field. It was church and human rights organizations that first stepped up.[16]

The first such ally was the Interfaith Center on Corporate Responsibility (ICCR), whose experience with South Africa, Farah, and J. P. Stevens had given it a strong background in shareholder resolutions and other methods of exerting economic pressure through the public shaming of companies. One of its members, the Sisters of Providence, in conjunction with Reverend Chuck Dahm (a former missionary to Latin America), contacted Coca-Cola headquarters in Atlanta upon hearing about the workers' plight. Coca-Cola's response—one that was repeated *ad nauseam* for the next decade—was that there was nothing in the contract between Coke-Atlanta and the bottling company in Guatemala that allowed Coke-Atlanta to intervene in a labor dispute between the bottling company and its workers.[17]

Receiving no reply from the bottling plant, the Sisters of Providence filed a shareholder resolution that demanded a full investigation of the Coke affiliate, ranging from alleged violence and human rights violations to low wages and financial improprieties. Tying the resolution to a set of moral and ethical concerns was still relatively new (especially for corporate executives), but the Sisters' argument was bolstered by the fact that social-moral concerns about apartheid in South Africa were having quite direct economic impacts on multinational corporations.[18]

By early 1978, the combination of the union's unrelenting struggle, Coke-Atlanta's pressure, and the impending visit by church shareholders, forced Trotter to come to an agreement that included better wages, working conditions, and ended the violence. Fearing that the bottling plant might close altogether, the unionists pushed Coke-Atlanta not to cut ties with Trotter (who preferred to close the plant than have a union), but to demand he make significant changes. Unfortunately, the union victory came at a moment when Guatemala was becoming more polarized as an increasingly organized left saw normal avenues for political participation cut off by an oligarchy that viewed any form of popular organization as a threat to their power and privilege. By late 1978, only months after the contract was signed, sectors in the Guatemalan military and oligarchy decided that the union must be destroyed.[19]

Guatemalans in exile started to push their cause, and the ICCR and workers found more international allies. Dan Gallin, general secretary of the International Union of Food and Allied Workers (IUF) went on an Amnesty International delegation, and this led to the union's deeper involvement.[20] However, international religious, human rights, and labor organizations would carry out a year-long global campaign. The pressure on the union only intensified in Guatemala. With repression at an all-time high and membership dropping dramatically, international allies decided to carry out a boycott—consumer, producer, and tourist—that eventually reached some 40 countries.[21]

By the mid-1980s, Coke-Atlanta had seen enough, and negotiated the sale of the bottling plant to a new set of owners who, although they accepted the union and rid the plant of violence, also ran the company into the ground, selling off assets, bankrupting the enterprise, closing the plant, and skipping town.[22] After a long struggle, the plant was eventually reopened with new owners, saving most of the jobs and guaranteeing the existence of the union.[23]

The Guatemalan Coke campaign is a remarkable and pioneering case of international solidarity in terms of the actors and resources that mobilized against a large multinational corporation and one of the most repressive governments in the world. International solidarity helped to diminish the level of repression and created a political opening for Guatemalan workers. This was not an easy task. International solidarity was sought and given in the first place because Coke workers in Guatemala, and the Guatemalan labor movement more broadly, were unable to shape corporate or state power sufficiently to protect even basic workers' rights. In this context, the campaign had necessarily limited goals—of keeping a small group of workers alive and creating space for them to organize—that were not designed to build a broader labor movement or turn the tide in Guatemala.

This speaks to the broader challenge faced by international campaigns that target a particular company in support of a specific group of workers. The Coke bottling company could get away with murder in the first place because the wider political context, characterized by a decimated labor movement, a repressive state, and a stacked political-legal system, was tilted so far in favor of corporate power and the Guatemalan oligarchy. This meant that a campaign focusing on one company had a slim chance of successfully helping even a single group of workers, and virtually no chance of altering the broader balance of forces. Sustaining a high-profile international campaign that serves to protect a small group of workers is extremely difficult in a context where domestic allies are exceptionally weak and opponents operate with near impunity. Following human rights solidarity, anti-corporate labor solidarity often flows to workers in the direst possible circumstances. It is sought and extended in truly desperate contexts, where the need is great, but where the possibilities for building lasting working-class power can be also quite limited.

In this particular case, there was no reason to think the Coke campaign would lead to a broader movement, or reshape the political situation in Guatemala in ways that might allow for something larger to emerge. It was not designed to, nor was this goal something international solidarity could possibly deliver. At the same time, there was no doubt a sense among international allies that something had to be done given the severity of the situation, and that this was the best solidarity had to offer at the time. As we will see, this sentiment has continued to drive anti-corporate labor solidarity as it became a central current of international solidarity in the neoliberal age of *maquiladoras* (foreign-owned exporters) and sweatshops.

Anti-Sweatshop Labor Solidarity in Central America

As the wars subsided in Central America, foreign corporations looking to extend the *maquiladora* model onto new terrain were attracted to a region where most of the left had been destroyed, labor unions had been decimated, neoliberalism had been firmly embraced by elites, and cheap labor was abundant. Consequently, the *maquila* sector rapidly expanded, and along with it the violation of workers' rights. This in turn led many of the same solidarity activists who had worked with Central Americans during the 1980s to return to the region to support workers' struggles. Solidarity that focused on human rights, US military aid, and promoting peace transitioned unevenly to free trade, US corporations, and workers' rights.

In Guatemala, there were only six *maquilas* in the country in 1984 when the workers at the Coke union were attempting to negotiate a contract. By 1992 there were 250, and over 700 about a decade later. Responding to this rapid transformation, and hoping to build on the solidarity of the Coke campaign, US activists, Guatemalan exiles, and members of the ACTWU created the U.S./Guatemala Labor Education Project (U.S./GLEP) in 1987, the first US-based NGO to explicitly support workers' struggles in Central American *maquiladoras*. The assumption behind U.S./GLEP's formation was that the situation in Guatemala was so dire, so violent, and so stacked against labor that it was impossible for Guatemalan workers to organize, improve wages or working conditions, or make gains of any kind without international solidarity.[24]

One of U.S./GLEP's most high profile cases—which preceded the student-centered anti-sweatshop movement of the late 1990s—involved an attempt by workers at a Philips Van-Heusen (PVH) plant in Guatemala to organize a union between 1991 and 1993. After establishing the union, workers asked the plant to enter into contract negotiations, which led the company's legal representative to tear up the worker's petition. In conjunction with U.S./GLEP, the workers and their allies then put pressure on the company in both Guatemala and the United States in order to bring the company to the negotiating table. The company refused, hired armed guards to monitor and intimidate the workers, and then argued—and the Guatemalan Ministry of Labor agreed—that the workers had not followed the necessary legal requirements to begin collective bargaining. U.S./GLEP then took the campaign to US textile unions and organized protests at PVH outlets across the United States. The International Labor Rights Fund, the International Ladies Garment Workers Union, the ACTWU, as well as other unions and solidarity organizations, became involved, at one point filing a labor rights petition asking the US trade representative to review Guatemala's trading privileges. The threat of losing its trading privileges with the United States forced the Guatemala government to recognize the first *maquila* union in over six years.[25]

By the time the four-year struggle to have the union officially recognized was over, however, the union itself was significantly weakened, and therefore had to go through another round of organizing in order to once again show that it had sufficient members to petition for collective bargaining. This required a renewed series of battles with the company, the Guatemalan state, and even the US embassy—all of whom stood on the side of PVH and the *maquila* industry. When U.S./GLEP learned that the chief executive of PVH was on the board of directors of Human Rights Watch, the organization planned a demonstration at a fundraising event involving the president. Sensing the potential for embarrassment, PVH agreed to have Human Rights Watch investigate the plant and the workers' claims, including whether the union now had enough members to allow for collective bargaining. After the Human Rights Watch report came out, and the company was sufficiently worried about its image, PVH entered contract negotiations, and three months later the Guatemalan workers ratified the only contract in the entire Guatemalan *maquila* industry.[26]

A single contract, though, could not address the structural inequalities that had led to the proliferation of Central American sweatshops. In the end, it could not even deliver lasting improvements to a single group of workers. Fifteen months after the contract was signed PVH closed down its unionized factory. This unexpected move left over 500 workers unemployed just two weeks before Christmas. PVH claimed that this decision was not a "union-busting" measure, but because the loss of an "important client" had left the company no other choice.[27]

An unprecedented victory had turned into a crushing defeat, and the Guatemalan *maquila* industry was once again union free.[28] The corporate tactic of granting (what appear to be) concessions in order to pacify and demobilize opponents, and then implementing a larger plan that negates the concessions and destroys unions, was used to great effect throughout the 1990s. As others have noted, globalization has weakened the potential power of the strike because it has made it easier for corporations to close plants which, in turn, makes the threat of plant closure all the more effective in squashing strikes.

International solidarity was one way that workers and unions sought to strengthen their hand.

The PVH campaign suggests, however, that not only is it difficult to sustain international solidarity over a long period of time, but an approach that targets one factory at a time has its limitations. For one thing, it is difficult to protect (let alone empower) even a small group of workers over a sustained period of time when the broader political environment is stacked so heavily against working people—when fundamental rights are routinely ignored, opponents operate with impunity, violence reigns, and popular organizations are exceptionally weak. Second, not only is it difficult for such campaigns to protect a particular set of workers, but they are often not equipped or designed to advance an effective labor movement with the capacity to shape political and economic power.

The Salvadoran Origins of the Anti-Sweatshop Movement

Many US activists working in solidarity with Salvadorans during the 1980s also made the shift to anti-corporate activism during the 1990s. The National Labor Committee (NLC) was formed by ten AFL-CIO federation presidents in 1981 with a fairly focused purpose: to challenge official AFL-CIO policy on El Salvador by influencing members of the Executive Council. In 1983 the NLC, with the help of NACLA staffers, made contacts with Salvadoran unionists and learned first hand about repression under Salvador's US-backed military regime. During the course of this trip and related investigations, the NLC also learned from Salvadoran unionists that US apparel companies had been established with the help of USAID and had proved impossible to organize. The NLC focused on human rights abuses against trade unionists during the rest of the 1980s, making numerous "rescue missions" to Central America during the worst of the violence. This initial trip both initiated important relationships for the organization and led the NLC to see US foreign policy and free trade in broader terms—as forces working to maintain low wages, undermine unions, and support US companies abroad.[29]

After the Salvadoran peace accords were signed in 1990, the NLC shifted its attention from human rights to workers' rights, arguing that workers' rights should be seen as a fundamental human right, and became an independent labor rights NGO. Adopting a human rights model that highlighted and publicized the most egregious violations of workers' rights, the NLC made fighting sweatshops its calling card. Charles Kernaghan, its charismatic director, was one of the earliest and most influential anti-sweatshop advocates, and is often associated with pioneering media-savvy tactics that target well-known brands and celebrities with wholesome images (Kathie Lee, The Gap, Wal-Mart, Disney, and so on). The Gap campaign in El Salvador was one of the NLC's earliest anti-sweatshop ventures. The NLC took many of the strategies developed there as it brought students into the anti-sweatshop movement at the end of the 1990s.

In 1995 the NLC was contacted by a union federation in El Salvador that was looking to garner international support for unionists who had been fired by a Taiwanese-owned *maquila* that produced clothing primarily for The Gap (as well as J.C. Penney and Eddie Bauer). The workers had attempted to organize in order to improve horrible working conditions. Kernaghan visited the plant, and launched a full-scale publicity campaign. Interestingly, although the Salvadoran campaign had focused on mistreatment of workers, unpaid overtime, and poor benefits, the US campaign, which eventually included students, unionists, and religious activists, focused on child labor, including a US speaking tour with teenage workers.

The first stop on the tour was the founding convention of UNITE.[30] UNITE subsequently launched a Stop Sweatshops Campaign, became a central player in the anti-sweatshop movement, and played a particularly important role in training students as the movement developed on university campuses. Back in El Salvador, the company intensified attacks against the workers. The Gap eventually conceded that there were violations of its code of conduct and declared it would no longer place orders at the plant. Northern activists quickly pressured the company to return production to the plant, determined to avoid a PVH-style outcome where organizing led to lost jobs.[31]

The Gap campaign eventually produced two agreements, one that forced the Salvadoran plant to meet with unionists, and the second committing The Gap to independent monitoring and to renewing its contract with the plant once it was sure that workers' rights, as defined by Gap's own code, would be protected. Salvadoran workers continued to be threatened, and played little role in negotiating the second agreement or the system of monitoring.[32]

The conditions at the factory improved, and independent monitoring earned a place in the solidarity toolkit. Workers starting getting paid according to the law, although they were still subject to high production quotas and saw few raises. The union never managed to win a collective bargaining agreement or demand wage increases. It was pressure by US groups that got The Gap to agree to independent monitoring of labor.[33]

Nevertheless, the tour of teenage Salvadoran workers in 1995 was not only crucial for the Gap campaign, it brought together the NLC and UNITE, put sweatshops on the front pages, and garnered interest in the issue among students. For 60 days Judith Viera and Claudia Molina travelled across the country, meeting with activists, journals, students, and unionists. UNITE members in Dallas, San Francisco, and New York turned out to support them at rallies in front of Gap stores. American high school and college students were particularly moved by the teenagers' stories.[34]

This momentum was furthered by two high-profile exposés coming just months after the Gap campaign. In August 1995 investigators raided a barbed wire enclosed apartment building in El Monte, California where they found 72 Thai workers. Armed security guards had held some captive for as long as seven years, where they worked 16-hour days, seven days a week, and earned 70 cents an hour while producing clothes for the likes of Nordstrom, Sears, and Target. The public was shocked to learn that growing immigration from Asia and the Americas, combined with overseas competition, a turn towards "flexible, just-in-time" production, and the power of a few major retail chains (led by Wal-Mart), had brought the sweatshop back into the United States in the form of underground establishments in major urban areas.[35]

Then, four months after the Gap agreement was signed, the NLC took on Wal-Mart by targeting its wholesome spokesperson Kathie Lee Gifford. During the Gap campaign, Kernaghan found the Kathie Lee line of clothing in a Honduran sweatshop. It was subsequently learned that the line was also produced in sweatshop conditions in

New York. After threatening to sue Kernaghan, and crying on national television, Kathie Lee and her husband, Frank Gifford, eventually handed out money to workers in New York and called on Wal-Mart to accept independent monitoring in Honduras.[36]

The sweatshop had captured public imagination, and unions and NGOS expanded a campaign that relied on consumer-public vigilance to insure that corporations complied with human rights as well as environmental and labor standards. The NLC led the charge against Kathie Lee, and perfected the practice of exposing sweatshop practices, generating public interest, and embarrassing corporations. With long-standing ties in Central America with trade unionists, leftists, churches, women's groups, and human rights organizations, the NLC had the capacity to obtain workers' stories and expose conditions that neither government inspectors nor corporate-friendly inspectors could access. In 1998 and 1999, the NLC enhanced its budding alliance with students by taking delegations to El Salvador, Nicaragua, and Honduras, and helped them produce reports and videos.[37]

These efforts exposed not only the sweatshops, but the inadequacy of codes of conduct that many corporations had adopted in response to earlier campaigns in South Africa and elsewhere. They convinced many people—including many brand-vulnerable corporations—that an industry-wide system of regulating corporate behavior was necessary if the garment industry was to shed the sweatshop label. As a result, in 1996 the Clinton Administration formed the Apparel Industry Taskforce (AIP), which included not only labor, human rights, religious and consumer organizations, but major garment manufacturers and retailers (The Gap, Liz Claiborne, PVH) as well as the US Department of Labor.[38] With an administration committed to free trade and a Congress hostile to unions, the goal quickly coalesced around an industry-wide code of conduct and monitoring system, whereby US companies would effectively regulate themselves (and thus be able to promote their companies as "sweatshop-free"). The taskforce was set up by the government, but the government would not play an enhanced role in regulating corporations or stopping sweatshop practices.

At this point, the emerging sweatshop movement went in two directions. The NLC took a pragmatic approach, reasoning that this was the best that could be achieved under current political conditions, and signed on to the Taskforce's Code of Conduct and became part of the Fair Labor Association—a governing body dominated by corporations that enforced the code. For critics, the code was plagued by weak labor regulations, an inadequate monitoring system, was controlled by industry, and did little to empower workers or protect their rights. As a result, when the NLC signed on it had a partial falling out with its trade union allies and the anti-sweatshop movement it had helped cultivate on university campuses.[39]

Students, with close connections to UNITE, responded to the FLA by creating their own code of conduct, which included the right to unionize, disclosure of factory locations, inspections by truly independent monitors, an end to child labor, workplace safety, and minimum wages. They also created United Students Against Sweatshops (USAS) in 1998, as well as the Workers Rights Consortium (WRC), an alternative to the FLA that was committed to independent monitoring and full disclosure of production sites. The move worked, and by 2003 the WRC had over 100 affiliated schools (with some being forced by students to leave the FLA).[40]

USAS has stayed away from boycotts and explicitly worked to counter plant closures, instead emphasizing the continuous improvement of working conditions and opening up spaces for workers and their allies to advocate on their own behalf. From its inception, student–labor solidarity has been central to its mission. By 2001, USAS defined itself no longer in terms of the garment industry, but as a vehicle for strengthening student–labor solidarity. The anti-sweatshop movement became defined in increasingly broad terms, with the sweatshop becoming a metaphor for, or way of talking about, social justice issues in relation to global capitalism.[41]

USAS has been quite successful in getting universities to commit to purchasing sweatshop-free clothing, and getting corporations to adopt more stringent codes of conduct. Monitoring and enforcing corporate practices on a global level without state involvement has proven more challenging, in part because the codes remain essentially voluntary and depend on continually mobilizing consumer/public opinion in order to enforce. Likewise, empowering workers throughout the world who produce high-profile branded athletic clothing, let alone extending the movement into the garment industry as a whole, has been a daunting task. Few garment factories in the Caribbean, Mexico, and Central America are unionized, and sweatshop conditions are the norm. Even in Los Angeles, serious violations were found at more than half of the most effectively monitored shops. The greatest impact of independent monitoring tends to be on the physical conditions of plants, and it rarely affects wages or unionization rights.[42]

The anti-sweatshop movement has also been criticized for its human rights-like emphasis on egregious cases of violation, rather than the structural inequalities that underlie these cases. As Daniel Bender captures:

> The focus on the sweatshop as the worst kind of workplace allows for an easy escape for corporations. They can make small improvements, like those Nike boasts about in its "Transparency 101" campaign. Not only does this blunt the force of consumer-oriented activism, but it also obscures the real problems of work as defined by the workers themselves .... Corporate campaigns, boycotts, even "sweat-free" shopping might solve the most egregious problems of the sweatshop, but they leave in place the global inequalities of wealth and local inequalities within families, communities, and nations.[43]

Conclusion

In much the same way that the fair trade movement educated broader publics about the inequalities inherent in global trade, and the Global Justice Movement highlighted the dark side of globalization and neoliberalism, the corporate campaign has taught us much about the global division of labor and the impact that globalization has on Third World workers. It has also done much to establish cross-national relationships between workers, labor unions, students, and the broader solidarity left. Raising awareness about these issues and establishing relationships no doubt provides building blocks for developing more effective solidarity in the future.

Yet in terms of building long-term international solidarity, corporate campaigns and anti-sweatshop activism have faced a number of challenges. First, in the simplest sense, because most corporate campaigns operate in contexts where the balance of forces is so heavily stacked against workers, it takes an incredible amount of resources to build and then sustain campaigns to help even a small group of workers. The Latin American workers who typically capture global attention do so because their situation is dire—because workers are being severely repressed and the right to organize is virtually nonexistent. Consequently, even heavily resourced and committed international actors often find it difficult to provide meaningful support when faced with powerful multinational corporations backed by local militaries, police, and corrupt judicial systems. In the absence of strong social movements and labor unions, and when confronted with an entrenched oligarchy and corporate power, it is hard for international solidarity to deliver even short-term gains to small groups of workers.

Second, and more importantly, it is unclear whether the corporate campaign as a mode of solidarity has the capacity to strengthen the labor movement or the left. Such campaigns are typically initiated with workers who are in such difficult situations that they are in no position to organize or defend themselves. The human rights-like focus on creating public awareness for such workers means that solidarity is often extended to those who have the greatest potential for garnering media attention—that is, to those who have suffered horribly at the hands of a high-profile corporation. There is a certain logic to this, and it is certainly admirable to help workers whose rights have been trampled on by US corporations (and firmly in line with a tradition of solidarity that helps the weakest among us), but this is not necessarily a very strategic practice. It selects workers based more on their victim status, and/or as producers of a branded commodity, than on their potential for establishing labor unions or strengthening a broader labor movement. As a form of solidarity, these top-down campaigns are typically run by professionals from unions, NGOs, churches, or even student organizations, and are less about building working-class organizations than about saving victims by shaming particular corporations. They may succeed in changing the practices of a company in ways that help small groups of workers (often for short periods of time), but such campaigns generally do not advance working-class power through the development of mass organizations. To be fair, this is not an easy task.

Third, in the same way that corporate campaigns often assume the absence of effective labor organizations, they also tend to enter into contexts where an effective state is not present. Nor are they equipped or designed to transform the state or bring it under popular control. Like fair trade, corporate campaigns essentially bypass the state in favor of third-party monitors who are expected—in the absence of state regulators—to ensure that corporations are respecting workers' rights to organize, providing reasonable working conditions, and paying appropriate wages. The problem, aside from the fact that third parties often lack the capacity for such work and tend to be co-opted by the very corporations they are monitoring, is that this is not a model that can realistically be scaled up beyond a handful of high-profile companies tied to foreign multinationals. At some point, the question of state power has to be addressed.

In this sense, it is not entirely surprising that corporate campaigns emerged in the United States during the 1970s, precisely when the labor movement was in decline, the human rights movement was on the rise, and the US government was retreating from its redistributive and regulatory past. The strategy of focusing on a particular corporation, and highlighting its abusive practices in order to shame it before a broader public, not only reflects the inability of the labor movement to shape corporate practices on its own, but adopts a model that shares much with human rights practice.

Conclusion

Although US imperial aggression has been openly challenged in the United States for well over a century, this opposition has been uneven for a variety of reasons, including in part because the relative force and intensity of solidarity has been closely tied to the ebbs and flows of US intervention. Conspicuously aggressive instances of US imperialism, by either the US government or American corporations, have provided the fuel for igniting and driving political opposition. Consequently, when the more visible expressions of empire are thwarted, fade away, or simply no longer capture international attention, solidarity has been more difficult to sustain. To an extent, this is no doubt inevitable.

Nevertheless, although the urgency associated with particularly horrific abuses can be quite effective in igniting US-based opposition, a mode of engagement that relies on moral outrage is not necessarily designed to sustain solidarity over a long period of time—that is, to develop the political infrastructure necessary for engaging in long-term struggles. A politics produced by solidarity that relies on crisis as fuel may be ill equipped to advance significant political transformation, in part because it was never designed to do so in the first place. In this sense, the question is not simply short-term versus long-term struggle, but developing and working from a strategic politics that guides—even if in some imperfect and imprecise way—the types of struggles, allies, and tactics one embraces.

This tension has been at the core of Latin American solidarity since its origins in the 1800s, and essentially hinges on two related sets of questions. First, how do we link short-term campaigns against particular expressions of empire to longer-term struggles against imperialism and capitalism? The primary challenge with this question has often been asking it in the first place—that is, to think and act strategically as the space for radical visions and projects has contracted during the post-Second World War period. The quite real

202

urgency surrounding especially horrific acts of US imperialism tends to produce an act-now-think-later approach designed to put an end to immediate expressions of US military aggression, human rights abuses, or corporate exploitation. In the context of crisis, it is often difficult to think long term.

Whatever its virtues, such an approach may not be what is required for challenging the very structures that make these more conspicuous manifestations of empire possible (and so common) in the first place. This is not entirely news to those on the left, many of whom have consistently insisted upon a politics that embraces a strategic understanding of the short term in relation to long-term visions and struggles. Even with this recognition, however, it has been a difficult path to forge, especially as the left—whose great strength has been to articulate alternative visions of the world—has disappeared from public life.

Second, and related, how do we understand US imperialism? Although this question has not always been front and center in solidarity circles, in part because many opponents of US intervention have not seen the United States as an imperial power, it speaks to a long-standing tension in Latin American solidarity. Do we understand visibly exploitative instances of US imperialism as the relatively isolated actions of an otherwise democratic power whose overall presence is benign or benevolent? Or do we see those actions as the more conspicuous manifestations of a broader project that imposes an imperial brand of capitalism, one that delivers extreme levels of inequality and violence to the hemisphere? And, from a strategic perspective, do we pursue a politics focused on stopping or ameliorating the most extreme abuses, perhaps because it is best we can do, or do we engage in and design struggles that advance longer-term projects? Or both?

Although these questions have not always been openly wrestled with, they nonetheless point to key tensions within the history of Latin American solidarity. The core of the anti-imperialist current that emerged in the 1800s and early 1900s around the invasion of Mexico, Cuban independence, the Mexican revolution, and the occupations of Haiti, the Dominican Republic, and Nicaragua, was largely animated by opposition to the formal establishment of colonies or the use of the military troops—the most visible expression of US empire. This opposition was motivated by a range of impulses, including economic and racist rationales against imperial expansion, as well as the belief that US intervention was a betrayal of the inherently anti-imperialist and democratic orientation of the United States.

The mainstream current in the anti-imperialist opposition did not typically understand US presence in terms of what we might now refer to as economic imperialism. The unrestrained pursuit of economic interests by the US government and American corporations was not conceptualized in imperial terms, but seen as part of a positive presence that brought progress, modernity, and democracy to the region (except on those rare occasions when rogue actors temporarily strayed from core American values).

There were, to be sure, more radical-left currents of anti-imperialism emerging during the early 1900s, propelled by African American and white leftists who actively worked in solidarity with Latin Americans against not only the US military presence or particularly horrendous expressions of US capital, but the broader system advanced by the United States. Put another way, a left strand within the broader current of anti-imperialism understood struggles against a particular expression of US empire in Mexico or Nicaragua as part of a larger struggle against US imperialism and the brand of capitalism it advanced. These activists were not simply trying remove the US military, or constrain a particular corporation. They were fighting with Latin American allies for a radically more equitable world.

From the start, this battle to develop and sustain a radical-left internationalism was an uphill one. The difficulties inherent in communication and travel, the moderate-conservative orientation of the AFL, and the often violent persecution of the left in both Latin America and the United States during the early 1900s, ensured that radical currents remained marginalized. And yet a vibrant and militant left was emerging in the Americas, and had sufficient institutional and ideological presence in and outside the US labor movement to nurture an embryonic left internationalism. It was the existence of both the left and labor, the budding relationship between the two, and the growing presence of a left in the US labor movement, that infused this period with so much promise.

The Second World War disrupted the development of the US left, and the Cold War ushered in its near complete demise in the late 1940s and 1950s. The dismantling of the US left, including its expulsion from the labor movement, and the near complete destruction of left internationalism following the Second World War, meant that there was something of a solidarity vacuum when US-backed Cold War violence swept Latin America in the ensuing decades. Latin Americans leftists, who were themselves under fierce attack, found few allies on the left in the United States. Human rights eventually filled this solidarity void.

The uneven ascendance of human rights as the dominant strand in a rapidly growing current of Latin American solidarity during the 1970s had numerous implications for internationalism, including the increasingly institutionalized focus on the egregious—on those acts of state violence that were so far beyond the pale that they could (in theory) be universally condemned. Human rights refocused solidarity on the extreme through a professional-legal approach which sought to remove politics from the equation, both in terms of the commitment to targeting victims and perpetrators regardless of political affiliation, and in the sense that human rights organizations openly distanced themselves from political projects—particularly projects on the left that sought to confront material inequality. This was a form of international solidarity rooted in urgency and crisis, whose important goal of identifying and stopping human rights abuses was actively disconnected from a politics that pursued deeper political-economic transformation.

It also contributed to a model of solidarity that tended to move from one fire to the next in a somewhat arbitrary fashion. Why did Chile receive so much solidarity while Paraguay and Uruguay captured relatively little attention? Why, a decade later, did El Salvador become a larger recipient of solidarity than Guatemala? The answers to such questions were of course tied to historical factors. Was a military regime conspicuously repressive? Was it able to "spin" or conceal its violence? Did the US military intervene directly, work through proxies, funnel military aid, or support repression in more subtle ways? Were Latin American "victims" sympathetic, or sufficiently sophisticated at cultivating contacts with international organizations? Was there an exile community? And so on.[1]

Arbitrariness aside, there was a certain logic to this emerging formula. During the 1970s and 1980s Latin American military regimes were exceptionally repressive, often for long periods of time, and were bolstered by rather conspicuous support from the US government. This mode of empire defined an entire era, and so it is hardly surprising that the opposition developed a routinized set of practices for challenging imperial aggression. That there was a certain arbitrariness to solidarity was also not especially surprising. Cold War imperial aggression was itself quite uneven. It was certainly unfortunate that some cases struggled for attention, but it still made sense that Chileans were requesting solidarity, that they were able to capture global attention, and that the international community responded. The problem, at least for some, was a question of resources and finding a way to extend human rights internationalism to all deserving cases.

However, once the Cold War ended, civilian governments returned to power in Latin America, and the United States began to operate through the "soft" power of the Washington Consensus, the limitations associated with a solidarity that relied on the crisis and urgency of human rights abuses and civil war became more apparent. For one, the arbitrariness of solidarity became more glaring as the focus shifted unevenly away from entire countries that had been subjected to state violence towards more local entities that suffered an array of problems under civilian regimes. Put another way, as both the source and expressions of empire became less conspicuous and more diffuse, an almost surreal state of affairs could develop in which local communities, groups of workers, NGOs, and others scrambled to make the "pitch" to international actors that their particular expression of the neoliberal crisis was worthy of attention and aid.

In the end, however, the real problem was more fundamental than a degree of arbitrariness. Solidarity that relied on crisis for fuel was not designed for the long-term struggle of bringing about transformational change. It was not simply that once a particular crisis subsided—after US military aid was withdrawn, repression stopped, or a corporation finally recognized a labor union—that the energy driving solidarity declined and activists moved on to more compelling causes. This certainly happened, and is built into the human rights model of internationalism. Yet short-term struggles with defined targets and goals have an important place in progressive politics.

The challenge has been to conceptualize and design such campaigns in relation to longer-term struggles and visions. The motivation for engaging in a particular campaign, or even determining its "worthiness," has often been tied not to an evaluation of its strategic effectiveness, but (increasingly) to its capacity to capture public attention. Broader strategic discussions about the potential for a particular campaign to not only achieve immediate goals, but advance the development of a left-labor movement with the capacity to shape or capture state power, were too infrequently part of the calculus. This lack of strategic orientation around a transformational politics is largely engrained in human rights, whose political end game was relatively limited. But this lack of strategy borne in part by a mode of solidarity fueled by crisis seeped into progressive politics more broadly, as we have seen with workers' rights activism around particular corporations and sweatshops.

This tendency evolved unevenly as modern Latin American solidarity itself emerged during and after the 1970s. That this was also the period that witnessed the broader decline of the US left and the emergence of neoliberalism is not entirely a coincidence, and helps explain why a mode of solidarity that was often fueled by crisis simultaneously began to move away from a politics aimed at building political movements with the capacity to capture or influence state power. To be sure, this anti-state shift has been uneven and never complete. Human rights activism may not have been concerned with capturing political power in the larger sense, but was always centered on the state—even if its overall focus was on restraining the power of government. Likewise, the labor-left opposition to NAFTA was necessarily focused on state power. But as oppositional movements with the capacity to shape political power on the national level faded during the 1970s and 1980s, and as neoliberalism reduced the state's capacity to intervene on behalf of working people, progressive politics moved away from the state as a site of struggle. This was particularly true in international solidarity, as we have seen in initiatives as diverse as Zapatista internationalism, the Global Justice Movement, fair trade, and much of anti-corporate and sweatshop activism.

All this is to say that it has not been an easy time for internationalism or internationalists. The Cold War conservatism of labor, the decline of the left, the rightward shift of American politics, and the neoliberal assault on the state all created a hostile climate for left internationalism and limited its range of possibilities, practices, and visions. The weakness of the broader US left has not only meant that the United States has been aggressively imperial in orientation, but that it has been very difficult to sustain even humanitarian forms of internationalism—and even more difficult to develop shared struggles to build political power and advance anti-capitalist projects in Latin America and the United States. Without a left that can capture, shape, or influence US state power, internationalists will find it difficult not only to constrain US imperialism, but to develop a more effective solidarity that reacts to crisis, helps allies, and strategically builds political power.

These are, however, the conditions we find ourselves in and from which we must work. Not only does the world need an effective US-based left internationalism in order to constrain American empire, the US left needs its internationalist expressions to rebuild. Left internationalism has always been crucial for thinking about how forms of liberation, oppression, and inequality are connected across time and space—how "our" liberation is linked to "their" liberation. In this respect, the value of solidarity between people across borders remains in its promise and potential for defining and advancing more equitable ways of ordering the world.

Notes

Introduction

1   The Cerrejon mine, which had been owned jointly by Exxon and the Colombian state, was sold to a European consortium in the early 2000s. For more information about the ongoing conflict and international solidarity, see Aviva Chomsky and Steve Striffler, "Labor environmentalism in Colombia and Latin America," *WorkingUSA* (December 2014), 491–508; Aviva Chomsky, Garry Leech, and Steve Striffler, *The People Behind Colombian Coal: Mining, Multinationals, and Human Rights* (Casa Editorial Pisando Callos, 2007); Aviva Chomsky, *Linked Labor Histories: New England, Colombia, and the Making of a Global Working Class* (Duke University Press, 2008).

2   These delegations have been run through Witness for Peace, one of the longest-standing Latin American solidarity organizations in the United States (see Chapter 5).

3   Quite the opposite, the Colombian state co-owned the mine with Exxon until the early 2000s and was an active agent in the destruction of the communities.

4   This book is not only selective in the cases it explores, but relatively narrow in its focus on US-based solidarity that in some way challenges US empire or presence in Latin America. Although the Latin American side of this history of solidarity is at times addressed, it is not the focus of the narrative. Nor is European solidarity around similar issues, or solidarity efforts within or between Latin American countries. More than this, the book does not begin to explore all of the humanitarian efforts, much of what we might call "development solidarity," or a whole host of other efforts that have defined more grassroots exchanges between people in the United States and those in Latin America. Likewise, the US immigrant rights movement, which can certainly be understood as international solidarity, is not dealt with here.

5   For example, see Christian Smith, *Resisting Reagan: The U.S. Central American Peace Movement* (University of Chicago Press, 1996); Ralph Armbruster-Sandoval, *Globalization and Cross-Border Labor Solidarity in the Americas: The Anti-Sweatshop Movement and the Struggle for Social Justice* (Routledge, 2004); Lesley Gill, "The limits of solidarity: labor and transnational organizing against Coca-Cola," *American Ethnologist*, Vol. 36, No. 4 (2009), 667–80; Richard Grossman, "Solidarity with Sandino: the anti-intervention and solidarity movements in the United States, 1927–1933," *Latin American Perspectives*, Vol. 36, No. 1 (2009), 67–79; Hector Perla, "Heirs of Sandino: the Nicaraguan Revolution and the U.S–Nicaragua

solidarity movement," *Latin American Perspectives*, Vol. 36, No. 6 (2009), 80–100; James Green, *We Cannot Remain Silent: Opposition to the Brazilian Military Dictatorship in the United States* (Duke University Press, 2010); Mark S. Anner, *Solidarity Transformed: Labor Responses to Globalization and Crisis in Latin America* (ILR Press, 2011); Roger Peace, *A Call to Conscience: The Anti-Contra War Campaign* (University of Massachusetts Press, 2012). Jessica Stites Mor (ed.), *Human Rights and Transnational Solidarity in Cold War Latin America* (University of Wisconsin Press, 2013). Van Gosse has written widely and insightfully on this topic, in both books such as *Rethinking the New Left: An Interpretive History* (Palgrave Macmillan, 2005) and *Where the Boys Are: Cuba, Cold War America, and the Making of a New Left* (Verso, 1993), and articles such as "'The North American Front': Central American solidarity in the Reagan era," in Mike Davis and Michael Sprinker (eds.), *Reshaping the U.S. Left: Popular Struggles in the 1980s* (Verso, 1988). See his website for a more complete list of work on the subject: www.vangosse.com. Patrick William Kelly has also published a number of excellent pieces, including: "Human rights and Christian responsibility: transnational Christian activism, human rights, and state violence in Brazil and Chile in the 1970s," in Alexander Wilde (ed.), *Religious Responses to Violence: Human Rights in Latin America Past and Present* (University of Notre Dame Press, 2015); "The 1973 Chilean coup and the origins of transnational human rights activism," *Journal of Global History*, Vol 8, No. 1 (2013), 165–86. See also his new book, *Sovereign Emergencies: Latin America and the Making of Global Human Rights Politics* (Cambridge University Press, 2018). See also Teishan A. Latner, *Cuban Revolution in America: Havana and the Making of a United States Left* (University of North Carolina Press, 2018). Dan La Botz has also written widely on the subject, including "American 'slackers' in the Mexican revolution: international proletarian politics in the midst of a national revolution," *The Americas*, Vol. 62, No. 4 (2006), 563–90; and "The Mexican Liberal Party, the American left, and the emergence of international solidarity," in the forthcoming book *Riding with the Revolution: The American Left and the Mexican Revolution, 1900 to 1929*.

6   Samuel Moyn's work has been key for rethinking human rights internationalism: *The Last Utopia: Human Rights in History* (Harvard University Press, 2010); *Human Rights and the Uses of History* (Verso, 2014); *Not Enough: Human Rights in an Unequal World* (Harvard University Press, 2018). See also Barbara J. Keys, *Reclaiming American Virtue: The Human Rights Revolution of the 1970s* (Harvard University Press, 2014); and Sarah B. Snyder, *From Selma to Moscow: How Human Rights Activists Transformed U.S. Foreign Policy* (Columbia University Press, 2018). For recent studies on Latin America see Patrick William Kelly's *Sovereign Emergencies* as well as William Michael Schmidli's *The Fate of Freedom Elsewhere: Human Rights and U.S. Cold War Policy toward Argentina* (Cornell University Press, 2013). On the human rights revolution and the role of Amnesty International in particular, see Kenneth Cmiel, "The emergence of human rights politics in the United States," *Journal of American History*, Vol. 86, No. 3 (1999), 1231–50; Tom Buchanan, "Amnesty International in crisis, 1966–7," *Twentieth Century British History*, Vol. 15, No. 3 (2004), 267–89; Tom Buchanan, "The truth will set you free: the making of Amnesty International," *Journal of Contemporary History*, Vol. 37, No. 4 (2002),

575–97; Sarah B. Snyder, "Exporting Amnesty International to the United States: transatlantic human rights activism in the 1960s," *Human Rights Quarterly*, Vol 34 (2012), 779–99. "Internationalism" more broadly has gone through a rethinking beyond human rights. See e.g. such differing works such as Paul Ortiz, *An African American and Latinx History of the United States* (Beacon Press, 2018); and Erez Manela, *The Wilsonian Moment: Self-Determination and the International Origins of Anticolonial Nationalism* (Oxford University Press, 2007).

7 For example, Penny M. Von Eschen, *Race Against Empire: Black Americans and Anti-colonialism, 1937–1957* (Cornell University Press, 1997); Minkah Makalani, *In the Cause of Freedom: Radical Black Internationalism from Harlem to London, 1917–1939* (University of North Carolina Press, 2011); Lara Putnam, *Radical Moves: Caribbean Migrants and the Politics of Race in the Jazz Age* (University of North Carolina Press, 2013); Carol Anderson, *Bourgeois Radicals: The NAACP and the Struggle for Colonial Liberation* (Cambridge University Press, 2015); Carol Anderson, *Eyes Off the Prize: The United Nations and the African American Struggle for Human Rights, 1944–1955* (Cambridge University Press, 2003); Hakim Adi, *Pan-Africanism and Communism: The Communist International, Africa and the Diaspora, 1919–1939* (Africa World Press, 2013); Brenda Gayle Plummer, *In Search of Power: African Americans in the Era of Decolonization, 1956–1974* (Cambridge University Press, 2013); Margaret Stevens, *Red International and Black Caribbean: Communists in New York City, Mexico and the West Indies, 1919–1939* (Pluto Press, 2017); Gaye Theresa Johnson and Alex Lubin, *Futures of Black Radicalism* (Verso, 2017).

8 A phrase borrowed from Adolph Reed's discussion of the US labor movement. Adolph Reed, Jr. "Why Labor's Soldiering for the Democrats is a Losing Battle," *New Labor Forum*, Vol. 19, No. 3 (2008), 9–15.

9 If we resist the well-established tradition of erasing Native American history, it becomes clear that the United States was an imperial power from its birth, in effect colonizing territories and nations as it expanded to the west during the 1700s and 1800s. Such expansion was not overseas, nor was there an understanding of it as imperialist. Likewise, solidarity with Native Americans was quite limited, and really only extended after it was in many ways too late (see Chapter 1).

10 For many African Americans, the Italian invasion highlighted the connection between US blacks and oppressed people abroad. See Stevens, *Red International and Black Caribbean*, 181–200.

11 Gosse, *Rethinking the New Left*, 10–15.

12 It is worth noting that there were intense debates among sectors of the left about whether to subordinate everything to the war effort, including giving up the right to strike or aggressively pursuing equality for African Americans.

13 The Taft–Hartley Act was passed in 1947 and, among other things, forced union officers to sign non-communist affidavits. Along with the broader anti-communism of the late 1940s and early 1950s, the Act encouraged (and gave cover for) top leaders within the AFL-CIO (which combined forces in 1955) to drive communists out of unions.

14 Moyn, *The Last Utopia*; Keys, *Reclaiming American Virtue*.

15 Following Samuel Moyn, among others.

16 Moyn, *The Last Utopia*; Cmiel, "The emergence of human rights politics."

17 This blame can be largely assigned to a Cold War assault that decimated the left during this period.

18 Steinar Stjernø, "The idea of solidarity in Europe," *European Journal of Social Law*, No. 3 (Sept. 2011), 156–76.

1 US Empire, Anti-Imperialism, and Revolution

1 Many authors have stressed the importance of the French revolution for Haiti, particularly in terms of how the notions of equality it embodied spread and inspired people across the globe. For Haiti, see C. L. R. James's classic: *The Black Jacobins: Toussaint L'Ouverture and the San Domingo Revolution* (Vintage, 1989 [1938]). Alejo Carpenter's novel, *El Siglo de Las Luces* (Seix Barral, 1970), captures the profound impact of the French revolution on the Caribbean in general.

2 Paul Ortiz, *An African American and Latinx History of the United States* (Beacon Press, 2018).

3 Ortiz, *An African American and Latinx History*, 16–18.

4 Michael O. West and William G. Martin, "Contours of the Black International: from Toussaint to Tupac," in M. O. West, W. G. Martin, and F. C. Wilkins (eds.), *From Toussaint to Tupac: The Black International since the Age of Revolution* (University of North Carolina, 2009), 5–7.

5 Michael O. West and William G. Martin, "Haiti I'm sorry: the Haitian revolution and the forging of the Black International," in West, Martin, and Wilkins (eds.), *From Toussaint to Tupac*, 72–104.

6 Ashli White, "The Saint Dominguan Refugees and American distinctiveness in the early years of the Haitian revolution," in David Patrick Geggus and Norman Fiering (eds.), *The World of the Haitian Revolution* (Indiana University Press, 2009), 248.

7 Caitlin Fitz, *Our Sister Republics: The United States in an Age of American Revolutions* (W.W. Norton, 2016), 3.

8 Sylvia Frey, "The American revolution and the creation of a global African world," in West, Martin, and Wilkins (eds.) *From Toussaint to Tupac*, 47–71, quote on 66.

9 Laurent Dubois, "Frederick Douglass, Anténor Firmin, and the making of the U.S-Haitian relations," in Elizabeth Maddock Dillon and Michael Drexler (eds.), *The Haitian Revolution and the Early United States* (University of Pennsylvania Press, 2016), 96.

10 West and Martin, "Haiti I'm sorry," 72–3. For the broader impact of the Haitian revolution on African Americans see Gerald Horne, *Confronting Black Jacobins: The United States, The Haitian Revolution, and the Origins of the Dominican Republic* (Monthly Review Press, 2015).

11 See Frey, "The American revolution," 67. See also Maurice Jackson and Jacqueline Bacon, "Fever and fret: the Haitian revolution and African American responses," in Maurice Jackson and Jacqueline Bacon (eds.), *African Americans and the Haitian Revolution: Selected Essays and Historical Documents* (Routledge, 2010), 13–14.

12 Ortiz, *An African American and Latinx History*, 28.

13 Quoted in Ortiz, *An African American and Latinx History*, 31.

14 It is worth noting that Haiti actively extended solidarity to black people around

the Atlantic and to anti-colonialists more broadly. Its first constitution defined the country as a "black" nation and offered citizenship to anyone of African or Native American ancestry. Haiti also supported independence movements in Spanish America including Venezuela (1806), Mexico (1816), and Simon Bolivar's expeditions in Venezuela (1816). West and Martin, "Haiti I'm sorry," 80.

15   David Brion Davis, "Impact of the French and Haitian revolutions," in David P. Geggus (ed.), *The Impact of the Haitian Revolution in the Atlantic World* (University of South Carolina Press: 2001), 4–5.

16   Abraham Bishop, "The rights of black men," *The Argus* (Boston, December 6, 1791), reprinted in Tim Matthewson, "Abraham Bishop, 'The rights of black men,' and the American reaction to the Haitian revolution," *Journal of Negro History*, Vol. 67, No. 2 (1982), 148–54, quote from p. 148.

17   Bishop, "The rights of black men," 151.

18   Bishop, "The rights of black men," 153.

19   Fitz, *Our Sister Republics*, 4.

20   This is only possible when we ignore the fact that events in Latin America were much more closely tied to the collapse of Spanish and Portuguese empires than to anything happening in the United States.

21   Fitz, *Our Sister Republics*, 9.

22   Fitz, *Our Sister Republics*, 7.

23   Fitz, *Our Sister Republics*, 5.

24   Fitz, *Our Sister Republics*, 1–13.

25   As Fitz demonstrates, this was an uneven process in which many in the United States continued to identify with and defend the new nations in Latin America. *Our Sister Republics*, especially Chapter 6.

26   Quoted in Ortiz, *An African American and Latinx History*, 36–7.

27   Ortiz, *An African American and Latinx History*, 36–53.

28   Piero Gleijeses, "A brush with Mexico," *Diplomatic History*, Vol. 29, No. 2 (2005), 223–54.

29   Thoreau's opposition led him to encourage people to resist the war by not paying taxes, as he did himself, and landed in jail. Lawrence A. Rosenwald, "The theory, practice, and influence of Thoreau's civil disobedience," in William E. Cain (ed.), *A Historical Guide to Henry David Thoreau* (Oxford University Press, 2000), 153–79.

30   John H. Schroeder, *Mr. Polk's War: American Opposition and Dissent, 1846–1848* (University of Wisconsin Press, 1973), 36.

31   Ortiz, *An African American and Latinx History*, 52.

32   *North Star*, January 21, 1848, cited in Foner, *US Labor Movement*, 4; see also Howard Zinn, *A People's History of the United States, 1492–Present* (new ed., HarperCollins, 2003), 157.

33   Quoted in Ortiz, *An African American and Latinx History*, 47.

34   Paul Foos, *A Short, Offhand, Killing Affair: Soldiers and Conflict during the Mexican-American War* (University of North Carolina Press, 2000), 8.

35   James W. Russell, *Class and Race Formation in North America* (University of Toronto Press, 2009), 56.

36   Louis A. Pérez, *The War of 1898: The United States and Cuba in History and Historiography* (University of North Carolina Press, 1998), 5.

37   Quote from Pérez, *The War of 1898*, 5.

38 Ada Ferrer, *Insurgent Cuba: Race, Nation, and Revolution, 1868–1898* (University of North Carolina Press, 1999), 1–10.

39 Ortiz, *An African American and Latinx History*, 72–4.

40 Ortiz, *An African American and Latinx History*, 74.

41 Ortiz, *An African American and Latinx History*, 75.

42 Johnetta B. Cole, "Afro-American solidarity with Cuba," *The Black Scholar*, Summer 1977, 73–80.

43 Pérez, *The War of 1898*, 12–16.

44 Pérez, *The War of 1898*, 14.

45 Louis A. Pérez, *Cuba in the American Imagination* (University of North Carolina Press, 2008), 3–6.

46 Pérez, *The War of 1898*, 16.

47 Philip S. Foner, *The Spanish–Cuban–American War and the Birth of American Imperialism, Volume 1: 1895–1898* (Monthly Review Press, 1972), 166–76; Lars Schoultz, *Beneath the United States: A History of U.S. Policy Toward Latin America* (Harvard University Press, 1998), 129–32.

48 Foner, *The Spanish–Cuban–American War*, 168, 170.

49 William Jennings Bryan, "The Savannah interview," in William Jennings Bryan et al., *Republic or Empire? The Philippine Question* (Chicago: Independence Company, 1899), 14–15.

50 Carl Schurz, "American imperialism," in Bryan et al., *Republic or Empire?*, 329–63.

51 Resolution cited in Samuel Gompers, *Labor and the Common Welfare* (New York: Dutton, 1919), 224.

52 *American Federationist* 2 (Feb. 1896), 22, cited in Foner, *U.S. Labor Movement*, 13. Gompers wrote these words with respect to a boundary dispute between Britain and British Guyana, but made the same general argument about military involvement in Cuba.

53 Cited in Foner, *U.S. Labor Movement*, 28–9.

54 An expanded notion of imperialism that went beyond diplomatic or military aggression to include economic imperialism started to really gain traction in the 1920s and 1930s. Scott Nearing and Joseph Freeman's *Dollar Diplomacy: A Study in American Imperialism* (B.W. Huebsch and Viking Press, 1925) was key in this respect, as were Charles David Kepner and Jay Henry Soothill's *The Banana Empire: A Case Study of Economic Imperialism* (Vanguard Press, 1935) and Charles David Kepner, *Social Aspects of the Banana Industry* (AMS Press, 1936).

55 This was especially true as Caribbean and African-American blacks fought in the First World War and migrated to London, Paris, and New York.

56 To be sure, more moderate sectors within the United States, especially among the political establishment, backed nationalist reformers who sought to remove Diaz. But such "solidarity" was essentially counter-revolutionary in that it sought to replace Diaz while keeping the basic system in place—that is, it tried to constrain the revolution.

57 See Juan Gómez-Quiñones, *Mexican American Labor, 1790–1990* (University of New Mexico Press, 1994).

58 Dan La Botz, "The Mexican Liberal Party, the American left, and the emergence of international solidarity," in *Riding with the Revolution: The American Left and the*

Mexican Revolution, 1900 to 1929 (forthcoming), 11; John Mason Hart, *Empire and Revolution: The Americans in Mexico since the Civil War* (University of California Press, 2002), 152.

59   Foner, *U.S. Labor Movement*, 97–8.

60   La Botz, "The Mexican Liberal Party," 11–12.

61   La Botz, "The Mexican Liberal Party."

62   George J. Sánchez, *Becoming Mexican American: Ethnicity, Culture, and Identity in Chicano Los Angeles, 1900–1945* (Oxford University Press, 1993), 230.

63   Devra Weber, *Dark Sweat, White Gold: California Farmworkers, Cotton, and the New Deal* (University of California Press, 1994), 86.

64   See David Struthers, "iww internationalism and interracial organizing in the Southwestern United States," in P. Cole, D. Struthers, and K. Zimmer (eds.), *Wobblies of the World: A Global History of the iww* (Pluto Press, 2017). Beyond this, as *Wobblies of the World* so ably documents, the iww had an astoundingly global reach in the first decades of the twentieth century, including a presence throughout the Americas in places like Argentina, Cuba, Chile, Ecuador, Uruguay, and Puerto Rico.

65   Foner, *U.S. Labor Movement*, 101.

66   Colin M. MacLachlan, *Anarchism and the Mexican Revolution: The Political Trials of Ricardo Flores Magón in the United States* (University of California Press 1991), 23–4; Foner, *U.S. Labor Movement*, 102.

67   Foner, *U.S. Labor Movement*, 102–3.

68   Foner, *U.S. Labor Movement*, 102.

69   *MacLachlan, Anarchism and the Mexican Revolution*, 24.

70   James D. Cockcroft, *Intellectual Precursors of the Mexican Revolution, 1900–1913* (University of Texas Press, 1968), 120–33; La Botz, "The Mexican Liberal Party," 29.

71   Foner, *U.S. Labor Movement*, 103.

72   MacLachlan, *Anarchism and the Mexican Revolution*, 24; Foner, *U.S. Labor Movement*, 105.

73   Foner, *U.S. Labor Movement*, 103.

74   Margaret Stevens, *Red International and Black Caribbean: Communists in New York City, Mexico, and the West Indies, 1919–1939* (Pluto Press, 2017).

2 The Caribbean under US Occupation

1   Alan McPherson, *The Invaded: How Latin Americans and Their Allies Fought and Ended U.S. Occupation* (Oxford University Press, 2013), 1; Hans Schmidt, *The United States Occupation of Haiti, 1915–1934* (Rutgers University Press, 1995), 4–6.

2   McPherson, *The Invaded*, 91.

3   McPherson argues persuasively that "the invaded resisted because of local autonomy rather than nationalism" in *The Invaded*, 9.

4   On black internationalism, the emergence of a sense of Afro-Caribbean commonality, and the increased oppression against blacks across the region, see Lara Putnam, "Nothing matters but color: transnational circuits, the interwar Caribbean, and the Black International," in West, Martin, and Wilkins (eds.), *From Toussaint to*

Tupac, 107–129. More broadly, see Minkah Makalani, *In the Cause of Freedom: Radical Black Internationalism from Harlem to London, 1917–1939* (University of North Carolina Press, 2011), and Lara Putnam, *Radical Moves: Caribbean Migrants and the Politics of Race in the Jazz Age* (University of North Carolina Press, 2013).

5 Outside of opposition to US interventions in the Caribbean, efforts by the Comintern (or communists outside of the Caribbean) to organize or support workers in the Caribbean during the 1920s and 1930s were limited for a variety of reasons, and rarely moved beyond the planning stage. See Hakim Adi, *Pan-Africanism and Communism: The Communist International, Africa and the Diaspora, 1919–1939* (Africa World Press, 2013), Chapter 8 in particular.

6 Robin D. G. Kelley, *Race Rebels: Culture, Politics, and the Black Working Class* (Free Press, 1994); Makalani, *In the Cause of Freedom*, 1–9; Stevens, *Red International and Black Caribbean*, 30–9.

7 On the relationship between the Comintern and Black International during this period see Hakim Adi, "The negro question: the Communist International and black liberation in the interwar years," in West, Martin, and Wilkins (eds.), *From Toussaint to Tupac*, 155–75. See also Stevens, *Red International and Black Caribbean*.

8 This was for a variety of reasons, including that many Dominicans blamed corrupt politicians for the political chaos and cycle of revolution that defined their country. Others simply hoped to benefit from the US presence: McPherson, *The Invaded*.

9 Eric Paul Roorda, *The Dictator Next Door: The Good Neighbor Policy and the Trujillo Regime in the Dominican Republic, 1930–1945* (Duke University Press, 1998), 16–17.

10 Calder. *The Impact of Intervention: The Dominican Republic during the U.S Occupation of 1916–1924* (University of Texas Press, 1984); Joseph Robert Juarez, "United States withdrawal from Santo Domingo," *Hispanic American Historical Review*, Vol. 42 (May 1962), 152–90; McPherson, *The Invaded*.

11 Calder, *The Impact of Intervention*, xiv.

12 Calder, *The Impact of Intervention*, xvi.

13 Juarez, "United States withdrawal from Santo Domingo"; Calder, *The Impact of Intervention*.

14 Ortiz, *An African American Latinx History*, 100–3; McPherson, *The Invaded*, 170–5.

15 Juarez, "United States withdrawal from Santo Domingo," 152–4.

16 McPherson, *The Invaded*, 170.

17 Juarez, "United States withdrawal from Santo Domingo," 154–8.

18 McPherson, *The Invaded*, 180.

19 Erez Manela, *The Wilsonian Moment: Self-Determination and the International Origins of Anticolonial Nationalism* (Oxford University Press, 2007).

20 Calder, *The Impact of Intervention*, 201.

21 Juarez, "United States withdrawal from Santo Domingo," 170.

22 Calder, *The Impact of Intervention*, pp. 202–9; Juarez, "United States withdrawal from Santo Domingo," 157–9.

23 Juarez, "United States withdrawal from Santo Domingo," 158.

24 The PAFL was seen by many in Latin America, especially those within the labor movement, as an effort by the AFL to shape labor organizations in the region while isolating them from anarchist and communist influence.

25 Robert J. Alexander, *International Labor Organizations and Organized Labor in Latin America: A History* (Praeger, 2009): 30–1; Calder, *The Impact of Intervention*, 183–212; Juarez, "United States withdrawal from Santo Domingo," 168; McPherson, *The Invaded*, 167–8.

26 Juarez, "United States withdrawal from Santo Domingo," 168.

27 McPherson, The *Invaded*.

28 Leon D. Pamphile, "The NAACP and the American Occupation of Haiti," *Phylon* Vol 47, No.1, (1986), 91.

29 *The World's Work*, Vol. 30, No. 6 (October 1915), 633. A shorter version of the quote was found in Pamphile.

30 Cited in Pamphile, "The NAACP," 91; quote comes from World's Work.

31 Laurent Dubois, *Haiti: The Aftershocks of History* (Metropolitan Books, 2012), 214.

32 Schmidt, *The United States Occupation of Haiti*, 10–11.

33 Schmidt, *The United States Occupation of Haiti*, 82–5.

34 McPherson, *The Invaded*, 22–33, 94, 172–76.

35 Dubois, *Haiti*, 220.

36 Plummer, "The Afro-American response," 125–6.

37 McPherson, *The Invaded*, 169; DuBois, *Haiti*, 220.

38 Plummer, "The Afro-American response," 142.

39 McPherson, *The Invaded*, 169; Adi, "The negro question," 157. Makalani, *In the Cause of Freedom*, 37, 45–69.

40 McPherson, *The Invaded*, 169.

41 Pamphile, "The NAACP," 92.

42 Herbert Seligman, "The conquest of Haiti," *The Nation*, Vol. 111, No. 2871 (July 10, 1920), 35–6.

43 McPherson, *The Invaded*, 172.

44 Ortiz, *An African American and Latinx History*, 111; Schmidt, *The United States Occupation of Haiti*, 120–123.

45 Dubois, *Haiti*, 214.

46 Pamphile, "The NAACP."

47 Dubois, *Haiti*, 228.

48 Quoted in Dubois, *Haiti*, 242–3.

49 Pamphile, "The NAACP," p. 94.

50 Pamphile, "The NAACP"; Schmidt, *The United States Occupation of Haiti*, 119.

51 Henry Lewis Suggs, "The response of the African American press to the United States occupation of Haiti, 1915–1934," *Journal of African American History*, Vol. 87 (Winter 2002), 70–82, 72.

52 Mary A. Renda, *Taking Haiti: Military Occupation and the Culture of U.S. Imperialism, 1915–1940* (University of North Carolina Press, 2001), 263–265.

53 Plummer, "The Afro-American response," 138.

54 Plummer, "The Afro-American response," 139.

55 Pamphile, "The NAACP," 96–7.

56 Plummer, "The Afro-American response," 139–43; Schmidt, *The United States Occupation of Haiti*; Stevens, *Red International and Black Caribbean*, chapter 2.

57 Richard Grossman, "Solidarity with Sandino: the anti-intervention and solidarity movements in the United States, 1927–1933," *Latin American Perspectives*, Vol. 36,

No. 6 (2009), 67–79; Van Gosse, *Where the Boys Are: Cuba, Cold War America and the Making of a New Left* (Verso, 1993), p. 16.

58 McPherson, *The Invaded*, 15.

59 McPherson, *The Invaded*, 85.

60 Quoted in McPherson, *The Invaded*, 195.

61 McPherson, *The Invaded*, 218–25. The international support was even felt in Sandino's fighting force, which included small numbers of Hondurans, Salvadorans, Guatemalans, Mexicans, Venezuelans, Colombians, Costa Ricans, Peruvians, and Dominicans.

62 Gosse, *Where the Boys Are*, 17.

63 Ortiz, *An African American and Latinx History*, 112.

64 Ortiz, *An African American and Latinx History*, 112–13.

65 McPherson, *The Invaded*, 195.

66 Gosse, *Where the Boys Are*, 18; McPherson, *The Invaded*, 203.

67 Gosse, *Where the Boys Are*, 17.

68 McPherson, *The Invaded*, 221–22; Gosse, *Where the Boys Are*, 18.

69 Gosse, *Where the Boys Are*, 16.

70 Grossman, "Solidarity with Sandino."

71 Grossman, "Solidarity with Sandino," 68–70.

72 Grossman, "Solidarity with Sandino," 70–3; McPherson, *The Invaded*, 221.

73 Grossman, "Solidarity with Sandino," 75. The opposition movement as a whole was relatively visible during the first years of the war (1927–28), but became less conspicuous as the United States turned over more of the combat to the Guardia Nacional. With fewer US citizens in harm's way, media and popular interest in the United States declined (especially after the Great Depression). Sandino also lost important support when Communist Party policy, emanating during this period from Moscow, shifted away from the strategy of a United Front. Communists were to work only with communists, and Sandino was abruptly abandoned.

74 For a broader history of efforts by communists (many of whom were West Indian) in the United States and the Caribbean to develop revolutionary movements within and across nations, see Margaret Stevens's excellent *Red International and Black Caribbean*.

3 The Cuban Revolution and the Cold War

1 Van Gosse, *Rethinking the New Left: An Interpretive History* (Palgrave Macmillan, 2005), 10–15.

2 Gosse, *Rethinking the New Left*, 10–15.

3 Penny M. von Eschen, *Race Against Empire: Black Americans and Anticolonialism, 1937–1957* (Cornell University Press, 1997), 69–75.

4 Von Eschen, *Race Against Empire*, 107.

5 Von Eschen, *Race Against Empire*.

6 Von Eschen, *Race Against Empire*, 3.

7 Carol Anderson, *Bourgeois Radicals: The NAACP and the Struggle for Colonial Liberation* (Cambridge University Press), 1–9.

8 Von Eschen, *Race Against Empire*, 1–6.

9   Sadly, Haiti served as an example of this process. In the decades before the Second World War, including through the 1940s, black journalists chronicled how the US government and American business had exploited the black nation and propped up authoritarian rule. By the early 1950s, just years into the Cold War, "African American critiques of the role of the American government and US corporations in Haiti" had disappeared, and "journalists were suggesting that black Americans could share in the fruits of exploitation." Haiti had become a virgin territory to be stabilized by the presence of US business. Von Eschen, *Race Against Empire*, 163–4.

10 Von Eschen, *Race Against Empire*, 186–7.

11 Gosse, *Where the Boys Are*, 13.

12 Piero Gleijeses, *Shattered Hope: The Guatemalan Revolution and the United States, 1944–1954* (Princeton University Press 1991), 367–72.

13 One interesting exception to this relative silence in the broad arena of US-based Latin American solidarity during this period revolved around a series of revolts for an independent Puerto Rico, which was led by Puerto Rican nationalists and supported by various groups in the United States. Although US Puerto Ricans (and often women) provided the core of this solidarity, Ruth Mary Reynolds founded the American League for Puerto Rican Independence and was subsequently imprisoned in Puerto Rico. Margaret Power, "Puerto Rican women nationalists vs. U.S. colonialism: an exploration of their conditions and struggles in jail and court," *Chicago-Kent Law Review*, Vol. 87, No. 2 (April 2012).

14 Perry Anderson, "Internationalism: a breviary," *New Left Review*, Vol. 14 (March–April 2002), 16.

15 Moyn, *The Last Utopia*, 116–20.

16 Gosse, *Rethinking the New Left*, 59.

17 Ian Lekus "Queer harvests: homosexuality, the US new left, and the Venceremos Brigades to Cuba," *Radical History Review*, Vol. 89, (Spring 2004), 57–91.

18 Van Gosse, *Rethinking the New Left*, 59–60.

19 Gosse, *Where the Boys Are*, 2–3.

20 William M. Leogrande and Peter Kornbluh, *Back Channel to Cuba: The Hidden History of Negotiations Between Washington and Havana* (University of North Carolina Press, 2015), 15.

21 Gosse, *Rethinking the New Left*, 59–60; Van Gosse, "The African-American press greets the Cuban revolution," in Lisa Brock and Digna Castañeda Fuertes (eds.), *Between Race and Empire: African Americans and Cubans before the Cuban Revolution* (Temple University Press, 1998), 266–80.

22 Latner, *Cuban Revolution in America*, 12–19.

23 Gosse, "The African-American press," 266.

24 On efforts by Cuba to develop relationships with US black radicals see Mark Q. Sawyer, *Racial Politics in Post-Revolutionary Cuba* (Cambridge University Press, 2006,) ch. 4. On attempts by Cuba to cultivate good relations with African Americans see Devyn Spence Benson, *Antiracism in Cuba: The Unfinished Revolution* (University of North Carolina Press, 2016), ch. 4.

25 Gosse, "The African-American press."

26 Gosse, "The African-American press."

27 Gosse, "The African-Americanpress," 268–72; Gosse, *Rethinking the New Left*, 60–2.

28 Gosse, "The African-American press," 277–8.

29 Latner, *Cuban Revolution in America*, 14–16.

30 Latner, *Cuban Revolution in America*, 8; Gosse, *Rethinking the New Left*, 49–50.

31 Latner, *Cuban Revolution in America*, 22. See also Timothy B. Tyson, *Radio Free Dixie: Robert F. Williams & the Roots of Black Power* (University of North Carolina Press, 1999).

32 Sawyer, *Racial Politics*, ch. 4.

33 Gosse, *Rethinking the New Left*, 59.

34 Gosse, *Where the Boys Are*, 138–59.

35 Latner, *Cuban Revolution in America*, 13.

36 Gosse, *Where the Boys Are*, 146.

37 Gosse, *Rethinking the New Left*, 59–61; Gosse, *Where the Boys Are*, 6, 146–65.

38 Gosse, *Where the Boys Are*, 6.

39 Latner, *Cuban Revolution in America*, 18–19; Gosse, *Rethinking the New Left*, 59–62. As it turned out, Oswald was unknown to the FPCC's national office and had been the lone member-founder of a branch in New Orleans.

40 Latner, *Cuban Revolution in America*, 18–19.

41 Not surprisingly, Cuba was often portrayed by leftists in idealized terms, and often with the purpose of making a critique of the United States.

42 Latner, *Cuban Revolution in America*, 1.

43 Latner, *Cuban Revolution in America*, 7–8.

44 Latner, *Cuban Revolution in America*, 8–9.

45 Lekus, "Queer harvests," 63.

46 Lekus, "Queer harvests," 63.

47 Latner, *Cuban Revolution in America*, 33.

48 Lekus, "Queer harvests," 63. As both Lekus and Latner document, and as participants attested, this diversity was a strength, but also a source of considerable friction and division, as men and women from different economic, racial, sexual, and political backgrounds all tried to live and work alongside each other under difficult conditions.

49 Latner, *Cuban Revolution in America*, 34–8; Lekus, "Queer harvests," 63–4.

50 Lekus, "Queer harvests," 57.

51 For reasons of space, our story about the Venceremos Brigades stops in the early 1970s, but it is important to note that they continue to run delegations to Cuba every year, as do other left-leaning organizations.

52 Latner, *Cuban Revolution in America*, 27–31; 68–72.

53 It is important not to idealize the economic impact of such work, which as Teishan A. Latner points out, probably never offset the considerable costs involved in hosting hundreds of foreigners in Cuba for weeks on end. The value of such work, in a sense, has always been more political than any material contribution that comes from harvesting sugar or constructing houses.

4 South American Dictatorships and the Rise of Human Rights

1 Keys, *Reclaiming American Virtue*. For a good discussion of human rights activism in relation to the Soviet Union see Snyder, *From Selma to Moscow*, ch. 1.

2   For a broader discussion of why people in the United States came to care about human rights in other countries during this period, see: Snyder, *From Selma to Moscow*, 3–15.

3   Keys, *Reclaiming American Virtue*; Moyn, *The Last Utopia*.

4   In this sense, if it is not clear by now, this work follows the lead of earlier ground-breaking scholarship by Samuel Moyn and Barbara Keys, as well as newer important scholarship by Patrick William Kelly.

5   Judy Tzu-Chun Wu, *Radicals on the Road: Internationalism, Orientalism, and Feminism during the Vietnam Era* (Cornell University Press, 2013), 29–30.

6   Moyn, *The Last Utopia*, 95.

7   Moyn, *The Last Utopia*; Keys, *Reclaiming American Virtue*.

8   Moyn, *The Last Utopia*; Keys, *Reclaiming American Virtue*.

9   Roger Peace, *A Call to Conscience*, 54.

10 Gosse, "'The North American front," 16–21; Van Gosse, "Active engagement: the legacy of Central American Solidarity," *NACLA Report* (March/April, 1995). 24–5.

11 James Green, "Clerics, exiles, and academics: opposition to the Brazilian military dictatorship in the United States, 1969–1974," *Latin American Politics and Society*, Vol. 45, No. 1 (2003), 87–117, quote from 92.

12 Gosse, *The North American Front*, 17.

13 Plummer, *In Search of Power*, 165–78.

14 Calandra, "The 'good Americans': U.S. solidarity networks for Chilean and Argentinean refugees (1973–1983)," *Historia Actual Online*, Vol. 23 (2010), 22.

15 Van Gosse, *The North American Front*, 16–17.

16 For an excellent discussion of the relationship between human rights and Christianity during the emergence of human rights in the 1960s and 1970s see Patrick William Kelly, "Human rights and Christian responsibility: transnational Christian activism, human rights, and state violence in Brazil and Chile in the 1970s," in Alexander Wilde (ed.), *Religious Responses to Violence: Human Rights in Latin America Past and Present* (University of Notre Dame Press, 2015).

17 See James Green's "Clerics, exiles, and academics" and *We Cannot Remain Silent*, as well as Kelly's "Human rights and responsibility."

18 Kelly, "Human rights and responsibility," 102.

19 Green "Clerics, exiles, and academics" and *We Cannot Remain Silent*; Kelly, "Human rights and responsibility."

20 Green, "Clerics, exiles, and academics."

21 Kelly, "Human rights and responsibility," 102–4.

22 Green, *We Cannot Remain Silent*, 3.

23 Vania Markarian, *Left in Transformation: Uruguayan Exiles and the Latin American Human Rights Network, 1967–1984* (Routledge, 2005): 99.

24 Quote in Markarian, *Left in Transformation*, 99.

25 As we will see, Patrick William Kelly suggests that Chilean leftists also wrestled with the place of human rights in a revolutionary politics while in exile, with some quickly embracing it as a useful tool while others remained far more suspicious. "The 1973 Chilean coup and the origins of transnational human rights activism," *Journal of Global History*, Vol 8, No. 1 (March 2013), 165–86.

26 Cmiel, "The emergence of human rights," 1234–8. Tom Buchanan, "Amnesty

International in crisis, 1966–7," *Twentieth Century British History*, Vol. 15, No. 3 (2004), 267–89; Tom Buchanan, "The truth will set you free: the making of Amnesty International," *Journal of Contemporary History*, Vol. 37, No. 4 (2002), 575–97.

27 Cmiel, "The emergence of human rights," 1234–8.

28 Cmiel, "The emergence of human rights," 1240.

29 Snyder, "Exporting Amnesty International," 780–8; Cmiel, "The emergence of human rights," 1240–1.

30 Cmiel, "The emergence of human rights," 1240–1.

31 Cmiel, "The emergence of human rights," 1240–5.

32 Keys, *Reclaiming American Virtue*, 265–6.

33 Moyn, *The Last Utopia*, 132.

34 As Tom Buchanan has shown, this tendency was built into the origins of Amnesty. "The truth will set you free."

35 Kelly, "The 1973 Chilean coup," 167.

36 Keys, *Reclaiming American Virtue*, 201.

37 Kelly, "The 1973 Chilean coup," 168.

38 Latin American activists, many of whom came out of a Marxist-left tradition, or at least were exposed to it, tended to have a much more critical and reflective stance with respect to human rights from the 1970s through the present. See Kelly's discussion of Chilean exiles in Mexico and their tentative embrace of human rights in "The 1973 Chilean coup."

39 For a variety of reasons, including the facts that European countries quickly denounced the coup, Allende and the Chilean left had developed strong ties with European leftists, and the United States supported Pinochet and made it difficult for Chileans to come there, many more Chilean exiles went to Europe than the United States. As a result, the dominant—and better established left—currents of international solidarity with Chile involved Europe and other countries in Latin America, especially Mexico. Nevertheless, because of the US government's global power and support for Pinochet, the United States remained an important site. See: Kim Christiaens, Idesbald Goddeeris, and Magaly Rodríguez García, *European Solidarity with Chile, 1970s–1980s* (Frankfurt am Main: Peter Lang, 2014).

40 Margaret Power, "The U.S. movement in solidarity with Chile in the 1970s," *Latin American Perspectives*, Issue 169, Vol. 36, No. 6 (November 2009), 46–66; Patrick William Kelly, "The 1973 Chilean coup," 165–86.

41 Keys, *Reclaiming American Virtue*.

42 Darren Hawkins, *International Human Rights and Authoritarian Rule in Chile* (University of Nebraska Press, 2002); Edward Cleary, *The Struggle for Human Rights in Latin America* (Prager, 1997); Hugo Frühling, "Resistance to fear in Chile: the experience of the Vicaria de la Solidaridad," in Juan E. Corradi, Patricia Weiss Fagen, and Manuel Antonio Garretón (eds.), *Fear at the Edge: State Terror and Resistance in Latin America* (University of California Press, 1992).

43 Frühling, "Resistance to fear"; Power, "The U.S. movement"; Hawkins, *International Human Rights*.

44 Frühling, "Resistance to gear," 121–41.

45 Hawkins, *International Human Rights*, 57.

46 Cleary, *The Struggle for Human Rights*, 10–11; Frühling, "Resistance to fear"; Hawkins, *International Human Rights*. As Patrick William Kelly shows, Chileans— particularly those in exile who tended to be firmly on the left—approached the emergence of human rights from a variety of perspectives, which ranged from relatively uncritical acceptance to deep suspicion. Kelly, "The 1973 Chilean coup."

47 Kelly, "Human rights and Christian responsibility," 110.

48 It was revealed that ITT conspired with the CIA to prevent Allende from assuming the presidency and then (when that failed) caused economic chaos in Chile in order to force him from office.

49 Van Gosse, "Unpacking the Vietnam syndrome: the coup in Chile and the rise of popular anti-interventionism," in Van Gosse and Richard Moser (eds.), *The World the Sixties Made: Politics and Culture in Recent America* (Temple University Press, 2003), 102–4.

50 Gosse, "Unpacking the Vietnam syndrome."

51 Tinsman, *Buying into the Regime*, 178.

52 Gosse, "Unpacking the Vietnam syndrome," 103–6; Calandra, "The 'good Americans.'"

53 Tinsman, *Buying into the Regime*, 180.

54 Victoria Goff, "The Chile solidarity movement and its media: an alternative take on the Allende and Pinochet years," *American Journalism*, Vol. 24, No. 4 (2007), 95–125.

55 Tinsman, *Buying into the Regime*, 178–95.

56 Tinsman, *Buying into the Regime*, 178–95.

57 Tinsman, *Buying into the Regime*, 178–95.

58 Gosse, "Unpacking the Vietnam syndrome," 100–2.

59 Keys, *Reclaiming American Virtue*; Moyn, *The Last Utopia*.

60 Thomas F. Quigley, "The Chilean coup, the church and the human rights movement," *America: The Jesuit Review* (February 11, 2002); Keys, *Reclaiming American Virtue*.

61 Hawkins, *International Human Rights*, 57–79.

62 Calandra, "The 'good Americans,'" 25; Quigley, "The Chilean goup."

63 Calandra, "The 'good Americans,'" 22–26; Quigley, "The Chilean goup,"; Lars Schoultz, *Human Rights and United States Policy toward Latin America* (Princeton University Press, 1981), 77–97.

64 Lars Schoultz, *Human Rights and United States Policy*, 77–97.

65 Keys, *Reclaiming American Virtue*, ch. 7; Hawkins, *International Human Rights*.

66 Keys, *Reclaiming American Virtue*, 148.

67 Hawkins, *International Human Rights*, 55–6.

68 Kelly, "The 1973 Chilean coup," 176.

69 Quoted in Kelly, "The 1973 Chilean coup," 173.

70 Kelly, "The 1973 Chilean coup," 174–6

71 The human rights activism that emerged around the 1976 coup and repression in Argentina is beyond the scope of this book, but was also driven by grassroots initiatives, human rights organizations such as Amnesty, D.C.-based NGOs, and policymakers in and around the Carter administration. See Schmidli, *The Fate of Freedom Elsewhere*.

72 Keys, *Reclaiming American Virtue,* 156.

73 Kelly, "The 1973 Chilean coup," 166.

74 Partly as a result, solidarity became far whiter than it had been in first half of
the twentieth century. This was to a certain extent inevitable given that the only
institutions less diverse than human rights groups and D.C. policymakers were
religious organizations—which in the United States remain deeply segregated.
Combined with the solidarity shift away from the "black Caribbean" and towards
South America and Central America in the 1970s and 1980s, the fact that (white)
faith-based groups were at the core of solidarity efforts necessarily meant that Latin
American solidarity as a whole became inevitably whiter—even as exiles remained
central to efforts, and African Americans (and increasingly immigrants) continued
to engage in internationalism. This is not to say that the longstanding tradition of
African American solidarity with Latin America disappeared. It was, in a sense,
marginalized by the overwhelming flow of resources and energy into South and
Central American solidarity—though even here African Americans remained an
engaged minority. See, for example, Omali Yeshitela, "The first conference in solidarity with Nicaragua," *The Black Scholar* (July/August 1981), 25–36. More than
this, the ongoing presence and importance of exiles in solidarity movements, and
the increasing importance of immigrants and diasporic solidarity, complicates the
racial-national makeup of solidarity. Solidarity with Puerto Rico, which includes
Puerto Ricans and their allies, further complicates the solidarity map. See e.g. Katherine T. McCaffrey, "Social struggle against the U.S. Navy in Vieques, Puerto Rico:
Two Movements in History," *Latin American Perspectives,* Vol. 33, No. 1 (2006),
83–101.

5 Central American Solidarity in Reagan's America

1   Christian Smith, *Resisting Reagan: The U.S. Central American Peace Movement*
(University of Chicago Press 1996), xvi.

2   Gosse, "Active engagement," 23.

3   Gosse, "Active engagement,"; Van Gosse, "El Salvador is Spanish for Vietnam:
the politics of solidarity and the new immigrant left, 1955–1993," in Paul Buhle and
Dan Georgakas (eds.), *The Immigrant Left* (SUNY Press, 1996); Perla, "Heirs of
Sandino."

4   For example, see Chapter 8's discussion of the Guatemala Coke campaign.

5   Gosse, "The North American front," 19–20.

6   Peace, *A Call to Conscience,* 65.

7   Gosse, "Active engagement," 25.

8   Gosse, "The North American front," 21; Van Gosse, "Active engagement," 25.

9   Peace, *A Call to Conscience,* 68.

10 Van Gosse, "Active engagement," 25.

11 Smith, *Resisting Reagan,* 141.

12 Gosse, "The North American front," 16–17.

13 Gosse, "The North American front," 17–25.

14 Peace, *A Call to Conscience,* 70.

15 Gosse, "Active engagement;" "The North American front," 23–4; 27.
16 Gosse, "The North American front," 23; "Active engagement," 27; Peace, *A Call to Conscience,* 71–3. Indeed, as Van Gosse has noted, despite a division in the early 1980s between leftists who wanted to actively support revolution, including armed insurrection, and anti-interventionists who simply wanted the United States to get out of the region, most within the movement recognized by the mid-1980s that ending US military aid/intervention would generate a range of consequences and support a variety of goals. Ending military aid would reduce the number of human rights abuses, facilitate Central American self-determination, and even open up the possibility of revolution.
17 Smith, *Resisting Reagan,* 151–152.
18 Quoted in Smith, *Resisting Reagan,* 18.
19 Smith, *Resisting Reagan,* 24–32.
20 The Contras were a right-wing rebel group funded by the United States in order to undermine and ultimately overthrow the Sandinistas.
21 Smith, *Resisting Reagan,* 24–32.
22 Smith, *Resisting Reagan,* 89.
23 Smith, *Resisting Reagan,* 95.
24 Iran-Contra was a political scandal during Reagan's second term in which members of his administration facilitated the sale of arms to Iran (which was under an arms embargo), and used money from those sales to fund the Contras (who had been prohibited from receiving additional funding by the Boland Amendment).
25 Smith, *Resisting Reagan,* 89–109.
26 Gosse, "The North American front."
27 Gosse, "Active engagement," 25.
28 Gosse, "The North American front"; "Active engagement"; Smith, *Resisting Reagan*; Peace, *A Call to Conscience.*
29 Gosse, "Active engagement," 23.
30 Gosse, "Active engagement," 23.
31 Carter had imposed an aid embargo on Guatemala because of its human rights record, which slowed Reagan's ability to funnel aid to the country. Smith, *Resisting Reagan,* 25–6; 35–41.
32 Smith, *Resisting Reagan,* 50–2; Peace, *A Call to Conscience,* 4.
33 Gosse, "Active engagement," 23.
34 Gosse, "Active engagement," 23.
35 Gosse, "Active engagement," 24.
36 Gosse, "Active engagement," 24.

6 NAFTA, Fair Trade, and Globalization

1 On the growth of human rights organization in relation to Colombia, see Winifred Tate's *Counting the Dead: The Culture and Politics of Human Rights Activism in Colombia* (University of California Press, 2007).
2 For a broader history of the AFL-CIO's internationalism see Kim Scipes, *AFL-CIO's Secret War against Developing Country Workers: Solidarity or Sabatoge* (Lexington

Books, 2010); Jack Scott, *Yankee Unions, Go Home: How the AFL Helped the U.S. Build an Empire in Latin America* (New Star Books, 1978).

3 In 1962, following the Cuban Revolution, the AFL-CIO opened the American Institute for Free Labor Development (AFLLD), which promoted the idea that labor, capital, and the state could live harmoniously, in effect spreading business-style unionism in order to undermine more radical labor movements.

4 See Chapter 8 for a discussion of the labor-led campaign in support of Coca-Cola workers in Guatemala during the late 1970s and early 1980s.

5 John D. French, "Labor and NAFTA: nationalist reflexes and transnational imperatives in North America, 1991–1995," in Ronaldo Munck (ed.), *Labor and Globalisation: Results and Prospects* (Liverpool University Press, 2004).

6 Joel Stillerman, "Transnational activist networks and the emergence of labor internationalism in the NAFTA countries," *Social Science History*, Vol. 27, No. 4 (Winter 2003), 577–601; Dan Crow and Greg Albo, "Neoliberalism, NAFTA, and the state of North American labour movements," *Just Labour*, Vols 6 & 7 (Autumn 2005), 12–22.

7 The alliance between the *Frente Autentico del Trabajo* and the United Electrical, Radio and Machine Workers of America (UE), which coordinated cross-border organizing against multinationals they shared in common, was probably the most notable instance of cross-border organizing.

8 French, "Labor and NAFTA," 160.

9 Jefferson Cowie, "Nationalist struggles in a transnational economy: a critical analysis of U.S. labor's campaign against NAFTA," *Labor Studies Journal*, Vol. 21 (1997), 3–32.

10 Stillerman, "Transnational activist networks," 577–601.

11 Cowie, "Nationalist struggles;" French, "Labour and NAFTA," 156–62.

12 Cowie, "National struggles," 4.

13 Cowie, "National struggles," 27.

14 John D. French, "From the suites to the streets: the unexpected re-emergence of the 'labor question,' 1994-1999," *Labor History*, Vol. 43, No. 3 (2002), 285–304.

15 This section on fair trade draws largely from Laura Raynolds, Douglas Murray, and John Wilkinson, *Fair Trade: The Challenges of Transforming Globalization* (Routledge, 2007), especially the second chapter by Laura Raynolds and Michael Long, "Fair/alternative trade: historical and empirical dimensions," as well as Daniel Jaffee, *Brewing Justice: Fair Trade Coffee, Sustainability, and Survival* (University of California Press, 2007). See also Global Anabaptist Mennonite Encyclopedia Online, "Byler, Edna Ruth (1904–1976)," http://www.gameo.org/encyclopedia/contents/B94.html; World Free Trade Organization (WFTO), "60 years of fair trade," www.wfto.com/index.php?option=com_content&task=view&id=10&Itemid=17; "Ten thousand villages," from 'the needlework lady' to today's craftswoman: a brief history," www.tenthousandvillages.com/php/about.us/history.php.

16 Some ATOs did move beyond handicrafts, selling for example "solidarity" coffee from Nicaragua in support of the Sandinistas.

17 Laura T. Raynolds and Michael A. Long, "Fair/alternative trade: historical and empirical dimensions," in Laura T. Raynolds, Douglas Murray, and John

Wilkinson (eds.), *Fair Trade: The Challenges of Transforming Globalization* (Routledge, 2007), 15–32.

18 Stephanie Barrientos, Michael E. Conroy, and Elaine Jones, "Northern social movements and fair trade," in Raynolds et. al., *Fair Trade*, 56–7.

7 Zapatistas and Global Justice

1 In the long term, the end of the Soviet bloc opened the door to a broader and productive rethinking of socialism. In the short term, however, it not only undermined efforts to advance anything vaguely resembling socialism, but reinforced the ideology that any efforts to restrain or regulate capitalism necessarily brought about negative consequences.

2 There is a wealth of literature on the Zapatistas. Thomas Olesen has written wisely on their relationship to international solidarity, including two useful articles, "'Globalising' the Zapatistas: from Third World solidarity to global solidarity?" *Third World Quarterly*, Vol. 25, No. 1 (2004), 255–67, and "Mixing scales: neoliberalism and the transnational Zapatista network," *Humboldt Journal of Social Relations*, Vol. 29, No. 1 (2005), 84–126. For a critical take on the Zapatistas, see Dan La Botz, "Twenty years since the Chiapas rebellion: the Zapatistas, their politics, and their impact," *Solidarity*, January 13, 2014. Abigail Andrews provides a very useful look into Zapatista transnational solidarity in two articles: "Constructing mutuality: the Zapatistas' transformation of transnational activist power dynamics," *Latin American Politics and Society*, Vol. 52, No. 1 (Spring 2010), 89–120, and "How activists 'take Zapatismo home:' South-to-North dynamics in transnational social movements," *Latin American Perspectives*, Vol. 38, No. 1 (January 2011), 138–52. See also Richard Stahler-Sholk, "Neoliberal homogenization: the Zapatista Autonomy Movement," *Latin American Perspectives*, Vol. 34, No. 2 (March 2007), 48–63; Bhaskar Sunkara, "Why we loved the Zapatistas," *Jacobin*, 2011, https://www.jacobinmag.com/2011/01/why-we-loved-the-zapatistas. There are also numerous book-length treatments of nearly every aspect of the Zapatista phenomenon.

3 La Botz, "Twenty years since the Chiapas rebellion."

4 Stahler-Sholk, "Resisting neoliberal homogenization."

5 Curry Stephenson Malott, "Conclusion: indigenous philosophy as twenty-first century lifeboat: the critical pedagogy of the Zapatistas," *Counterpoints*, Vol. 324; *A Call to Action: An Introduction to Education, Philosophy, and Native North America* (2008), 209–23.

6 Olesen, ""Globalising the Zapatistas"; Olesen, "Mixing Scales"; Andrews, "Constructing mutuality"; Andrews, "How activists."

7 Andrews, "Constructing mutuality"; Andrews, "How activists"; Stahler-Sholk, "Resisting neoliberal homogenization."

8 Andrews, "Constructing mutuality."

9 Subcomandante Marcos, "Marcos to NGOs: Zapatistas don't want charity, but respect," August 6, 2003. www.narconews.com/Issue31/article833.html

10 Andrews, "How activists."

11 There is an immense literature on the Global Justice Movement. For the privileged

place of Zapatismo in the broader movement see Olesen, "Globalising the Zapatistas"; Peter Rosset et al., "Zapatismo in the Movement of Movements," *Development*, Vol. 48, No. 2 (2005), 35–41; Luis Hernández Navarro, "The global Zapatista movement," *Global Exchange*, January 16, 2004. For a good introduction, see Liz Highleyman, "The Global Justice Movement," in Immanuel Ness (ed.), *Encyclopedia of American Social Movements* (M.E. Sharpe, 2004); Geoffrey Pleyers, "The Global Justice Movement," *Global Studies Journal*, July 1, 2010. For a good review of the literature, see Helen Hintjens, "Appreciating the movement of the movements," *Development in Practice*, Vol. 16, No. 6 (November 2006), 628–43; France Curran, "What Happened to the Global Justice Movement," *International Viewpoint*, November 25, 2007; Dan La Botz, "The New Movement for Global Justice," *Against the Current*, Sept./Oct. 2008.

12 Olesen, "Globalising the Zapatistas"; Rosset, "Zapatismo in the movement of movements"; Hernández Navarro, "The global Zapatista movement."

13 Boaventura de Sousa Santos, *The Rise of the Global Left: The World Social Forum and Beyond* (Zed Books, 2006).

14 Olesen, "Globalising the Zapatistas"; Rosset, "Zapatismo in the movement of movements"; Hernández Navarro, "The global Zapatista movement."

15 Rachel Neumann, "Out of step: labor and the Global Social Justice Movement," *New Labor Forum*, Vol. 11 (Fall/Winter 2002), 38–47. Highleyman, "The Global Justice Movement"; Pleyers, "The Global Justice Movement."

16 Highleyman, "The Global Justice Movement"; Pleyers, "The Global Justice Movement."

17 Highleyman, "The Global Justice Movement"; Pleyers, "The Global Justice Movement."

18 Neumann, "Out of step," 41.

19 Curran, "What Happened to the Global Justice Movement."

8 Corporate Campaigns and Sweatshop Activism

1 For an excellent discussion of international solidarity around CAFTA see Mary Finley-Brook and Katherine Hoyt, "CAFTA opposition: divergent networks, uneasy solidarities," *Latin American Perspectives*, Issue 169. No. 6 (2009), 27–45.

2 It is worth noting that only the FTAA was defeated, and that was less owing to international solidarity than to the rise of the Latin American left.

3 Kepner and Soothill, *The Banana Empire*; Kepner, *Social Aspects of the Banana Industry*.

4 To be sure, many of these tactics and strategies have earlier origins, and other campaigns and movements have been central in refining and popularizing them. But it is hard to overemphasize the importance of the Farm Workers' movement for international solidarity or the left in general. Not only did the UFW put Latin America, or at least Mexico, on the map for a new generation of progressives at a time when US foreign policy was becoming the subject of increased public scrutiny, it also created "the nation's leading organizer training school." A significant cadre of individuals trained by the UFW transitioned into the solidarity left and went on

to create and staff Latin American solidarity organizations of the 1980s, 1990s, and beyond. Randy Shaw, *Beyond the Fields: Cesar Chavez, the UFW, and the Struggle for Justice in the 21st Century* (University of California Press, 2008), 6.

5   Jarel B. Manheim, *The Death of a Thousand Cuts: Corporate Campaigns and the Attack on the Corporation* (Lawrence Earlbaum Associates, 2001), 47–9.

6   By 1971, the NCC had created the Corporate Information Center, which merged in 1974 with the Interfaith Center on Social Responsibility, forming the Interfaith Center on Corporate Responsibility (ICCR) – the major religious organization targeting corporations. Manheim, *Death of a Thousand Cuts*, 48.

7   Manheim, *Death of a Thousand Cuts*, 49.

8   Manheim, *Death of a Thousand Cuts*, 56

9   Manheim, *Death of a Thousand Cuts*, 56.

10   The North American Congress on Latin America (NACLA) was formed in the mid-1960s, with support from the Methodist and Presbyterian churches and the National Council of Churches.

11   Stephen Kinzer, *Overthrow: America's Century of Regime Change from Hawaii to Iraq* (Times Books: Henry Holt and Company, 2006), 188.

12   Brent Fisse and John Braithwaite, *The Impact of Publicity on Corporate Offenders* (SUNY Press, 1983), 124.

13   Paul Buhle and Dan Georgakas, *The Immigrant Left in the United States* (SUNY Press, 1996), 310, 312. See also Van Gosse and Richard R. Moser, *The World the Sixties Made: Politics and Culture in Recent America* (Temple University Press), 109.

14   Gosse, *The World the Sixties Made*, 111.

15   Henry Frundt, *Refreshing Pauses: Coca-Cola and Human Rights in Guatemala* (Greenwood, 1987) 13–16.

16   Frundt, *Refreshing Pauses*, 17–27.

17   Frundt, *Refreshing Pauses*, 28–41.

18   Frundt, *Refreshing Pauses*, 28–41.

19   Frundt, *Refreshing Pauses*, 42–55.

20   Peter Waterman, *Globalization, Social Movements, and the New Internationalisms* (Continuum, 2001), 69; Frundt, *Refreshing Pauses*, 91.

21   Frundt, *Refreshing Pauses*, 105–22.

22   Frundt, *Refreshing Pauses*, 173–86.

23   Frundt, *Refreshing Pauses*, 187–99

24   Deborah Levenson-Estrada and Henry Frundt, "Toward a new internationalism: lessons from the Guatemalan labor movement," *NACLA Report on the Americas*, 28: 5 (March–April 1995), 18–19.

25   Levenson-Estrada and Frundt, "Toward a new internationalism," 19. Armbruster-Sandoval, *Globalization and Cross-Border Solidarity*, 29–40.

26   Armbruster-Sandoval, *Globalization and Cross-Border Solidarity*, 37–52.

27   Armbruster-Sandoval, *Globalization and Cross-Border Solidarity*, 52–7.

28   Armbruster-Sandoval, *Globalization and Cross-Border Solidarity*, 35–7.

29   Kitty Krupat, "From war zone to free trade zone: a history of the National Labor Committee," in Andress Ross et al. (eds.), *No Sweat: Fashion, Free Trade, and the Rights of Garment Workers* (Verso, 1997), 65–70.

30   In 1995 the International Ladies Garment Workers Union (ILGWU) merged with the

Amalgamated Clothing and Textile Workers Union to form the Union of Needle-trades, Industrial and Textile Employees (UNITE).

31 Jill Esbenshade, *Monitoring Sweatshops: Workers, Consumers, and the Global Apparel Industry* (Temple University Press, 2004), 169–74.

32 Esbenshade, *Monitoring Sweatshops*, 169–74.

33 Esbenshade, *Monitoring Sweatshops*, 169–74.

34 Esbenshade, *Monitoring Sweatshops*, 170–1; Armbruster-Sandoval, *Globalization and Cross-Border Solidarity*, 76–7; Krupat, "From war zone," 54–5.

35 Eileen Boris, "Consumers of the world unite! Campaigns against sweating, past and present," in Daniel Bender and Richard Greenwald (eds.), *Sweatshop U.S.A.: The American Sweatshop in Historical and Global Perspective* (Routledge, 2003), 213–14. Armbruster-Sandoval, *Globalization and Cross-Border Solidarity*, 2–3.

36 Krupat, "From war zone," 58–63.

37 Boris, "Consumers of the world," 214–16; Liza Featherstone and United Students Against Sweatshops, *Students Against Sweatshops* (Verso, 2002), 90.

38 Armbruster-Sandoval, *Globalization and Cross-Border Solidarity*, 11.

39 The NLC played a key role in cultivating student interest in sweatshops during 1998 and 1999—just as United Students Against Sweatshops was forming—when it took delegations of students to El Salvador, Nicaragua, and Honduras and helped them produce reports and videos. Featherstone, *Students Against Sweatshops*, 90.

40 Boris, "Consumers of the world," 214–18.

41 Boris, "Consumers of the world," 217–18. "By early 2003, it [USAS] had chapters in over 200 universities. At its national conference in Los Angeles that February, over a hundred students met to strategize not only how to stop sweatshops and fight the institutions of global capitalism (the WTO, IMF, and Free Trade Association of the Americas) but also how to provide solidarity for farmworker struggles, win living wages in their communities and on campuses, and support immigrant rights." Boris, "Consumers of the world," 218.

42 Esbenshade, *Monitoring Sweatshops*, 198–201.

43 Bender, *Sweated Work, Weak Bodies*, 195–6.

Conclusion

1 The bar for moral outrage, public attention, and the call to action was, of course, always changing. It was not simply that what shocked, appalled, captured attention, or generated moral outrage changed over time or was shaped by a whole series of factors. It was also that the US government, military regimes, and political actors in both Latin America and the United States all became increasingly sophisticated at negotiating the process. If the presence of US troops draws too much attention, operate through military aid. If military aid proves too explosive, find ways to conceal it. If torturing or falsely imprisoning enemies of the state captures unwanted attention, then use death squads to simply disappear them while denying involvement. If Americans are not moved by one type of level of atrocity, then focus on another.

Index

Johnson, James Weldon, 58–60, 62
Johnson, Lyndon B., 101
Jones, Leroi, 85

K
Kelly, Patrick William, 103, 110, 122
Kennedy, Edward, 121
Kennedy, John F., 86–7
Kepner, Charles, 183
Kernaghan, Charles, 195, 197
killings
 by death squads in El Salvador, 138
 of Romero and others, 129–31
 of Salvadoran college students, 128
 of Sandino, 67
 by US forces in Haiti, 60
 by US forces in Nicaragua, 64
King, Martin Luther Jr, 30, 76
Kirkpatrick, Jeanne, 133
Kissinger, Henry, 121
Ku Klux Klan, 86
Kunhardt, José Eugenio, 53–4

L
La Guajira, Colombia, 1
labor movements/solidarity, 8, 9, 10–11,
 14, 76–7
 attempts to influence, 53–4
 conservatism of, 11, 208
 purge of left from, 10–11, 76–7
 see also trade unions
labor, transportation of (to undercut
 terms), 42
Lansing, Robert, 56
Latin America
 attitudes to US interventions, 21–2
 shortage of allies during Cold War,
 81, 107
 US 19th-century views of, 29
 US interventions in, 37–8
 see also Caribbean, individual
 countries by name
Latin American Strategy Committee,
 119
Latner, Teishan, 90
lawyers and human rights, 118

Lawyers Committee for Human Rights,
 117–18
left, the
 in the 1960s, 97, 98
 articulating different visions, 203
 decline of, 7, 13–14, 143, 203–5
 efforts to reconstitute, 20
 in Europe, 222n4–39
 global, 168, 179
 and labor movements, 9–11, 204
 left internationalism, 5–6, 12–13, 20,
 81, 208
 New Left, 185
 persecution of, 72–3, 96, 107, 113, 204
 radical, 48–9
 in South America, 96, 106, 112–13, 143
 in the USA, 5–7, 10, 72–3, 98, 203–8
Lenin, Vladimir I., 52
Levinson, Sandra, 90–1
liberals
 distancing from left, 72–3, 76
 and human rights, 119–20
 uneasy alliance with left, 44
lobbying, 109, 121, 127, 132, 136, 152
Locker, Michael, 185

M
Magón, Ricardo Flores, 41
Mannheim, Jarol, 186
maquilas/maquiladoras, 191–5
marches/demonstratons, 136
Marcos (Rafael Sebastián Guillén
 Vicente), 171
Markarian, Vania, 106
market–based politics, 161
Martí, José, 32
Martin, William, 27
Marx, Karl, 23
Matthewson, Tim, 27–8
Mayfield, Julian, 85
McCarthyism, 10
McCay, Claude, 58
McKinley, William, 33, 36
McPherson, Alan, 46, 52, 58
media
 attitudes of US, 51–2, 63–4, 82, 84, 134

trade unions
  attacks on, 152
  attitudes to foreign policy, 149–50
  business-friendly, 77
  and campaigns against businesses,
    184–6
  early organization of, 40
  in Guatemala, 188–93
  and mass movements, 184
  progressive focus on issues of, 15
  supporting Mexican workers, 40–2
  see also labor movement, individual
    unions by name
Trotter, John, 188–9
Trujillo, Rafael, 54
Truman Doctrine, 74
Trump, Donald, 155
Turner, John Kenneth, 42
Twain, Mark, 65

U
u.s./Guatemala Labor Education Project
  (U.S./GLEP), 192
Union of Needletrades, Industrial and
  Textile Employees (UNITE), 151, 195–6,
  229–30n8–30
United Auto Workers, 115, 129, 150, 151
United Electrical, Radio and Machine
  Workers (UE), 150, 151
United Farm Workers, 172, 184, 228n8–4
United Fruit Company, 63–4, 183, 187
United Mine Workers, 66
United Nations, 114, 120, 122
United States
  alternatives to use of troops, 69–70,
    135
  civil war, 22–3
  covert interventionism, 76
  economic domination, arguments
    for, 35
  empire, opposition to, 5–6
  exceptionalism, 29
  foreign policy in 1930s, 71
  foreign policy in 1950s and 60s, 87,
    97, 98
  foreign policy in 1980s, 122–3, 133–6

formation of, 24–5
  forms of solidarity in, 4
  government, 6
  interventionism, local attitudes to, 46,
    50–1, 59, 71
  interventionism, us attitudes to, 36–8,
    47–9, 52, 64–9, 71, 87, 100–2, 116,
    125
  the left in, *see under* left
  military interventions in Latin
    America, 21, 136
  military occupations in Caribbean, 9,
    37, 45–70
  opposition to interventionism, 46–7,
    71, 225n5–16
  perceived as essentially benevolent
    (or not), 21–2, 36–7, 49, 52, 56,
    116–17
  power of, 5–6, 10
  seeking global domination, 35, 74,
    99
  and white exceptionalism, 29, 37
United States–Colombia Trade
  Promotion Agreement (CTPA), 182
United Students Against Sweatshops
  (USAS), 198, 230n8–39, 230n8–41
Universal Negro Improvement
  Association, 48, 63
UP, 57, 52
Uruguay, 106–7
us Catholic Conference, 131–2
USAID, 194
USAS, 198, 230n8–39, 230n8–41

V
Venceremos Brigades, 82, 88–91,
  220n3–51
Venezuela, 144
Vesey, Denmark, 27
Vicaría de la Solidaridad, 114
Viera, Judith, 196
Vietnam War, 82, 89, 98, 99, 120
  protests against, 85
violence
  accompanying us interventions, 60–1
  in Central America in 1980s, 138